EAT, SHRINK & BE MERRY!

**Great-tasting food
that won't go
from your lips to your hips!**

EAT, SHRINK & BE MERRY!

**Great-tasting food
that won't go
from your lips to your hips!**

Janet & Greta Podleski

Cartoons by Ted Martin

GRANET
PUBLISHING INC.

PR#1 US

Cartoons by Ted Martin
Edited by Fina Scroppo
Design and production by Matrix Four Limited
Printed in Canada

Design consultants: Matthews Communications Design Inc.
Food photography and cover photo by Colin Erricson
Food styling by Terry Schacht

All inquiries should be addressed to:

Granet Publishing Inc.
1241 Weber Street E., Unit #2
Kitchener, Ontario N2A 1C2
1.800.470.0738

E-mail: janetandgreta@eatshrinkandbemerry.com

www.eatshrinkandbemerry.com

If you're interested in bulk purchases of **Eat, Shrink & Be Merry!** for your employees or other premium uses, please call us at 1-800-470-0738. We offer a very aggressive discount schedule and would be happy to answer any questions you may have.

The following product and company names appearing in the book are trademarks or trade names of their respective companies:

7-Eleven, Aero, All My Children, Armani, Aunt Jemima, Batman, Betty Crocker, Birkenstock, Boca Ground Burger, Bonanza, Bugs Bunny, Butterball, Calgon, Campbell's, Chia Pet, Club House, Coca-Cola, Coffee Crisp, Coke, Colgate, Cream of Wheat, Crisco, Danone, Dog Chow, Domino's Pizza, Dove Dark Chocolate Bar, Drano, Egg Beaters, Flintstones, General Hospital, Gummy Bears, Hershey's Kisses, Hostess Ding Dong, Humpty Dumpty, I Dream of Jeannie, Jeopardy, Kit Kat, Kraft Dinner, Krispy Kreme, La-Z-Boy, Little House on the Prairie, Lundberg Family Farms, Martha Stewart, Milky Way, Mrs. Butterworth, Nature's Path, Nokia, NutraSweet, Ocean Spray, Oprah, Oreo, Pepsi-Cola, Pepsodent, PEZ, Philadelphia Dips, Pillsbury Doughboy, Ponds, Pop-O-Matic Trouble, Pop Rocks, Popsicle, Prada, Quarter Pounder, Reader's Digest, Red Rose, Ron Popeil's Pocket Fisherman, Seinfeld, Snickers, S.O.S. Pads, SPAM, Splenda, Starbucks, Survivor, Swansons, Swiffer Mop, The 700 Club, The Bionic Woman, The Hamburglar, The Incredible Hulk, The Six Million Dollar Man, ThighMaster, Turtles, Twinkies, Wheaties

Recipe analysis calculated using Nutribase Professional Nutrition Manager software (Cybersoft, Inc.). When a choice of ingredients is listed, analysis is calculated using the first ingredient. Optional ingredients are not included in the analysis.

To our beloved father, John Podleski (1923-1991)

When our first cookbook, *Looneyspoons*, debuted on the national bestseller list in December 1996, the newspaper made a very unusual error in reporting our names. Much to our disbelief, in plain black and white for the whole country to see, was the title *Looneyspoons*, not "by Janet and Greta Podleski," but "by John Podleski." It's true! We're not making this up!

No one at the newspaper could explain the mistake. Not only did they swap two names for one, but also they mysteriously inserted the name of our father who had passed away in 1991 after battling lung cancer. Even though we corrected the error, his name reappeared on the list for two more weeks!

Since we dedicated *Looneyspoons* "to our mother, who still to this day insists that Polish sausage is a health food," we figured this was our father's way of getting in on the action. More than likely, dad wanted us to know that he was watching from above, steering us in the right direction, laughing at our corny jokes, and nodding in approval.

The Globe and Mail, Saturday, December 14, 1996

THE GLOBE AND MAIL
National Bestseller List

In Paper

1 **Song Of Solomon**, by Toni Morrison (Penguin, $15.99) — 2/4

2 **The English Patient**, by Michael Ondaatje (Vintage Canada, $14.50) — 1/37

3 **A Hundred Secret Senses**, by Amy Tan (Random, $8.99) — 7/4

4 **The Horse Whisperer**, by Nicholas Evans (Dell, $9.99) — 3/10

5 **The Book Of Ruth**, by Jane Hamilton (Doubleday, $16.95) — 6/3

6 **Cry Of The Halidon**, by Robert Ludlum (Bantam, $9.99) — 8/6

7 **Shock Wave**, by Clive Cussler (Pocket, $9.99) — 4/3

8 **Primary Colours**, by Anonymous (Warner, $8.99) — 3

9 **Come To Grief**, by Dick Francis (McClelland & Stewart, $8.99) — 5/3

10 **Snow Falling On Cedars**, by David Guterson (Vintage Canada, $16.95) — 9/39

Special Interest

1 **1997 Friendship Book**, by Gay Francis (J. Wiley & Son, $9.95) — 1/4

2 **Looneyspoons**, by John Podleski (Granet, $24.95) — 2/2

3 **Chicken Soup For The Soul**, by Jack Canfield (Health Communications, $19.95) — 6/91

4 **It's A Magical World**, by Bill Watterson (Andrews & McMeel, $20.95) — 4/9

5 **Men Are From Mars, Women Are From Venus**, by John Gray (HarperCollins, $18) — 3/46

Contents

The best six doctors anywhere
And no one can deny it
Are sunshine, water, rest, and air
Exercise and diet.
These six will gladly you attend
If only you are willing
Your mind they'll ease
Your will they'll mend
And charge you not a shilling.

Nursery rhyme quoted by Wayne Fields,
What the River Knows, 1990

Our Sorta Kinda Introduction

A Tale of Two Sisters

Hi! We're sisters Janet and Greta Podleski. Pleased to meet you. There! Now that the formal "introduction" is out of the way, we can move on to the informal introduction, which really isn't an introduction at all, but a little story. A little story that's a little long-winded, mind you (we love to babble!), but a story that we hope will inspire you to achieve your goals, whatever they may be. Whether you're trying to change your eating habits, lose weight, launch a new career, or even become a better parent, the journey we're about to describe will show you that, when you dream big, set goals, work hard, refuse to quit, and let passion be your guide, just about anything is possible. We'll also explain how *Eat, Shrink & Be Merry!* came to be, and why we believe, with all our hearts, that this book can help you to feel better, look better, and cook better! If you're one of the millions of people who doesn't have a clue what to eat anymore (Are carbs okay? Will fat make me fat? Is protein a magic weight-loss aid?), we can help. We *want* to help! But first, we'd like you to get to know us a little better. What would possess two sisters from St. Thomas, Ontario, to mix pots and pans with pens and puns in an effort to improve people's eating habits? Just sit right back and you'll hear a tale…

Twelve years! Hard to believe that so much time has passed since we wrote and self-published our first cookbook, *Looneyspoons: Low-Fat Food Made Fun!* It seems like only yesterday that we were sequestered in the basement of our tiny bungalow, holed up in our claustrophobic, makeshift office, with unopened Visa, MasterCard, and utility bills piling up (why bother opening them when you can't pay them?) alongside a stack of rejection letters from publishers. Greta, an avid cook since the age of five, was dreaming up delicious, low-fat recipes while Janet, the domestic nightmare, was researching and writing lifestyle tidbits and food trivia that would liven up the margins alongside the recipes.

Look out *Sports Illustrated Swimsuit Edition!* Here we are in the '70s after just two weeks on the high-protein Scarsdale Diet.

Only a year apart in age, we had been sibling rivals all our lives. So, when we think back to those trying times, we marvel at how we worked together in (almost!) perfect harmony in that musty, sparsely furnished basement—despite having risked everything, despite being flat broke, and despite having to cope with the stress of not knowing whether our stack of loose pages would ever become a "real" book on bookstore shelves. Oh, yeah…and despite having made a pact to keep the whole project a secret, vowing not to tell even our mother or four older sisters! Forget sibling rivalry. At that time, we felt more like conjoined twins, inextricably linked at the brain! Two sisters sharing one passion—to help people eat more healthfully.

It all started in early 1995. Inspired by Greta's love of cooking, Janet's knack for writing, and both of our corny senses of humor, we came up with the idea to create a zany, one-of-a-kind, low-fat cookbook. Actually, we pictured it being more than just a cookbook—it would be a lifestyle guide that would bring clarity (and fun) to the confusing, intimidating, and often boring world of nutrition and dieting. "Everyone loves to eat and everyone loves to laugh," we reasoned. "Why not combine the two?" So we did. We wrapped the entire cookbook in humor—silly cartoons, corny jokes, and "punny" recipe titles like *Jurassic Pork, Miss American Thigh,* and *Chili Chili Bang Bang*—to make the normally dry subject of nutrition easier to digest. Pun intended, of course! We were sure there was nothing like it on the market, and we passionately believed that this book would make a real difference in people's lives, helping them to lose weight, feel great, and live longer.

We literally went for broke to get our beloved cookbook on store shelves. Greta had already moved into Janet's modest basement, and then,

just one month after hatching our "brilliant" plan, we decided to quit our secure full-time jobs—on the same day, no less! To fund our project, we cashed in all of our retirement savings (we didn't have much) and sold our possessions at an "everything-but-the-kitchen-sink" yard sale. We sold furniture, TVs, stereos, clothing, and unopened infomercial purchases like our Ron Popeil Pocket Fisherman, Chia Pet, and ThighMaster—basically anything that wasn't nailed down. In the heat of the moment, Janet drove her car onto the front lawn, tied balloons to the antenna, and sold it for $5,000! We went 14 months without any income while writing the book, living off proceeds from the yard sale, credit-card advances, personal loans, and the occasional bake sale or bottle drive (seriously!). We would have resorted to panhandling had Greta not needed every single one of our pans to develop recipes!

> ❝ **For motivation, we clipped the national bestseller list from the newspaper, whited out the name at the top, and typed in *Looneyspoons, by Janet and Greta Podleski.*** ❞

For motivation, we clipped the national bestseller list from the newspaper, whited out the name at the top, and typed in "*Looneyspoons,* by Janet and Greta Podleski." In bestseller fantasyland, we appeared ahead of blockbusters such as *Chicken Soup for the Soul* and *Men Are From Mars, Women Are From Venus.* We tacked that list to our office wall (right onto the yellow-painted paneling!) and stared at it day and night, visualizing ourselves as regular guests on *Oprah.* Then, on our office chalkboard (we weren't very high-tech back then), we scribbled "*Looneyspoons*: One million copies sold!" (We later discovered that 10,000 copies sold would be considered a bestseller in Canada. Oh well. Go big or go home.) To avoid the naysayers—people who would certainly discourage us by calling us "nuts" or by saying, "The last thing the world needs is another low-fat cookbook," we decided to keep the venture to ourselves. We declared it our "secret basement project."

When our bank accounts dwindled to a paltry $1.17 between the two of us, we optimistically mailed our manuscript to the largest New York publishers. It wasn't long before every single one of them bluntly turned us down. To them, we were simply two unknown "would-be" authors without a track record, without an agent, without a hope. And our work was too much of a break from tradition. "A cartoon-illustrated cookbook? You must be joking!" Actually, we *were* joking! That was the point! Jokes and food...food and jokes! But they didn't get our point and, at that time, we were $80,000 in debt, unemployed, and starting to get on each other's nerves.

Desperate, but undaunted, we solicited the help of David Chilton, author of Canada's all-time bestselling book, *The Wealthy Barber*, and host of the popular PBS television series of the same name. How we managed to woo Dave is another story in itself, but, in a nutshell, it was his cookbook-loving mother who convinced him to get involved. He dropped off sample pages of *Looneyspoons* at her house and asked her to try out a few of the recipes. After a week of cooking and taste-testing, she told Dave it was the best food she'd ever eaten! "You mean the best low-fat food?" he asked. Dave's mom replied, "No. The best food, period!" Well, that was good enough for Dave and he offered to finance our entire project right then and there. Truthfully, we think he felt sorry for us, too. We were completely broke

and Janet had by then resorted to using her credit card to pay her mortgage. Dave wrote us a personal check for $2,000 to "help us out" and told us we could repay him "someday." We never did. The three of us formed our own publishing company, Granet Publishing Inc. (we spliced our names together but somehow forgot to include Dave's. Oops!) and, thanks to Mrs. Marjorie Chilton, *Looneyspoons* officially hit bookstore shelves in September 1996.

In its first year, beyond our wildest dreams, *Looneyspoons* sold a whopping 325,000 copies, making it, according to "people in the know," one of the fastest-selling books in Canadian publishing history. Wow! The publishers who rejected us offered to "take the book off our hands." We declined, as we were having way too much fun! Since then, we've sold about 850,000 copies in Canada alone (with one-tenth of the US population!), which they say is unheard of for a self-published book. After all, we're just Janet & Greta, not Simon & Schuster! Our "secret basement project" spent 85 consecutive weeks on Canada's national bestseller list. We should know, since our mom checked the list and phoned us every single Saturday. Guess you could say we wrote a book in our basement and it became a best *cellar*!

While selling lots of books was certainly exciting (paying off our massive debts felt pretty good,

8/18/95

Dear Greta & Janet.
    Sorry, No. I'm serious about food and cook-books and low fat ones are at the moment coming over the transom, under the door, through the window. What have you got against P. NUT BUTTER? Then put it in beef stir fry?! Hope you have better luck next time. But thanks for asking
NEW YORK, NEW YORK
RP

No one wanted to publish *Looneyspoons*! We were even rejected by a literary agent, who "scolded" us for telling people the number of fat grams in a tablespoon of peanut butter! We cried for days.

too!), we can honestly say that what thrilled and motivated us more than anything was the feedback we received from readers. Thousands of letters, e-mails, and phone calls came pouring in from everywhere and everyone—men, women, busy mothers, single fathers, seniors, teenagers—all eating more healthfully and having fun doing it. "I lost 50 pounds!"; "I dropped four dress sizes!"; "My doctor can't believe how my cholesterol levels have improved!"; "My finicky kids are finally eating vegetables!"; "The food was so good, I got healthy by accident!" We would read each and every letter, and we'd literally dance around our office, high-fiving each other with excitement. (To this day, we still respond to every single e-mail. If you don't believe us, just test us!) We were really pumped to hear that our book was making a difference and impacting people's lives. Our fax machine would be humming with orders from bookstores, and we would react with, "Hey, that's great...but did you read that letter from Mrs. Sims from Chicago who said that her meat-and-potatoes husband drools over our vegetarian lasagna and lost 20 pounds by using our book? Cool!" (We'd often pick up the phone and end up chatting with people like Mrs. Sims for an hour!)

We eventually sold *Looneyspoons* into the U.S. marketplace and embarked on a whirlwind book tour: 20 cities in 30 days! It almost killed us. We lived in airports and hotels, traveled with one suitcase each, and changed cities just about every day, saving weekends for doing laundry and crying. We were exhausted, but excited. We'd often do 10 interviews in one day, five or six of them involving cooking demonstrations (poor Greta!). One highlight of our tour was making an appearance on *The 700 Club*, a popular religious show out of West Virginia. We're often asked, "Why would *The 700 Club* invite two Canadian cookbook-writing sisters to be guests on their

program?" Well, when Janet phoned the producers to ask if we could appear on their show, she mentioned that we were sisters—and we're pretty sure they thought we were nuns! Yes, *that* kind of sister! We showed up with low-fat cheesecake and stacks of cookbooks and vowed to change people's habits, though we weren't wearing them!

> " We would read each and every letter, and we'd literally dance around our office, high-fiving each other with excitement. To this day, we still respond to every single e-mail."

Within a year of the book's release, readers started asking for more. After what we'd just been through, the thought of writing another book was overwhelming, to say the least. And frankly, we were certain that we'd drained our brains on *Looneyspoons*. How could we come up with another 150 ridiculous recipe titles like *Veal of Fortune, I Yam What I Yam,* and *The Way We Stir*?

But the letters and phone calls just kept coming. And you know, when people are pouring out their hearts, taking the time and effort to write very personal, emotional letters explaining how your book has changed their lives for the better, it's pretty tough to ignore. We were spurred into action, motivated and determined to give our readers what they were asking for. Dave Chilton, our super-talented partner, great friend, and president of Granet Publishing Inc. (we made him president to make up for the whole Granet naming boo-boo) challenged us not just to match the quality and appeal of *Looneyspoons*, but to surpass it.

After accepting his challenge, we sequestered ourselves once again, this time for well over a year. Greta no longer lived in Janet's basement (thank heavens!) and we didn't have to resort to yard sales to raise money, either. Phew! The result was *Crazy Plates: Low-Fat Food So Good, You'll Swear It's Bad For You!*, published in 1999. Dave's mom, our most important critic, said everything about it was just plain better! We're very proud of that book and we still chuckle every time we read the goofy recipe titles— *Mercedes Buns, Celine Dijon Chicken,* and *Love Me Tenderloin,* to name a few.

We were blown away by the response from readers. Not only were there wonderful tales of weight loss, improved fitness, and better health, but also fans told us they were reading *Crazy Plates* when cooking was the last thing on their minds—in cars, in planes, in trains, in beds, in living rooms, in cottages, at the beach. Heck, we even had an 80-year-old man tell us that he kept *Crazy Plates* in his bathroom, he thought it was so funny! (We took it as a compliment and reminded him that that's where the fiber ends up anyway.) In its first 12 months, *Crazy Plates* sold 350,000 copies, shocking all of us by beating *Looneyspoons'* first-year sales. We even sold *Crazy Plates* on the big, U.S. shopping channel (QVC), where we spoke a mile a minute, doing our best Ivana Trump and Joan Rivers imitations. Can we talk? Yes, we can—faster than auctioneers, if we have to! Also, our book was one of the finalists for the prestigious James Beard Foundation Cookbook Awards. While that was truly an honor, nothing was more exciting than attending the fancy, shmancy awards ceremony in Times Square, where we met two of our childhood television idols: The Fonz and Jack Tripper (a.k.a. Henry Winkler and John Ritter)! Those were *Happy Days*!

All in all, we felt blessed and deeply grateful that we were able to realize our dreams. Who'da thunk that *The Leaning Tower of Pizza* and *Itsy Bitsy Teeny Weeny Colored Polka Dot Rotini* would help so many North American families to eat well and laugh their way to good health? Plus, tacked onto the wall next to our phony national bestseller list (the one with the whited-out number-one spot), we posted the real bestseller list, with our names at the very top...no liquid paper required! What a thrill!

In 2001, we made a huge leap from the publishing business to the frozen-food business with the introduction of Crazy Plates Meal Kits, based on our favorite recipes. Our meal kits were designed to help busy people eat healthfully when they don't have the time or energy to cook. Our

Our mom always made us pose with our
bowling trophies when we were little. Fast forward 30 years
and here we are again, this time with our Grand Prix Awards for our Crazy Plates Meal Kits.
(Since we eat right and exercise regularly, we could still fit into the same clothes! Well, sorta.)

slogan, "It's cooking from scratch, but we do the scratching!" struck a chord with consumers as they conveniently prepared meals like *Worth Every Penne* and a chicken stir-fry called *Stir Crazy*. At a glitzy soirée in Whistler, BC, we were stunned when our meal kits were voted "Best New Grocery Product of the Year" by the Canadian Grocery Industry. Yee-ha! We love trophies! Thank goodness we received two, otherwise Janet's mantel would still be empty.

So there! Now you're somewhat acquainted with our story. And that's important, because everything you've just read has everything to do with the book you're holding in your hands. *Eat, Shrink & Be Merry!* is the culmination of our experiences over the last 12 years. What inspired us to cook up our meatiest, juiciest, most flavorful batch of pots and puns ever? Once again, it all boiled down to passion.

In 2002, Janet decided to go back to school, studying at the Canadian School of Natural Nutrition to become a Registered Nutritionist. She did it because she truly loves the subjects of health, fitness, and nutrition. In fact, she can't get enough of them! On her bedside table, you won't find a Harlequin romance, *The Kite Runner,* or even *The Wealthy Barber.* Nope. Each night, she curls up with the likes of *The Encyclopedia of Natural Healing, Fat Wars, Healthy Fats for Life, Food and Mood,* and *Eating Alive: Prevention Thru Good Digestion.* Enough to put anyone to sleep, huh? (She does flip through the occasional *Men's Health* magazine, too. She likes the "pictures!")

Janet's experience at school was life-changing. Learning in depth about the value of eating nutrient-

From stockbroker to stock boy: *The Wealthy Barber* has his assets frozen in the grocery store thanks to our venture into the food business.

filled foods—how it affects our cells, our organs, our bodies, and ultimately, our lives—was really eye-opening. She applied new concepts to the way she ate and the way she exercised, and saw dramatic improvement in her own life. After that, she was driven—obsessed, actually—to share her recent enlightenment with everyone. Janet couldn't wait to teach our mom, sisters, and friends everything she had learned about healthy living. The seams of Janet's brain were literally bursting with excitement! (Good thing jugs of shampoo were on sale at Costco!)

Learning all the "latest and greatest" in nutrition made Janet realize, "Wow! An awful lot has changed since we wrote *Looneyspoons* back in 1996!" We're the first to admit that some of the information in our first book is a little outdated (but the recipes still rock!). Low fat isn't the main focus now, though it's still important. *Good* fats are. Eggs, nuts, and avocados are back in. Processed, refined foods (bad carbs) are out. There have been great strides and advancements in the study of weight loss, metabolism, trans fats, cholesterol, blood sugar, anti-oxidants, heart disease—you name it, researchers have discovered more about it. With so much new information out there, Janet felt compelled and obligated to bring the fans of *Looneyspoons* and *Crazy Plates* (and anyone else who would listen!) up to speed.

That's when she knew she had to call Greta. "Greta," she said. "We really *must* write another book! I'm bursting at the brain seams!" Much to Janet's surprise, Greta replied, "Funny you should say that. So am I." You see, she had just had her own epiphany of sorts.

On one of her regular grocery-store trips, Greta was approached by a male acquaintance in the bakery section and was asked her opinion about a new low-carb bread. "Yeah," Dan bragged, "I'm all over this low-carb-diet trend. Got me a case of low-carb beer and I'm just lovin' it. I used to drink six cans a week of the old stuff, but now I'm up to 12 cans and I don't even need to worry about it, since it's good for me." Yikes. He could tell by the stunned look on Greta's face that she didn't exactly approve of his new-found "health" kick. "And I got rid of the apples in my kids' lunches, too. I had no idea I was poisoning them with all those carbs!" It was more than Greta could take. Beer: good. Apples: bad. Is that what it's come to? She politely informed her friend that perhaps he was a little misguided in his approach and presented him with some simple facts about proper nutrition and the benefits of eating fruit, including the occasional Golden Delicious. She had no idea that during her 10-minute, healthy-eating soliloquy, someone was attentively eavesdropping, and that same someone just happened to be an employee of the low-carb bread company! "Geez," replied the bread salesman, "I don't mean to interrupt, but you really seem to know what you're talking about. You should write a book about that stuff to help people like me— I don't have a clue what I'm supposed to eat anymore." "Good idea," was Greta's reply.

Though 12 years had passed since our first cookbook debuted and nutrition science had advanced, some things hadn't changed at all. As Greta's "close encounter of the grocery-store kind" revealed, when it comes to health and nutrition— especially the subject of weight loss—most people are still confused and intimidated. Many don't even know where to start. There's so much conflicting information, so many fads, myths, and misconceptions, it's hard to figure out who to

believe and who to trust. What really works? How can I safely lose weight and keep it off forever? Low fat, no fat, high fat, high protein, no carb, low carb, bad carb, good carb—good grief!

We had a long talk about the low-carb craze, its pros and cons (it isn't all bad!), and the reason why diets, in general, fail. The truth is, no matter how much people say they care about their health, no matter how much someone wants to lose weight, no one wants to give up their favorite foods or sacrifice the pleasures of eating. And who can blame them? Pizza tastes better than celery sticks any day! Regardless of your goal—whether it's to lose weight, lower your cholesterol, or increase your energy levels—bland, flavorless, diet food is just not going to cut it. Not for the long haul, anyway. Whether it's low fat or low carb, great taste is a must. Are you really going to eat low-carb tortillas that taste like sawdust just because they contain only 6 grams of net carbs? Likewise, how long can you eat steak, bacon, and cheese before you're sick of them and sick *from* them?

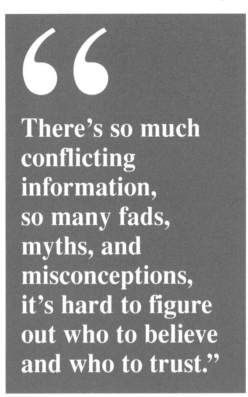

"There's so much conflicting information, so many fads, myths, and misconceptions, it's hard to figure out who to believe and who to trust."

We felt compelled to *step up to the plate* and give people the tools they need to make healthy eating both scrumptious and satisfying. Both of us desperately wanted to make sense of the fad diets that had people shunning apples and guzzling low-carb beer, clear up some of the myths and misconceptions about losing weight, make the subject of nutrition easier to understand, and most importantly, teach people how to *eat* instead of how to diet. Plus, we really needed an outlet for our endless supply of stupid jokes!

"That's it! We have to do something!" Greta announced. "Let's create the first-ever *know-carb, know-fat* cookbook!" And because she's the bossy one, that's the exact moment *Eat, Shrink & Be Merry!* was born. To say we were passionate about it would be an understatement. For the next two years (double the time we spent on either *Looneyspoons* or *Crazy Plates*), we literally lived, breathed, and slept this book. As Willy Nelson (kinda) said, "It was always on our minds."

Before writing a single word, Janet spent six months researching and compiling health and lifestyle information, aiming not only to educate readers, but also to entertain and motivate them. She asked herself, "What would I want my 74-year-old Polish mother to know so she'll be dancing to Bobby Vinton songs at the age of 100? What tips would I want to share with my sisters, Donna, Theresa, Margie and Helen, or with my best friend, Leanne? What information would improve their health, their hips, their energy levels, their quality of life?" That's the stuff we packed into this book.

Then there was the food. Greta, who Dave calls "The Rainman of Healthy Cooking," was at her obsessive-compulsive, perfectionist best, chaining herself to her stove for well over a year, painstakingly creating 150 brand-new recipes that wouldn't sacrifice taste or sabotage waists. You would have loved being one of Greta's test-kitchen dummies. She'd pull into their driveways at dinner time, delivering her culinary experiments right to their front doors. "Here comes Meals on Heels!" they'd shout with glee. Only when recipes received an enthusiastic double-thumbs-up did they qualify for entry into the cookbook. Greta shopped at one grocery store and spent nearly $10,000 on ingredients. (She accumulated so many customer-loyalty points, she'll never need to buy windshield-washer fluid again!) She vowed to stick with her original *Looneyspoons* recipe-development philosophy: "If I can't find the ingredients at my local grocery store, then I'm not putting them in the book," reasoning that people are too busy nowadays to shop at two or three different stores searching for exotic ingredients. Humbly stated, the recipes in *Eat, Shrink & Be Merry!* are Greta's best work yet! Some of our personal favorites include *Dilly Beloved* (page 90), *Chicken Littles*

(page 20), *Feast from the East* (page 40), *Turk du Soleil* (page 134), and *Girl-Guy Cookies* (page 168). All of the taste, but not on your waist—we guarantee it!

In *Eat, Shrink & Be Merry!*, you'll notice some general themes sprinkled throughout the pages. Calories count. Portion sizes matter. Dieting stinks! Making small, gradual changes to your lifestyle and eating habits is much more effective than making sweeping overhauls. Healthy eating isn't all or nothing. It's what you do consistently, over the long haul, that matters most. Do the best you can most of the time and, once in a while, treat yourself so you won't feel deprived. In fact, *make sure* you indulge every now and then! How's that for "dieting" advice? We *need* comfort foods like chocolate, pizza, cheesecake, and ice cream. Those foods are happy foods, emotional foods. They stave off irritability, depression, and anxiety. Our brains need them. They make us smile.

> "Healthy eating isn't all or nothing. It's what you do consistently, over the long haul, that matters most."

Unfortunately, the concept of "moderation, balance, and variety" sounds pretty boring to most people. It's not the latest Hollywood fad, it's not sexy enough, scientific enough, effortless enough, or fast enough. Most people are looking for that instant, don't-lift-a-finger, miracle ACME Blubber-Busting Solution that will magically obliterate fat (overnight, if possible!).

Which brings us to our next point: The truth is, if you want to lose weight, you've gotta eat less and move more. Sorry. Someone had to tell you and it might as well be us! There's no easy way around it. If a revolutionary, miraculous weight-loss potion or formula actually existed, we'd be reading about it on the front page of every newspaper, no one would be overweight, and all those Sunday morning infomercial hosts would be out of jobs (no more Blubber-Busting Solution!). No matter how you dress it up or how you label it—low carb, low fat, high protein—in the final analysis, losing weight is about burning off more than you chew. (That's why we've included motivating little tidbits called The Ex Files to encourage you to make exercise a daily habit.)

Sure, healthy living takes some discipline and commitment, but you're worth it, aren't you? If we were to achieve only one goal by writing this book, it would be to convince you that what you eat really does matter. We'd be thrilled to hear that you're taking better care of yourself and that you've made a commitment to eat more healthfully because of something we've said or written. Please feel free to contact us! We love hearing personal success stories from readers.

Since it was our dream to make *Eat, Shrink & Be Merry!* the best cookbook we could possibly write, we spent two full years on it, sacrificed our social lives, and nearly drove each other crazy. We added fabulous food photos to each chapter, plus some cool stitching to the binding so your pages won't fall out when you're making *Chicken Teriwacky* for the 500th time. We even used extra-

special, super-high-quality paper so the book would feel good in your hands. We sweated the small stuff, big time, to make this book the best it could be, hoping our efforts and our words would motivate you to become the best *you* can be.

So, now that we're finally finished babbling, what are you waiting for? *Eat, Shrink & Be Merry!*

Sincerely,

Janet & Greta

Janet & Greta
Sisters, but not nuns

Our Polish mother, Alfreda, was thrilled about our new book but confused by the title.
"Eat, Shrink & Be Married! You girls are so funny!"

Chicken Littles

Japanese rumaki: bacon-wrapped,
ginger-marinated chicken bites and water chestnuts

Someone run and tell the king, our chicken bites are the greatest thing! Who would believe that bacon-wrapped chicken morsels could be so tasty without tons of fat? They may be little, but their flavor's huge!

¼ cup reduced-sodium
  soy sauce
2 tbsp brown sugar
1 tbsp grated gingerroot
1 tsp grated orange zest
¼ tsp each ground coriander
  and curry powder
1 tsp minced garlic
2 large boneless, skinless
  chicken breasts
  (about 12 oz)
12 whole water chestnuts (canned)
12 slices bacon, cut in half crosswise
24 round wooden toothpicks

The fat is falling! The fat is falling!

- To make marinade, combine soy sauce, brown sugar, gingerroot, orange zest, coriander, curry, and garlic in a small bowl. Set aside.

- Cut chicken breasts into 24 bite-sized pieces. Cut water chestnuts in half. Combine chicken, water chestnuts, and marinade in a shallow glass baking dish (a pie plate would work) or in a large, heavy-duty, resealable plastic bag. Mix well to coat chicken and water chestnuts with marinade. Marinate in refrigerator for at least 1 hour. (You can marinate overnight for even better flavor.)

- To make rumaki, lay one half-strip of bacon on work surface. Place chicken piece in center of bacon strip and top chicken with water chestnut. Fold over ends of bacon to cover chicken and water chestnut. Secure with toothpick. Make sure toothpick pierces water chestnut, or the water chestnut will fall out (probably when you're eating it!).

- Place rumaki on a wire rack on a baking sheet. (Using a rack prevents the food from soaking in the bacon drippings.) Bake at 400°F for 20 to 25 minutes, until chicken and bacon are cooked through. Serve warm.

Makes 24 pieces

PER PIECE							
calories	total fat	saturated fat	protein	carbohydrate	fiber	cholesterol	sodium
40	1.8 g	0.6 g	4 g	1 g	0.3 g	11 mg	106 mg

Cooking TIP

If you're having a large party, you should double this recipe. Everyone goes crazy for this appetizer and there's no such thing as leftover rumaki. Each guest will eat between three and 300 of them, so make lots! When they're almost ready, you'll probably find everyone gathered around the oven, wondering what smells so good. Most traditional rumaki recipes are made with chopped chicken livers, but we prefer chicken breasts. If you like, you can substitute 24 sea scallops for the chicken breasts.

THE E FILES

For many people, the mere sight of a swimming pool triggers negative twinges (unless it's the kind with a swim-up bar!). Too cold, too wet, too much water in my ears, too hard on my hair color, etc. And that's too bad. Swimming provides a great cardiovascular workout with none of the joint-jarring effects of running. Take the plunge and you'll burn roughly the same number of calories per minute as you would biking, without having to dodge cars and swallow bugs. Plus, swimming zeroes in on your core muscles, which means you could end up with a super-sculpted back and six-pack abs. Talk about skinny dipping! For an even better workout, try running in the pool. It's a lot tougher than it looks, and it's not just for seniors and patients in surgery rehab, either. Lots of professional athletes do it—basketball and hockey players, Olympic skaters, and even dancers. Sure makes you want to *tread* water, not *dread* it!

A woman is like a tea bag—only in hot water do you realize how strong she really is.

Eleanor Roosevelt

HEY, HEY...WE'RE THE MUNCHIES!

Hello, My Name is Betty and I'm Dehydrated

Do you have a drinking problem? Well, if you're serious about losing fat, you really *should* get sloshed. What's on tap? Water! If you're not downing 8 to 10 glasses of water per day, you could be dampening your weight-loss efforts. Without water, your body can't metabolize stored fat efficiently. In fact, even mild dehydration can slow your metabolism by 3%. If you weigh 150 pounds, that's 45 fewer calories burned each day, and over the course of a year, that 45 calories can amount to five pounds of stubborn fat strapped to your middle. Bartender! Gimme a double shot of H2O—on the rocks! Water is the ultimate liquid asset, making up more than 50% of our bodies. It regulates body temperature, keeps blood volume up, carries nutrients and oxygen to the cells, promotes proper digestion, tones muscles, and gets rid of toxins. Imagine! Drink like a fish and detox at the same time! Plus, water is energizing, and that makes you want to move. When you're dehydrated, you feel sluggish and tired, which usually sends you crawling to the cookie jar. A water shortage makes the body cling to every last drop, and that shows up as swollen feet, legs, hands, and eyelids, inflating your weight by as much as 5 to 15 pounds! Ironically, you should drink more water, not less, to beat the bloat. So sneak in some extra H2O whenever you can. Drink socially! Drink alone! Drink heavily! Join a 12-sip program!

I'm on a low-carb diet. Whenever I feel low, I eat carbs!

Bewedged

Baked whole wheat pita wedges with Parmesan and rosemary

Darrin to be different in the appetizer department? Concocting a spellbinding snack is as easy as wiggling your nose and sprinkling on some rose (mary, that is).

1 ½ tbsp dried rosemary
⅔ cup grated Parmesan cheese
3 6-inch whole wheat, flax, or multigrain pita rounds (with pockets)
1 tbsp olive oil
1 tbsp butter, melted
¼ tsp each garlic powder and onion powder

- Preheat oven to 350°F.

- Crush the dried rosemary with your fingers and combine it with the Parmesan cheese in a small bowl. Set aside.

- Using a sharp knife or kitchen scissors, cut each pita round into 6 equal wedges. Peel back the layers and cut each wedge again, so you end up with 12 wedges from each pita (36 wedges total).

- Place the wedges, rough side up, on a large baking sheet. Do not overlap wedges. (You will need to cook 2 separate batches.)

- In another small bowl, combine olive oil, melted butter, garlic powder, and onion powder. Using a pastry brush, lightly brush mixture onto rough side of wedges. Sprinkle with Parmesan-rosemary mixture.

- Bake on middle oven rack for 10 to 14 minutes. Important: Keep an eye on them so they don't burn! One minute they may look pale, and the next minute they could be black so don't wander away from the kitchen for too long. They should be lightly browned. Cool on a wire rack before serving.

Tip: You can substitute Asiago or Romano cheese for Parmesan.

Makes 36 wedges

			PER WEDGE				
calories	total fat	saturated fat	protein	carbohydrate	fiber	cholesterol	sodium
29	1.4 g	0.6 g	1 g	3 g	0.5 g	2 mg	51 mg

Yummus

Our version of traditional chickpea hummus gets rave reviews

You're the chick for me!

This is no ho-hum hummus! It's a real humdinger— the yummiest of the yummies— and it only takes a couple of minutes to prepare. *Yummust* try it!

1 can (15.5 oz) chickpeas, drained and rinsed
¼ cup light sour cream
2 tbsp tahini (sesame seed paste)
2 tbsp freshly squeezed lemon juice
1 tbsp olive oil
2 tsp minced garlic
1 tsp grated lemon zest
1 tsp honey
½ tsp salt
⅛ tsp each ground cumin and ground coriander
Pinch freshly ground black pepper

- Place all ingredients in the bowl of a food processor and whirl until smooth. Serve with warmed whole wheat pita wedges or crisp vegetables for dunking (or both!).

Makes about 1¾ cups

PER SERVING (¼ CUP)

calories	total fat	saturated fat	protein	carbohydrate	fiber	cholesterol	sodium
122	5 g	0.7 g	4 g	16 g	3 g	1 mg	247 mg

Cooking TIP

The sour cream is an unusual addition to traditional Middle Eastern hummus, but it adds back the creaminess that would otherwise be lost when the amount of high-fat tahini is reduced. (Traditional hummus recipes use up to ½ cup tahini.) To keep the carb count down, try surrounding the bowl of hummus with a colorful arrangement of thickly sliced bell pepper strips in every color you can find: red, yellow, orange, and green!

Ask Janet

What causes a beer belly?

The obvious answer would be too many brewskies, but it actually has more to do with hormonal imbalances and with the most overworked and underappreciated organ in the body—the liver. Like Rodney Dangerfield, the liver gets no respect. And that's a shame. While you kick back with a six-pack, your liver is busy processing an astounding 182 pints of blood every hour, filtering toxins, producing bile to break down fats, and disposing of excess hormones and cholesterol. But your liver isn't bulletproof. Pummel it each day with junk food, pharmaceutical drugs, caffeine, artificial sweeteners, and alcohol, and the poor thing becomes congested, fatty, and generally dis-*organ*-ized. When that happens, it drops the ball on some of its jobs, one of them being fat metabolism. In addition, excess hormones aren't flushed from the body properly, leading to a whole slew of complications, including the protruding, rock-hard, about-to-give-birth-to-twins type of beer gut. You see, when hormones are out of whack, yeast (candida) that's already in the intestinal tract tends to rise to the occasion, multiplying, thriving, and eventually driving your waistband outward. Did you know that your colon can expand up to five times its size in order to house flourishing yeast colonies? Yowch! The fact that beer actually contains yeast doesn't exactly help the overpopulation crisis, either. As you can see, a growing gut will be the *yeast* of your worries unless you treat your liver with respect. Shower it with things it loves: lemons, onions, garlic, eggs, cruciferous vegetables like broccoli and cauliflower, leafy greens, and lots of water. And go easy on the toxic stuff. To nip your beer belly in the bud, limit the crud!

The hostess must be like the duck— calm and unruffled on the surface, and paddling like hell underneath.

Anonymous

Go Ahead—Havacado!

Avocado, the fruit formerly known as full o' fat, has had its case reopened and reexamined, and is making a healthy comeback. Turns out the experts now give the "butter pear" triple-thumbs-up for its nutritional benefits. Yes, avocados are high in fat—about 30 grams in each, to be exact—but it's mostly the good, monounsaturated kind that helps our tickers keep on tickin'. Avocados are an excellent source of another heart helper, the B vitamin folate, which helps reduce your risk of heart disease. Plus, they're rich in phytosterols, which lower cholesterol, and they're a good source of potassium, which is helpful in lowering high blood pressure. No wonder health experts are singing the praises of this saintly, do-gooder. Holy guacamole!

S.O.S. pads, the pre-soaped scrubbers used to clean pots, were invented in 1917.

S.O.S. stands for...

a) Soapy Oven Scrapers
b) Suds Or Salmonella
c) Stinky Odor Stoppers
d) Save Our Saucepans

Answer: (d) Ed Cox from San Francisco created S.O.S. pads during the First World War and his wife came up with the clever name.

Honey, why are you staring at that can of orange juice?

'Cause it says 'concentrate'

The Big Dipper

Tasty and addictive layered shrimp dip

We didn't want this popular layered party dip to be *meteorcre*, so we added some chopped shrimp. Now it's a real star—the best dip in the universe! Forget about the lousy *constellation* prize. Our scrumptious shrimp dip is an astronomic gastronomic winner!

1 tub (8 oz) light garden vegetable spreadable cream cheese (such as Philadelphia)
2 cups light sour cream
1½ cups chunky-style salsa (mild, medium, or hot)
1 cup packed shredded light medium cheddar cheese (4 oz)
1 cup chopped romaine hearts or crunchy lettuce
1½ cups coarsely chopped cooked large shrimp (about 8 oz)
½ cup diced tomatoes
⅓ cup chopped green onions
¼ cup chopped pitted black olives (optional)

- Beat together cream cheese and sour cream on medium speed of electric mixer until smooth. Spread mixture evenly over bottom of a serving platter. (You could use a glass lasagna dish if you don't have a fancy platter.)

- Spoon salsa over sour cream layer and spread to edges, leaving a ½-inch border. Top salsa with shredded cheese, then chopped lettuce, followed by shrimp. Sprinkle tomatoes, green onions, and black olives (if using) over shrimp.

- Cover loosely with plastic wrap and refrigerate for at least 1 hour before serving. Serve with baked tortilla chips or with thick slices of colorful bell peppers and cucumber rounds if you're watching your carbohydrate intake. Multigrain melba toast rounds are also a tasty, crunchy accompaniment.

Tip: Choose a thick sour cream for this dip, so the bottom layer will better support the other ingredients. If the salsa is too runny, you may want to drain some of the liquid before spreading it over the sour cream layer. Use large shrimp for this recipe, even though you're chopping them—they'll look much nicer and more impressive than if you use teensy, weensy shrimp.

Makes 12 servings

PER SERVING

calories	total fat	saturated fat	protein	carbohydrate	fiber	cholesterol	sodium
142	5.8 g	3.4 g	12 g	8 g	0.8 g	59 mg	473 mg

HEY, HEY...WE'RE THE MUNCHIES!

Hokey Smokey Salmon

Impressive (but easy!) layered smoked salmon and cream cheese torta

♫ You put your left fin in...

You put the light cheese in,
You leave the fat cheese out,
You put the fresh dill in,
And you spread it all about,
You add the hokey smokey,
And you turn it upside down,
That's what it's all about!

**1 pkg (8 oz) light cream cheese
(at room temperature)**
**1 tub (8 oz) light garden vegetable spreadable
cream cheese (such as Philadelphia)**
1 cup light ricotta cheese
2 tbsp hot or mild seafood cocktail sauce
Grated zest of 1 lemon
8 oz smoked salmon
1 bunch fresh dill sprigs
Cheesecloth for lining pan (see tip below)
Sliced lemon twists for garnish (optional)

- Beat together both cream cheeses, ricotta cheese, cocktail sauce, and lemon zest on high speed of electric mixer until smooth. Set aside.

- Place a dampened piece of cheesecloth in an 8 x 4-inch loaf pan, extending cloth over edges of pan. Layer half the salmon in bottom of pan, right to edge and completely covering bottom. Cover salmon with some of the dill sprigs. Spoon half the cheese mixture evenly over dill and spread to edges. (Hint: It's easiest if you spoon lots of small blobs in the pan, then spread them with the back of a warm spoon.) Repeat layering: salmon, dill sprigs, cheese mixture. Fold cheesecloth over filling, cover pan with plastic wrap, and refrigerate for at least 8 hours or overnight.

- To serve, unfold cheesecloth and place a small serving platter over loaf pan. Invert torta onto serving platter and gently remove cloth. Garnish with more fresh dill sprigs and lemon twists, if desired. Serve with multigrain crackers or multigrain melba toast rounds.

Tip: Cheesecloth is a lightweight, natural cotton cloth with a fine weave that won't fall apart when wet and won't flavor food it touches. It's cheap and most well-stocked grocery stores sell it in small bags, usually in the housewares or cookware section.

Makes 24 servings

PER SERVING (3 TBSP)

calories	total fat	saturated fat	protein	carbohydrate	fiber	cholesterol	sodium
72	4.4 g	2.6 g	4 g	2 g	0 g	20 mg	242 mg

"SAY IT AIN'T SO!"

Look out Sister, look out Jack, you've got pop-o-matic trouble! Back when we were kids, a family-sized bottle of Coke lasted Mom, Dad, Sis, and Junior from one week's grocery run to the next. Nowadays, a "single serving" Double Gulp at 7-Eleven convenience stores is packed with an unthinkable, sugar-filled 64 ounces! That's eight cups of pop—the same amount found in that family-sized bottle of days gone by. Gulp! If you don't want to double your pant size, try giving your waistline (and your bladder) a break and settle for the 12-ounce "kiddie" size. Or better yet, drink a bottle o' water instead of that pail o' pop. With all those empty calories and enough sugar to sweeten a three-tiered wedding cake, drinking a bucket of pop can make you turn *pail*!

Funky Factoid

Did you know that a person who's lost in the woods and starving can obtain nourishment by chewing on his shoes? It's true! Leather has enough nutritional value to sustain life for a short time. And you thought putting your foot in your mouth was a *bad* thing! It's also why people with really small feet should always carry a compass.

You're the spitting image of your father!

Crash Test Dumplings

Chicken-stuffed, steamed wontons with a
sesame-ginger dipping sauce

We're no *dummies*...we know you love Chinese food but appreciate healthier renditions, like these dumplings that are steamed and not fried. It's not like we created these by *accident*, though. Many thoughts *collided* to make this recipe *smashingly* good.

Filling

8 oz extra-lean ground chicken

¼ cup each minced red bell pepper, minced green onions, and finely diced water chestnuts

1 tbsp minced fresh cilantro

1 tbsp cornstarch

2 tsp reduced-sodium soy sauce

2 tsp toasted sesame oil

1 tsp grated gingerroot

1 tsp granulated sugar

1 tsp minced garlic

¼ tsp salt

Dipping Sauce

½ cup chicken broth

2 tbsp each reduced-sodium soy sauce, brown sugar, and freshly squeezed lemon juice

2 tsp each grated gingerroot, toasted sesame oil, and cornstarch

¼ tsp crushed red pepper flakes

24 to 28 square wonton wrappers (3½ x 3½ inch—see tip below)

- Combine all filling ingredients in a medium bowl and mix well. Cover and refrigerate while you make the dipping sauce.

- Whisk together chicken broth, soy sauce, brown sugar, lemon juice, gingerroot, sesame oil, cornstarch, and crushed red pepper flakes in a small saucepan. Heat over high heat, whisking constantly, until sauce comes to a boil and thickens. Remove from heat.

- To make dumplings, lay one wonton wrapper at a time on work surface with one of the pointed ends toward you so it looks like a diamond. Spoon 1 tsp or so of filling in middle of wrapper and shape it into a tiny log about 1½ inches long. Fold bottom edge up over filling, fold in sides, and roll up tightly like a cigar. Moisten edge with water and press to seal. Repeat with remaining wrappers and filling. Place filled wontons on a plate and cover with a damp tea towel to prevent them from drying out. This part is a little fiddly and time-consuming, but once you get the hang of it, it's pretty easy.

- To cook dumplings, add 1 inch of water to a large pot and insert a metal steamer basket. Spray steamer basket lightly with cooking spray. Bring water to a boil. Place half the dumplings in the basket in a single layer (don't burn yourself!). Cover with a tight-fitting lid and steam for 6 minutes, until meat is cooked through. Remove dumplings and keep warm. Repeat with remaining dumplings, adding a bit more water if necessary. Serve warm dumplings with dipping sauce.

Makes 24 to 28 dumplings and 1 cup dipping sauce

PER SERVING (1 DUMPLING & 2 TSP SAUCE)							
calories	total fat	saturated fat	protein	carbohydrate	fiber	cholesterol	sodium
52	1.5 g	0.3 g	2 g	7 g	0.3 g	7 mg	121 mg

Cooking **TIP**

Wontons, pot stickers, and dumplings are Chinese specialties consisting of paper-thin dough wrappers (sometimes called wonton skins) that are stuffed with ground or minced meat and vegetables, then steamed, boiled, or fried and served as an appetizer or side dish with a dipping sauce. Look for wonton wrappers in small packages in the produce department of your grocery store.

Chic to be Greek Dip

Lemon-dill white-bean hummus topped with chopped veggies and feta cheese

Opa! We hopa you like our fancy layered Greek dip. It's chic and sleek!

White-Bean Hummus

1 can (15.5 oz) white kidney beans (cannellini), drained and rinsed
¼ cup light sour cream
2 tbsp freshly squeezed lemon juice
2 tbsp tahini (sesame seed paste)
1 tbsp minced fresh dill
1 tsp minced garlic
1 tsp liquid honey
1 tsp grated lemon zest
¼ tsp salt
Pinch black pepper

½ cup diced tomatoes
½ cup seeded and diced English cucumber
⅓ cup chopped green onions
¼ cup crumbled basil-and-tomato feta cheese (1 oz)
2 tbsp chopped black olives

- To make hummus, place all hummus ingredients in the bowl of a food processor and whirl until smooth.

- Spread bean mixture evenly over bottom of an 8- or 9-inch casserole dish or pie plate. Top with tomatoes, cucumber, green onions, feta cheese, and black olives. Cover with plastic wrap and refrigerate for at least 1 hour before serving. Serve with baked pita wedges (page 21) or homemade baked tortilla chips (see recipe in margin).

Makes 10 servings

PER SERVING (⅓ CUP)

calories	total fat	saturated fat	protein	carbohydrate	fiber	cholesterol	sodium
91	3.5 g	0.3 g	4 g	11 g	2.8 g	4 mg	240 mg

To make baked tortilla chips, preheat oven to 350°F. Cut six 6-inch, whole wheat flour tortillas into 6 wedges each (for a total of 36 wedges). In a small bowl, mix together 1 tbsp olive oil, 1 tbsp melted butter, 1 tsp dried Italian seasoning, and ¼ tsp each garlic powder and onion powder. Arrange tortilla wedges in a single layer on a cookie sheet (you will need to make a couple batches). Using a pastry brush, lightly brush tortillas with olive oil-herb mixture. Bake for 10 minutes, until golden brown and crispy. Cool before serving.

RETURN TO SLENDER

Polishing off your plate is a good idea, but only if you're doing the dishes! According to a 2004 survey, 27% of North Americans said they finish their entire meal, no matter what the size. In 2000, the figure was 20%. Obviously, our *figures* are growing. Remember, just because a restaurant or your mother-in-law throws 4,325 calories in front of you doesn't mean you have to eat *all* of them. So, when you start feeling full, exercise restraint. Or, better yet, try this exercise: Push your chair away from the table. If you're serious about changing your eating habits for better health or to shed a few pounds, this little rule can make a big difference: Stop eating when you're full and never eat when you aren't hungry. Go on and try it—it's better than a diet!

If you get a gift basket from your psychiatrist, chances are it will be shrink-wrapped.

This should help you live in the present.

Tartlett O'Hara

Warm mini crab and cheese tartlets

These scrumptious tartlets will play a *starring* role on your appetizer table. So tasty, they'll be *Gone with the Wind*!

These will Rhett your appetite.

1 tsp butter
1 cup finely chopped mushrooms
1/3 cup minced shallots or onions
1 tsp minced garlic
1 can (4 oz) lump crabmeat, drained
1/2 cup packed shredded light old (sharp) cheddar cheese (2 oz)
1/4 cup grated Parmesan cheese
3 tbsp light cream cheese
1 tbsp freshly squeezed lemon juice
1 tbsp chopped fresh parsley
1 tsp Dijon mustard
1/4 tsp each salt and freshly ground black pepper
1 can (8 oz) Pillsbury Crescent Rolls

- Preheat oven to 375°F. Spray two 12-cup mini muffin pans with cooking spray and set aside.

- To make filling, heat butter in a small, non-stick skillet over medium heat. Add mushrooms, shallots, and garlic. Cook and stir until vegetables are tender, about 4 minutes. Remove from heat and let cool slightly. When cooled, combine mushroom mixture with remaining ingredients, except crescent rolls, in a medium bowl. Mix well.

- Unwrap crescent rolls and lay entire rectangular "sheet" on a lightly floured surface to prevent sticking. Do not separate dough at perforations. Instead, pinch together perforations with your fingers. Using a very sharp knife, cut the rectangle into 24 perfect squares by first cutting the dough into 6 equal, short strips, then into 4 equal, long strips. Place dough squares into mini muffin cups. The 4 points of each square will be sticking up—perfect! Fill each cup with crab mixture. Bake for 12 to 14 minutes, until dough is puffed up and golden around the edges. Let tarts cool for a few minutes before serving. They're hot!

Makes 24 tartlets

			PER TARTLET				
calories	total fat	saturated fat	protein	carbohydrate	fiber	cholesterol	sodium
54	2.8 g	1.2 g	3 g	4 g	0.2 g	10 mg	159 mg

Low-carb products can make you gain weight.

Fat or Fiction?

Just like the fat-free craze of yesterday, today's obsession with low-carb products has people overindulging—and bulging! But the "low carb" claim on food packaging is not your license to fill. Low fat, and now, low carb, doesn't necessarily mean low calorie, and in the big, fat scheme of things, it's excess calories that make or break your waistline. As far as low-carb products go, not only do they carry a heftier price tag than standard fare, but also some have higher fat and calorie counts, depending on how they've been doctored up to reduce the carbs. Many products aren't much lower in carbs than their original versions, either. For example, low-carb peanut butter has 5 grams of carbs per serving. Regular peanut butter has 7 grams. Worth the extra cash? *Nut* really. Low-carb products can be valuable if they help you reduce calories, because that's what it takes to lose weight. But if you end up eating low-carb chips and candy bars instead of fruits and vegetables, you're not doing your hips or your health any favors. Yes, there are some nutritious, low-carb products on store shelves. And boosting the protein and fiber content in products like bread, for instance, is a boon to weight loss and overall health. But don't go out of your way to buy packaged, processed low-carb foods thinking they're the magic bullet to weight loss. They aren't. And please don't eat them with reckless abandon, the way we used to eat fat-free cookies (remember those days?). When given the choice, you're almost always better off eating a natural food (like fruit, nuts, or a salad) than you are choosing processed, refined foods with additives, preservatives, and artificial sweeteners (like energy bars). Make smarter choices and your weight-loss efforts won't collapse like a house of *carbs*!

If Aunt Jemima wrote a cookbook would it sell like hotcakes?

Funky Factoid

Seems like getting married is *knot tied* to keeping slim: In a 10-year study, men who married gained about 11 pounds. Those who stayed single during the same period gained just five pounds. Wedded bliss hit women's waistlines even harder: The single women in the study gained about six pounds while those who married gained a whopping 14. Holy *Fat*rimony!

All Choked Up

An edible thistle that was prized by the Romans as food of nobility, the artichoke is as nutritious as it is delicious. *Choke*-full of fiber, vitamin C, folate, and a gold mine of minerals, the healing qualities of the artichoke were well-recognized in ancient times, when it was used as an aphrodisiac, diuretic, breath freshener, and even as a deodorant. Today, natural practitioners recommend artichokes for lowering cholesterol and stabilizing blood sugar. Plus, recent research shows that an active compound in artichoke, called silymarin, is a powerful antioxidant and may help regenerate the liver. After a few too many margaritas, *thistle* really help you! What won't help you, or those around you, is undercooking artichokes, especially Jerusalem artichokes. That can cause flatulence, or as Englishman John Goodyer wrote in 1617, they "...can cause a filthy, loathsome, stinking wind within the body." Oh, those artsy, fartsy culinary writers!

Doctor, my husband thinks he's a stick of margarine!

Don't worry. I'll make him butter.

The Choke's On You

Hot baked artichoke dip topped with crumbled bacon

Ha! Ha! Fooled ya! Betcha thought a dip made with artichokes couldn't be so delicious, but our dreamy dip is loaded with good stuff and stands up to the taste test. And that's no *choke!*

- **1 can (15.5 oz) white kidney beans (cannellini), drained and rinsed**
- **1 tbsp freshly squeezed lemon juice**
- **1 can (14 oz) artichoke hearts (not marinated), drained and chopped**
- **1 cup packed shredded light Swiss or Monterey Jack cheese (4 oz)**
- **½ cup grated Parmesan cheese**
- **½ cup light sour cream**
- **⅓ cup light mayonnaise or Miracle Whip**
- **2 tsp minced garlic**
- **1 tsp Worcestershire sauce**
- **3 to 4 dashes hot pepper sauce**
- **¼ tsp freshly ground black pepper**
- **4 slices bacon, cooked and crumbled**
- **2 tbsp chopped green onions**

- Preheat oven to 350°F.

- Purée white beans and lemon juice in the bowl of a food processor until smooth. Transfer mixture to a medium bowl and stir in remaining ingredients, except bacon and green onions. Mix well.

- Spoon artichoke-bean mixture into a medium casserole dish that has been sprayed with cooking spray. Sprinkle crumbled bacon and green onions over top. Bake, uncovered, for about 25 minutes, until dip is hot and bubbly. Let cool slightly before serving, as mixture will be very hot. Serve with baked pita wedges (page 21), warm, unbaked pita triangles, or multigrain melba toast rounds.

Makes 4 cups

PER SERVING (⅓ CUP)

calories	total fat	saturated fat	protein	carbohydrate	fiber	cholesterol	sodium
121	5.9 g	2.8 g	8 g	10 g	2.6 g	14 mg	362 mg

HEY, HEY...WE'RE THE MUNCHIES!

Lord of the Wings

Boneless, skinless chicken "wings" in a gooey, yummy sauce

They're the wings that everyone's *Tolkien* about! They sure are *hobbit*-forming. No bones about it!

12 large boneless, skinless chicken thighs (about 2½ lbs)
⅓ cup your favorite barbecue sauce
2 tbsp reduced-sodium soy sauce
2 tbsp Dijon mustard
2 tbsp liquid honey (see tip below)
2 tbsp freshly squeezed lemon or lime juice
2 tsp minced garlic
1 tsp chili powder
4 to 5 dashes hot pepper sauce (optional)
1 tsp cornstarch

- Preheat oven to 400°F. Spray a 9 x 13-inch baking pan with cooking spray and set aside.

- Trim any visible fat from chicken thighs. Cut each thigh in half and place cut pieces in a single layer in prepared baking pan. Fold or roll them up a bit so they resemble the shape of a chicken wing. They should just fit in pan (3 rows of 8 "wings").

- Whisk together barbecue sauce, soy sauce, mustard, honey, lemon juice, garlic, chili powder, and hot pepper sauce (if using) in a small bowl. Spoon sauce evenly over chicken pieces.

- Bake, uncovered, for 35 to 40 minutes, until chicken is cooked through and sauce is bubbly. Arrange chicken on a serving platter and keep warm. Pour sauce from pan into a small pot. Combine cornstarch with 2 tsp water and mix until smooth. Stir cornstarch mixture into sauce. Bring to a boil and whisk constantly until mixture has thickened (it won't take long). Serve "wings" with extra sauce for dipping.

Tip: If you're using a barbecue sauce that already has honey in it or a sauce that's quite sweet, you may want to reduce the honey in this recipe from 2 tbsp to 1 tbsp.

Makes 24 "wings"

PER SERVING (1 WING WITH 1 TSP SAUCE)

calories	total fat	saturated fat	protein	carbohydrate	fiber	cholesterol	sodium
56	1.7 g	0.4 g	7 g	2 g	0.1 g	31 mg	114 mg

(Note: If you skip the extra dipping sauce, the carb count is reduced to about 1.3 g and the sodium drops to about 75 mg)

Think exercise can't possibly burn off enough calories to nix the six Oreos you had for breakfast? Some people mistakenly believe that exercise is not worth the effort because of the relatively small number of calories it burns. Think again! The numbers on a treadmill's or stairstepper's electronic readout can be discouraging and misleading. You may have only burned 160 of the Oreos' 320 calories during your workout, but the calorie burning doesn't stop when your legs do. One of the great secrets behind vigorous exercise is its "residual effect": it boosts your metabolic rate so you can burn calories for hours after your workout. How's that happen? Well, when you jog or lift weights, you break down a large number of muscle fibers. These broken fibers have to be repaired (that's how you build and grow muscle) and all this rebuilding takes energy (calories!). You also have to replace the glycogen (muscle fuel) that was used up during exercise—again, more energy required! So, when all is said and done, you haven't burned just 160 calories, you've burned 250, 300, maybe even 375 calories! In fact, one study showed that more than two-thirds of fat-burning activity takes place *after* the actual exercise session. That phenomenon is technically known as PECBO (post-exercise calorie burn-off). Actually, Greta just made up that term!

Gimme all the cashew have!

Dunk 'n' GoNuts!

A trio of simple dips for slim dunking

Dip, dip hooray! These skinny dips won't end up on your hips. And when you start dippin', your taste buds'll be flippin'!

Quickie Nacho Dip
2 cups light sour cream
4 oz light cream cheese, softened
¼ cup light Miracle Whip
1 envelope (1.4 oz) Knorr vegetable soup mix
1 cup chunky-style medium salsa

- Beat together all ingredients using medium speed of electric mixer. Refrigerate for 2 hours before serving. Serve with baked nacho chips. Option: Spread dip in a casserole dish or on a fancy platter. Top with shredded light cheddar cheese, chopped green onions, chopped tomatoes, and chopped olives.

Makes about 4 cups

PER SERVING (¼ CUP)
calories	total fat	saturated fat	protein
60	2.7 g	1.3 g	3 g
carbohydrate	fiber	cholesterol	sodium
6 g	0.5 g	8 mg	299 mg

The Tastiest Shrimp Cocktail Sauce
¾ cup tomato-based chili sauce (such as Heinz)
¼ cup prepared horseradish
1 tbsp freshly squeezed lemon juice
1 tsp grated lemon zest
1 tsp granulated sugar
½ tsp Worcestershire sauce

- Combine all ingredients in a medium bowl. Mix well. Refrigerate until ready to serve. Sauce may be stored for up to 2 weeks in the fridge. If you like *hot* cocktail sauce, add a bit more horseradish or a few drops of hot pepper sauce.

Makes 1 cup

PER SERVING (1 TBSP)
calories	total fat	saturated fat	protein
15	0 g	0 g	0 g
carbohydrate	fiber	cholesterol	sodium
4 g	0.3 g	0 mg	173 mg

Holy Guacamole!
2 medium avocados, halved, seeded, and diced (see tip below)
2 tbsp freshly squeezed lemon or lime juice
½ cup minced red onions
½ cup diced tomatoes
1 tbsp minced fresh cilantro
1 to 2 tsp minced garlic
1 jalapeño pepper, seeded and minced, or a couple shakes of hot pepper sauce

- Combine all ingredients in a medium bowl. Cover and refrigerate until serving time. Guacamole will keep for about 3 days in the fridge.

Makes about 2½ cups

PER SERVING (2 TBSP)
calories	total fat	saturated fat	protein
55	4.7 g	0.7 g	1 g
carbohydrate	fiber	cholesterol	sodium
4 g	1.8 g	0 mg	62 mg

Cooking TIP

Unlike many other fruits, avocados don't ripen on the tree. They must be picked before the ripening process can start. For guacamole, choose avocados that yield to gentle pressure. Unripe avocados make horrible guacamole! To speed the ripening process, place avocados in a paper bag with a ripe apple or ripe banana. Store at room temperature and check daily to see if the fruit has softened. To seed an avocado, cut the avocado in half lengthwise and wiggle both halves to separate them. Tap the big seed with a sharp knife and when the blade catches, rotate the knife and lift out the seed. Scoop out the flesh using a small spoon. Dice or mash as directed in the recipe.

Havin' a Ball

Creamy salmon ball rolled in chopped nuts and parsley

*Gill*friends coming over for dinner? You can't strike out with *this* ball. Our easy salmon appetizer is always an *o-mega* hit!

- **2 cans (6 oz each) skinless salmon, drained and flaked**
- **1 pkg (8 oz) light cream cheese (see tip below)**
- **2 tbsp finely minced onions or shallots**
- **1 tbsp freshly squeezed lemon juice**
- **1 tsp prepared horseradish or cocktail sauce**
- **½ tsp salt**
- **¼ tsp freshly ground black pepper**
- **¼ cup finely chopped walnuts or pecans**
- **¼ cup finely minced fresh parsley**

- Mix together salmon, cream cheese, onions, lemon juice, horseradish, salt, and pepper in a medium bowl. You can use an electric mixer if it's easier. Cover salmon mixture and refrigerate for 1 hour so it firms up a little bit.

- Meanwhile, mix together nuts and parsley in a shallow bowl or pie plate. Remove salmon from fridge and form mixture into a ball (using your hands works best, even though it's a little messy). Roll in nut-parsley mixture so outside of ball is completely coated. Cover with plastic wrap and refrigerate for at least 4 hours.

- To serve, place ball on a small platter and surround with multigrain crackers or melba rounds, thick red bell pepper strips, and thick cucumber slices.

Tip: For this recipe, buy cream cheese in a brick, not in a tub. The spreadable cream cheese (tub) is too soft to hold its shape when you roll the mixture into a ball. However, if you want to make a salmon spread instead of a ball, then the softer cream cheese is just fine.

Makes one 2-cup ball

PER SERVING (2 TBSP)

calories	total fat	saturated fat	protein	carbohydrate	fiber	cholesterol	sodium
74	5 g	2.3 g	6 g	1 g	0.2 g	22 mg	195 mg

You should take up drinking red wine for its health benefits.

Fat or Fiction?

If media reports about the health benefits of red wine are driving you to drink, you should know that not everything about de*wine* is de*vine*. Yes, there's plenty of research praising the nectar of the Gods' antioxidant properties. The perceived health blessings revolve around a plant chemical called resveratrol, found in grape skins and seeds. When scientists saw promise for resveratrol in preventing heart disease and cancer in animal studies, Merlot mania was uncorked. Before having *grape* expectations, don't forget the damage that alcohol and its empty calories can cause. Booze, whether in beer, vodka, or wine, raises blood sugar, spurs appetite, and slows fat burning. If you're trying to lose weight, better go on a *low-cab(ernet)* diet! Because alcohol in any form is tough on the liver, and even moderate amounts have been linked to breast and colon cancers, bone loss, and other health problems, medical experts suggest if you sip on Shiraz, make it one drink per day for women and two drinks per day for men, max. Fortunately, there are plenty of other, less risky ways to give your heart a boost: Eat garlic, fish, and olive oil; curb the junk food; quit smoking; hug your kids; pet your dog; stop and smell the roses; be kind to strangers; give to a charity—none of which will leave you with a hangover!

"SAY IT AIN'T SO!"

Just a spoonful of sugar helps the medicine go down? Think again, Sugar. If you're in the habit of *merrily poppin'* sweet nothings in your mouth, you might find yourself needing medical attention too often. Studies have shown that eating too much white sugar and other sweets can, in effect, "paralyze" the white blood cells of the immune system for half an hour or more, making you more susceptible to disease. Better practice moderation, since *sugarcalafragilisticmakesyourcellsatrocious*!

HEY, HEY...WE'RE THE MUNCHIES!

Deviled eggs aren't exactly the fanciest hors d'oeuvres going, but they're always gobbled up ahead of the ritzy appetizers at family gatherings. Because of their health properties (see page 83), try using omega-3 eggs when you make this recipe. For perfectly hard-boiled eggs, place the eggs in a single layer in a large saucepan, then add cold water to cover eggs by 1 inch. Bring to a boil over high heat. Remove the saucepan immediately from the heat, cover, and let eggs stand for 15 minutes. Using a slotted spoon, transfer eggs to a "bath" of ice cold water. Let them sit in cold water for 5 minutes before peeling.

RETURN TO SLENDER

Burn the midnight oil and you'll likely run out of gas—and get fat! Ever notice you're a lot hungrier on days when you haven't had enough sleep? That's because your body's crying out for more energy. As your energy plummets, so does your mood, and that's a prime-time trigger for bingeing on sugar-loaded snacks. Most importantly, it's during deep sleep that feel-good brain chemicals like serotonin are replenished. But when you're sleep-deprived, your body tries boosting serotonin by making you crave sugary and starchy carbohydrates. Need another reason to replace the late-night news with more snooze? Chronic sleep deprivation is a major stressor on the body. Your body instinctively perceives lack of sleep as a legitimate threat to its well-being and it reacts by raising levels of stress hormones like cortisol. When lack of quality shut-eye becomes chronic, the extra cortisol can cause our bodies to store fat—and it's usually around the gut. So, if you're losing sight of your belly button, try hitting the snooze button!

Why did the cooks play poker? Because they wanted to win some pots.

Deviled in Disguise

Not-so-traditional deviled eggs, flavored with smoked salmon and dill

We took plain ol' deviled eggs and transformed them into a heavenly, *sinsational* treat. They're a *helluva* lot better than the boring deviled eggs of the past. Really *eggceptional*!

8 omega-3 eggs, hard-boiled and peeled (see tip in margin)
¼ cup minced smoked salmon (about 1 oz)
2 tbsp light mayonnaise
1 tbsp freshly squeezed lemon juice
1 tbsp honey mustard
1 tbsp minced fresh dill, or ½ tsp dried (fresh is best!)
¼ tsp each salt, black pepper, and hot pepper sauce
Paprika for garnish (optional)

- Carefully slice cooked eggs in half lengthwise and remove yolks. Place yolks in a medium bowl and mash well using a fork. Add remaining ingredients and mix well. Using a small spoon, fill centers of eggs with egg mixture, mounding slightly. Sprinkle filling with paprika, if desired. Cover loosely with plastic wrap and refrigerate for at least 1 hour before serving.

Tip: If you have a pastry bag with a large tip, you can use it to pipe the filling into the centers of the eggs. The smoked salmon will clog a small tip, so make sure you use a larger one.

Makes 16 deviled eggs

PER SERVING (1 EGG)

calories	total fat	saturated fat	protein	carbohydrate	fiber	cholesterol	sodium
46	3 g	0.9 g	3 g	1 g	0 g	107 mg	103 mg

I'll see your skillet and raise you two slow cookers.

For Pizza Sake!

An appetizer for the kids: Hot pizza dip with turkey pepperettes

It's a funky dunky that won't make them chunky! Your kids will devour this scrumptious, hot pizza dip—and it's easy to make, for pizza sake!

1 cup finely chopped mushrooms
½ cup minced red onions
½ cup thinly sliced or chopped turkey pepperettes
   (see tip below)
1 tbsp chopped fresh oregano, or ½ tsp dried
1 tub (8 oz) light ranch-flavored cream cheese
   (such as Philadelphia)
½ cup light sour cream
1 cup packed shredded light Monterey Jack or
   mozzarella cheese (4 oz)
½ cup your favorite pizza sauce
2 tbsp minced green onions

- Preheat oven to 350°F. Spray an 8- or 9-inch casserole dish with cooking spray and set aside.

- Spray a small skillet with cooking spray. Cook mushrooms, onions, turkey pepperettes, and oregano in skillet over medium heat until vegetables are softened, about 5 minutes. Remove from heat and set aside.

- In a medium bowl, beat together cream cheese and sour cream on medium speed of electric mixer until smooth. Stir in shredded cheese. Spread cheese mixture evenly over bottom of casserole dish. Spread pizza sauce over cheese layer. Spread vegetable-pepperette mixture over sauce. Sprinkle with green onions.

- Bake, uncovered, for 25 to 30 minutes, until mixture is hot and bubbly. Let cool for 5 minutes before serving (it's hot!). Serve with toasted whole wheat or multigrain pita wedges.

Tip: Look for bags of turkey pepperettes (mini pepperoni) where packaged cold cuts are sold at your grocery store.

Makes 12 servings

PER SERVING (¼ CUP)

calories	total fat	saturated fat	protein	carbohydrate	fiber	cholesterol	sodium
96	5.7 g	3.2 g	7 g	5 g	0.4 g	30 mg	447 mg

He Who Laughs, Lasts

According to experts, a child laughs between 200 and 400 times per day. Adults, a mere 15 times. We're not kidding, and that's too bad. Laughter does your body good, inside and out. In fact, if you're unable to exercise for whatever reason—illness, injury, sports bra's in the wash—laughter's not a bad substitute. Like exercise, it brings more oxygen to your lungs, lowers blood pressure, protects your heart's lining from inflammation and boosts your immune system so viruses, bacteria, and tumors won't get the best of you. No wonder George Burns lived to be 100! Plus, when you laugh out loud, your abdomen and diaphragm contract, your liver gets a massage, your facial muscles stretch, and your back and shoulders un-kink. It's like a half-day spa visit for your upper body and it doesn't cost a cent! And just to prove that laughter really is the best medicine, consider the following: Why do people dip bread into melted cheese? Because it's *fonduing* it! See, don't you feel better already?

Contrary to popular belief, the strongest muscle in the body is not the heart—it's the tongue! And it's no wonder. Most people exercise it far too much! And bet you didn't know that tongue prints are as unique as fingerprints. Could this be another way to *lick* crime?

Who invented the potato chip?

a) Harriet Ruffle
b) Valerie Pringle
c) H. Dumpty III
d) George Crum

Answer: (d) In 1853, while working as a chef in Saratoga Springs, NY, Crum unintentionally invented potato chips in response to a fussy, dissatisfied customer's complaint that the chef's French fries were cut too thick. He whittled the potatoes paper thin, deep-fried them, and sent them back out to the customer, hoping to annoy him. Surprisingly, the customer loved Crum's nearly translucent "fries," and potato chips were born!

Titanic Salad with Iceberg Lettuce

Layered potluck salad with tons of crunchy good stuff

The traditional version of this popular salad is *drowning* in as much as 40 grams of fat per serving—a *boatload* of fat on a *crash* course to your hips! You can avoid that *sinking* feeling with our slimmed-down, nutrient-packed version. Our hearts will go on...beating, that is, since we haven't gone *overboard* with fatty ingredients.

Dressing

1¹/₂ cups light mayonnaise
  (not fat-free)
¹/₂ cup light
  sour cream
1¹/₂ tbsp granulated
  sugar
1 tbsp freshly
  squeezed lemon juice
¹/₄ tsp salt

Salad

1 large head iceberg lettuce (see tip in margin)
1¹/₂ cups very thinly sliced baby carrots
1¹/₂ cups thinly sliced celery
1¹/₂ cups diced red bell pepper
1 cup frozen green peas
¹/₂ cup cooked, crumbled bacon
3 cups chopped cooked chicken breast (see tip in margin)
³/₄ cup packed shredded light medium or old (sharp)
  cheddar cheese (3 oz)
¹/₄ cup chopped green onions

- To make dressing, whisk together all dressing ingredients in a medium bowl. Cover and refrigerate until ready to use.

- To assemble salad, tear (don't chop) the lettuce into bite-sized pieces and spread evenly in serving dish. (Use a dish that's about 9 x 12 inches in size, and at least 3¹/₂ inches deep. A standard glass lasagna dish is too shallow.) Top lettuce with carrots, celery, red pepper, peas, bacon, and chicken, in that order.

- Spread dressing evenly over chicken layer and spread to edges, like you're icing a cake. Sprinkle cheese over dressing and top with green onions.

- Cover and refrigerate overnight. Serve cold.

Cooking TIP

Because the classic version of this salad tends to be loaded with high-fat mayonnaise, it can wreak havoc on your waistline. We've used light mayo to cut the fat by more than 50%, and we've added chopped, cooked chicken breast to make this impressive salad a complete meal. Make sure you refrigerate it overnight before serving— this gives the salad fairies a chance to work their magic. For some reason, this salad just isn't the same when you substitute romaine lettuce for the ordinary iceberg kind. We realize iceberg lettuce doesn't have a heck-of-a-lotta nutritional value, but, oh well! There are lots of other goodies in this salad to make up for it. Also, we like using the meat from a store-bought, rotisserie chicken to make preparation as easy as possible. If you want, you can add a layer of sliced, hard-boiled eggs.

Become a Stalker

Got high blood pressure? Then *stalk* up on celery! Researchers at the University of Chicago Medical Center showed that a very small amount of a compound in celery called 3-n-butyl phthalide (don't worry, this will *not* appear on your final exam!) can lower blood pressure in animals by 12 to 14%. That's a lot! The study was inspired by the father of one of the researchers, who, after eating about two stalks of celery every day for one week, was pumped to see his blood pressure drop from 158 over 96 to a normal reading of 118 over 82. Want a hot *stalk* tip? Don't leave out the leaves! Celery leaves are actually the most nutritious part of the plant, containing more calcium, iron, potassium, and vitamins A and C than the stalks. You can use the leaves in soups, chilies, salads, and other recipes that are enhanced by the flavor of celery.

Laughter is brightest where food is best.

Irish Proverb

Makes 12 servings

PER SERVING

calories	total fat	saturated fat	protein	carbohydrate	fiber	cholesterol	sodium
259	11.8 g	3.4 g	24 g	14 g	2.6 g	67 mg	549 mg

THE E FILES

If you want great things to happen to your body, pick up a dumbbell today! No, we're not endorsing Internet dating. We're talkin' about lifting weights, doing repetitions, building muscle...*that* kind of dumbbell! Not only does lifting weights work wonders for your physique, but also it can turn back the aging clock. It's true! Studies involving postmenopausal women suggest the body can appear 15 to 20 years younger after just one year of strength training. Forget the liposuction! Toss the ACME age-defying cream! Flush the human growth hormone pills down the toilet! The cheapest, most effective form of droop therapy is within your grasp!

"SAY IT AIN'T SO!"

Buffalo wings. Now there's a good example of what's cuckoo about the high-protein craze. Suddenly, some misguided folks actually think chicken wings will help them lose weight. Come on...don't be a wing nut! An average 12-wing order dipped in the blue-cheese dressing that comes with it is soaring with more than 1,000 calories and more saturated fat than you'd get in an entire rotisserie chicken! By the way, did wings really originate in Buffalo, or is that what your silhouette resembles when you eat them?

Aren't you taking this "living off the land" a bit too far?

Do the Chunky Chicken

High-protein, chunky chicken salad with chopped vegetables and a creamy dill dressing

Wanna ruffle some feathers at your next *potluck* luncheon? Don't show up with the same ol' song and dance—try this little number: A sensational and satisfying chicken salad that'll have everyone flapping their arms with joy.

Dressing

¾ cup lemon-flavored
    yogurt (see tip below)
¼ cup fat-free mayonnaise
3 tbsp white vinegar
2 tbsp minced fresh dill
1 tbsp Dijon mustard
½ tsp salt
¼ tsp freshly ground black pepper

Salad

4 cups chopped cooked chicken breast
1 ½ cups diced celery
1 cup chopped red bell pepper
½ cup chopped green onions (with white parts)
½ cup sliced almonds, toasted (optional)
½ cup frozen green peas, thawed
⅓ cup chopped fresh parsley
4 hard-boiled eggs, sliced

- To make dressing, whisk together all dressing ingredients in a medium bowl. Cover and refrigerate until ready to use.

- Combine all salad ingredients in a large bowl. Mix well. Add dressing and toss gently. Cover and refrigerate for at least 1 hour before serving.

Tip: If you can't find lemon yogurt, use plain yogurt (not vanilla!) in its place, and add 1 tbsp lemon juice plus 1 tbsp granulated sugar to the dressing.

Makes 6 servings

PER SERVING							
calories	total fat	saturated fat	protein	carbohydrate	fiber	cholesterol	sodium
250	7.2 g	1.9 g	34 g	11 g	1.9 g	214 mg	461 mg

Red, White, and Yahoo!

Grape tomatoes, fresh mozzarella, and chickpeas
tossed with fresh basil and balsamic vinegar

Yippee! This super-easy, flavorsome
salad is really a dandy.
First you're hit by the color,
then you're wowed by the taste.
Only a yahoo wouldn't like it!

- 1 can (15.5 oz) chickpeas,
  drained and rinsed
- 1 pint grape tomatoes,
  halved (about 2 cups)
- 1 cup mini fresh mozzarella balls,
  halved (4 oz—see tip below)
- 1/3 cup minced red onions
- 1/3 cup chopped fresh basil leaves
- 1 tbsp olive oil
- 1 tbsp balsamic vinegar
- 1 tbsp freshly squeezed lemon juice
- 1/2 tsp salt
- 1/4 tsp freshly ground black pepper

- Place ingredients in a large bowl in the order listed and mix well.
  May be served immediately, or salad can stand at room temperature
  for up to 1 hour before serving. Since tomatoes tend to lose their
  flavor when refrigerated, we recommend you add them at the last
  minute if you're preparing this salad in advance.

*Tip: Look for fresh mini mozzarella balls, called "mini bocconcini," in small,
cottage-cheese-like containers where you buy specialty cheeses at your grocery
store or ask for them at the deli-cheese counter. Fresh mozzarella is completely
different than regular mozzarella. It's very soft, white, and mild, and we know
you'll love it!*

Makes 5 servings

PER SERVING

calories	total fat	saturated fat	protein	carbohydrate	fiber	cholesterol	sodium
211	9.4 g	4 g	10 g	23 g	4.4 g	20 mg	432 mg

Ask Greta

I keep seeing the term "net carbs" on product labels. What does that mean?

Net carbs or net impact carbs are the latest dieting buzz words, popularized by Dr. Atkins and now adopted by food manufacturers. Basically, they refer to the number of so-called "bad carbs" (the ones that quickly raise blood-sugar levels and supposedly make us fat) in a food product. Manufacturers calculate this figure by taking the total grams of carbohydrates, then subtracting the fiber and sugar-alcohol numbers. Apparently, these subtracted carbs "don't count" because they have a minimal impact on blood sugar and, therefore, won't interfere with our weight-loss efforts. But that's misleading. These subtracted carbs still contain calories. And extra calories, no matter what you call them, usually result in extra pounds. The fact is, if your body's taking in too many calories, it won't need to use up the body's stored fat. Plus, unlike the terms "low fat" and "low calorie," there are currently no federal regulations defining net carbs or any of the other carb claims used on food labels. Those will surely come, but basically, these terms are marketing gimmicks. Net carbs means net profits for food manufacturers. Don't obsess over the numbers, and don't load up on low-carb products simply because you think they'll help you lose weight. They probably won't. Unless a low-carb product has fewer calories or more fiber (and tastes great!), why bother doling out the extra cash for it?

What's the difference between
a potato farmer and a baseball fan?
One yanks the roots and the other
roots for the Yanks.

To save some time, use bagged, pre-washed, pre-cut lettuce. This salad tastes best when the beef mixture is warm or at room temperature. Try to assemble it just before serving for the best flavor. If you like salad dressing with your taco salad, try mixing 1 cup Catalina or ranch salad dressing with 2 tbsp hickory-flavored barbecue sauce.

You can lose fat by eating fat.

Lose fat by eating fat? We know what you're thinking: Fat chance! Though you may find it hard to believe, omega-3 fatty acids—the kind found in fish and flaxseed oil—can actually speed up fat-burning. Like other fats, they contain nine calories per gram, but your body prefers not to store them as fat. Instead, they're used for important hormonal, structural, and cellular functions. And when these fats make up 12 to 15% of your total daily calorie intake, they can send your fat-burning engine off to the races. *Omegod*, that's good news! Omega-3's also help your kidneys flush out excess water held in tissues, acting as a *bloatation* device. That's important, because for many folks, water retention can dampen weight-loss efforts by adding serious poundage to the bathroom scale—10, 15, even 20 extra pounds! Plus, having the right fats in your diet helps slow digestion, making you feel fuller longer. Good fat can also be your weight-loss friend because it increases energy levels. And the more energy you have, the more active you'll be, and we all know that's the surest, most direct route to Slim City.

Herb gardeners who work on weekends get thyme-and-a-half.

Na-cho Ordinary Taco Salad

Layered taco salad, without the tacos!

It's *buenos* without the *nachos*! Toss the tacos and you can say *adios* to bad fat and bad carbs. What's left is all good: A *mexy*, mouthwatering, multi-level salad ideal for a hot summer night or a backyard party. Olé!

Beef Mixture

1 1/2 lbs extra-lean ground beef
1 cup chopped onions
1 large jalapeño pepper, seeded and minced
2 tsp minced garlic
1 tbsp chili powder
2 tsp ground cumin
2 cups quartered grape tomatoes
1/3 cup ketchup
1/2 tsp salt
1/4 tsp freshly ground black pepper

Salad

12 cups torn romaine and iceberg lettuce (see tip in margin)
1 cup canned whole-kernel corn, drained
1 cup canned black beans, drained and rinsed
1/2 cup diced green bell pepper
1 cup packed shredded light old (sharp) cheddar cheese (4 oz)
1 cup quartered grape tomatoes
1/3 cup chopped green onions
1 small ripe avocado, peeled and sliced (optional)
1 cup each light sour cream and medium salsa

- Heat a large, non-stick skillet over medium-high heat. Add beef, onions, jalapeño pepper, and garlic. Cook and stir until beef is no longer pink, breaking up any large pieces. Add chili powder and cumin. Cook 1 more minute. Add grape tomatoes, ketchup, salt, and pepper. Cook and stir for 2 more minutes. Remove skillet from heat and set aside.

- To assemble salad, spread lettuce over bottom of a serving platter. (If you want to make individual salads instead of one large salad, spread lettuce over bottom of individual-sized plates or shallow bowls.) Top with beef mixture, followed by corn, beans, green pepper, cheese, tomatoes, green onions, and avocado slices (if using), in that order. Top with sour cream and salsa just before serving.

Makes 8 lunch/6 dinner servings

PER SERVING (BASED ON 8 SERVINGS)

calories	total fat	saturated fat	protein	carbohydrate	fiber	cholesterol	sodium
279	11.1 g	6.1 g	25 g	22 g	5.7 g	65 mg	700 mg

Feast from the East

Asian beef-noodle salad with grilled sirloin and a
zesty sesame-orange dressing

Feast your eyes on this! East *meats* West when oodles of beef and
noodles are paired with colorful veggies and a lip-smacking Asian
dressing. Lotsa fiber and lean protein make it a *waist*-watcher's
dream. Even after a heaping helping, you'll still fit into your
Beijing suit!

Dressing

½ cup chicken broth
⅓ cup hoisin sauce
2 tbsp reduced-sodium
    soy sauce
2 tbsp seasoned rice vinegar
    (see tip below)
1 tbsp toasted sesame oil
1 tbsp grated gingerroot
2 tsp grated orange zest
1 tsp minced garlic
¼ tsp each salt, freshly
    ground black pepper, and
    crushed red pepper flakes

Chow time !

ORIENT EXPRESS

OE

Salad

8 oz uncooked whole wheat spaghetti
1 lb sirloin steak, grilled and cut into strips
2 cups small broccoli florets
1 cup thinly sliced red bell pepper
1 cup peeled, seeded, and diced cucumber
1 cup grated carrots
1 cup frozen green peas, thawed
½ cup chopped green onions
⅓ cup chopped fresh basil leaves

• Whisk together all dressing ingredients in a small bowl and
  refrigerate until ready to use.

• Cook spaghetti according to package directions. Drain. Rinse
  well with cold water and drain again. Transfer spaghetti to a
  large salad bowl and toss with remaining ingredients. Add
  dressing just before serving and toss again.

*Tip: Rice vinegar is mild, slightly sweet, and comes in regular and seasoned
varieties. Seasoned rice vinegar has a little salt and sugar added.*

Makes 6 lunch/4 dinner servings

PER SERVING (BASED ON 6 SERVINGS)

calories	total fat	saturated fat	protein	carbohydrate	fiber	cholesterol	sodium
340	7.6 g	2.1 g	25 g	46 g	6.3 g	46 mg	619 mg

40

RETURN TO SLENDER

When you get the urge to splurge (and we
all do!), don't waste valuable calories and
stomach space on tasteless, mediocre
treats. As a rule of tongue, before any high-
fat, high-calorie, belt-busting food crosses
your lips, make sure it's "splurge-worthy."
Rate the indulgent food from 1 to 10. If it
isn't a 9 or a 10, don't bother—it's not
worthy! Who really wants to gorge on 600
sugar-loaded, headed-straight-to-your-hips
calories in the form of Gram and Gramps'
70th anniversary sheet cake? Be polite,
enthusiastically taste a small forkful, then
slip the rest to Aunt Gertrude's Pomeranian.
Same goes for your mother-in-law's
fruitcake, chock-full of those scrumptious
artificial fruit globules and the ever-so-tasty
FD&C red #3. It's not worthy! Repeat: Not
worthy! Every single high-calorie
indulgence should have a high "worth it"
factor and should be a food that you
absolutely love, love, love. For Greta, it
would be pizza or gooey chicken wings.
For Janet, just about anything chocolate
would do. There's nothing worse than
having to loosen your belt after eating a
meal or a food that you didn't really enjoy.
Talk about *waisting* calories!

Funky Factoid

Dying for a cheeseburger, fries, and a
chocolate shake? In 2004, an Indiana
coffin manufacturer reported selling four or
five triple-wide caskets per *month* compared
with only one per *year* in the late 1980s.
Remember the old proverb: Don't dig your
grave with a knife and fork.

*Exercise is a dirty word. Every
time I hear it, I wash my mouth
out with chocolate.*

Author Unknown

Let It Bean

Easy, colorful, high-fiber, multi-bean salad

When we found ourselves in times of trouble trying to concoct a great-tasting, nutritious salad, our mother, Alfreda, came to us, speaking words of wisdom, and said, "Let it bean." Realizing that a high-fiber diet is the cornerstone of good health, she's been eating this salad regularly and recommended that we include her scrumptious recipe in our cookbook so that you can be regular, too.

Salad

2 cups fresh or frozen cut green beans, cooked (see tip below)

1 can (15.5 oz) chickpeas, drained and rinsed

1 can (15.5 oz) black beans, drained and rinsed

1 can (15.5 oz) red kidney beans, drained and rinsed

1 can (11 oz) whole-kernel corn, drained

1 cup diced red onions

1 cup diced red or orange bell pepper

½ cup chopped fresh parsley

Dressing

¼ cup safflower oil or light olive oil

¼ cup cider vinegar or white vinegar

2 tbsp granulated sugar

1 tsp Dijon mustard

½ tsp celery seed

¼ tsp each salt and freshly ground black pepper

- Combine all salad ingredients in a large bowl. Mix well.

- Whisk together oil, vinegar, sugar, mustard, celery seed, salt, and pepper in a small saucepan. Bring to a boil. Remove from heat and pour over bean mixture. Stir gently. Cover and refrigerate overnight for the best flavor. Stir occasionally if possible. (We think this salad tastes great as soon as it's made, but our mom insists you wait 'til tomorrow. Darn.)

Tip: Steam or boil the green beans just until they're tender. Be careful not to overcook them. Some people use canned green beans in their bean salad, but they're a little on the mushy side and have a faded green color, so we don't recommend them for this salad.

Makes 6 to 8 servings

PER SERVING (BASED ON 8 SERVINGS)

calories	total fat	saturated fat	protein	carbohydrate	fiber	cholesterol	sodium
253	8.1 g	0.6 g	9 g	40 g	9.6 g	0 mg	357 mg

THE E FILES

If we can put a man on the moon, certainly we can come up with a simple formula to help prevent the dreaded midlife metabolic meltdown. Well, NASA researchers in Houston, Texas, have met the challenge. Houston! We have a problem…solved! They've been tracking a group of roughly 500 employees (average age 40) to find out how much physical activity it takes to stop the scale from rising along with the number of candles on the birthday cake. That magic number seems to be about two-and-a-half miles of walking each day. If you prefer exercise that can't be measured in distance, such as tennis, step class, or yoga, the space men determined that five to seven hours of exercise per week would prevent your derriere from…well…taking up more space. One small step for man, one giant step for man's hind!

Pop Quizine

In 1905, 11-year-old Frank Epperson invented…

a) soda pop
b) Pop Rocks
c) lollipops
d) Popsicles

Answer: (d) Frank mixed some soda water powder to drink, but left it on the back porch overnight with a stir-stick in it. It froze solid, and the *Epsicle* was born. The name was later changed to Popsicle.

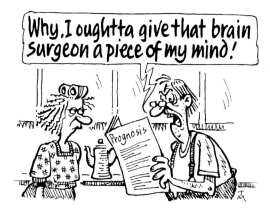

Why, I oughtta give that brain surgeon a piece of my mind!

Dressed to Thrill

Ultra-flavorful, reduced-fat salad dressings

Nowadays, salads cloaked in bad fats are not in *vogue*. Fortunately, there *Armani, mani* ways to design sensational, heart-healthy salad dressings that you can be *Prada*. Try *modeling* your homemade dressings after any one of these slimmed-down, enticing creations.

Cheater's Creamy Parmesan Italian

- 1 cup bottled fat-free Italian dressing
- 2 tbsp light mayonnaise
- 2 tbsp grated Parmesan cheese
- 1 tbsp balsamic vinegar
- 1 tbsp liquid honey
- ¼ tsp each dried oregano and freshly ground black pepper

Oriental Sesame

- ¾ cup hoisin sauce
- ¼ cup olive oil
- 3 tbsp red wine vinegar
- 2 tbsp seasoned rice vinegar
- 1 tbsp Dijon mustard
- 1 tbsp freshly squeezed lime juice
- 1 tbsp toasted sesame oil
- 1 tbsp grated gingerroot
- ⅛ tsp freshly ground black pepper

Maple-Balsamic Vinaigrette

- ⅓ cup balsamic vinegar
- ¼ cup olive oil
- ¼ cup apple juice
- 3 tbsp pure maple syrup
- 2 tbsp minced shallots
- 2 tbsp freshly squeezed lemon juice
- 1 tbsp Dijon mustard
- 1 tbsp chopped fresh dill
- 1 tsp minced garlic
- ¼ tsp each salt and freshly ground black pepper

- Directions for all dressings: Whisk together all ingredients and store in an air-tight container in the refrigerator for up to 1 week. Mix well before using.

Makes about 1⅓ cups

PER SERVING (2 TBSP)

calories	total fat
30	1 g
saturated fat	protein
0.3 g	1 g
carbohydrate	fiber
4 g	0 g
cholesterol	sodium
2 mg	274 mg

Makes about 1½ cups

PER SERVING (2 TBSP)

calories	total fat
90	6.3 g
saturated fat	protein
0.9 g	1 g
carbohydrate	fiber
8 g	0.5 g
cholesterol	sodium
1 mg	266 mg

Makes about 1 cup

PER SERVING (2 TBSP)

calories	total fat
95	6.9 g
saturated fat	protein
0.9 g	0 g
carbohydrate	fiber
8 g	0 g
cholesterol	sodium
0 mg	85 mg

Funky Factoid

According to researchers at Johns Hopkins University, music affects how fast we eat. The average diner eats five mouthfuls per minute when listening to lively music, four mouthfuls per minute when eating without music, and three mouthfuls per minute when listening to a slow melody. So, listening to slow tunes means it'll take you longer to finish your meal and you'll likely eat less, since it takes about 20 minutes for your stomach to tell your brain that it's had enough. Translation: A Lovin' Spoonful of Meatloaf with Cranberries and Bread served on The Platters with a glass of April Wine won't make you a Chubby Checker!

Grainman

Light-tasting, colorful bulgur salad with dried cranberries, walnuts, and fresh mint

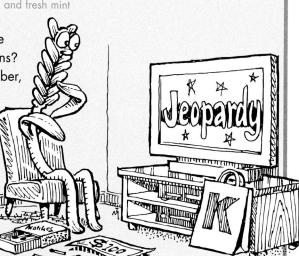

Cruisin' for new recipe ideas with whole grains? Well, this nutty, high-fiber, bulgur salad is sheer *genius!* It's so scrumptious and so healthy, even if you haven't used a pot in years, it's worth *Dustin off, man.*

1 cup orange juice
1 cup bulgur (see tip in margin)
½ cup chopped dried cranberries
½ cup each diced celery and peeled, diced English cucumber
¼ cup minced red onions
¼ cup chopped walnuts, pecans, or natural almonds
⅓ cup chopped fresh parsley
2 tbsp chopped fresh mint leaves
1 tbsp olive oil
1 tbsp freshly squeezed lemon juice
1 tsp grated lemon zest
¼ tsp salt
⅛ tsp freshly ground black pepper

- Combine orange juice and 1 cup water in a medium saucepan. Bring to a boil over high heat. Reduce heat to low and stir in bulgur. Simmer, covered, for 5 minutes. Remove from heat and let stand, covered, until bulgur has absorbed all of the liquid, 15 to 20 minutes.

- Meanwhile, place cranberries, celery, cucumber, red onions, and nuts in a large bowl. Add cooked bulgur, parsley, mint, olive oil, lemon juice, lemon zest, salt, and pepper. Mix well. Cover and refrigerate for at least 2 hours before serving.

Makes 6 servings

PER SERVING

calories	total fat	saturated fat	protein	carbohydrate	fiber	cholesterol	sodium
191	5.7 g	0.6 g	5 g	33 g	5.6 g	0 mg	112 mg

What do you call a parrot in a raincoat?
Polly Unsaturated.

Cooking TIP

What the heck is bulgur? It's a nutritious grain that's created when whole wheat kernels are steamed, dried, and crushed.

It has a nutty flavor and chewy texture when cooked and is primarily used in pilafs and salads. Look for bulgur in well-stocked supermarkets (check the bulk-food section) and natural/health-food stores.

RETURN TO SLENDER

Think you're a dietary saint because you've been drizzling fat-free dressing on your salad? Well, we hate to put a crimp in your halo, but the latest research shows that "no fat" might be no good—and we're not talkin' flavor, either. Nope, we're talkin' vitamins, minerals, and nutrients, and how your body absorbs them from the foods you eat. Turns out that some of the healthy stuff in vegetables, like beta-carotene, lycopene, and even calcium, can only be absorbed in the presence of fat. Now, that doesn't mean you should soak your salad with vats of full-fat dressing or sauté your veggies in gobs of butter. It's all about balance and moderation. To get the most nutritional bang for your buck, top your naked salad with low-fat or reduced-fat dressings or add some olive oil, low-fat cheese, a sprinkling of nuts, or sliced avocado. If you wanna *dress* for success, a little fat'll do ya!

She's seen "Dry Dry Birdie" at least a dozen times.

Are You a Craving Lunatic?

If constant cravings for sugary treats are driving you wild, you (and your hips!) will appreciate these tips to help curb the urge to splurge: (1) Keep in mind that most cravings last only about 10 minutes and then subside. Cravings are often your body's cries for water and oxygen, so wait 10 minutes, drink a glass of water with lemon (for an energy boost), and take a few deep breaths. You might try changing activities to clear your mind, too. Go for a walk, take a shower or hot bath, or phone a friend (thanks, Regis!). (2) Rate your hunger on a scale of 1 to 10. Unless you're a 9 or 10, fight the urge. Still uncontrollably ravenous? Give in to your craving, but don't go nuts. Ideally, your "craving cure" should set you back no more than 150 calories. (3) Eat foods containing tryptophan. Say what? Tryptophan is an amino acid that your body uses to make the feel-good brain chemical, serotonin. When serotonin levels are down, we feel down, and the body's way of lifting serotonin, and our spirits, is to load up on sugary or starchy foods. But if you eat foods high in tryptophan (turkey, bananas, milk, pineapple, chicken, whey protein, or yogurt), your body can replenish serotonin, preventing you from going on a hip-wrecking carb binge. (4) Brush your teeth! Sometimes the flavor of toothpaste can take the edge off a sugar craving. After all, Colgate and Coffee Crisp aren't exactly complementary flavors, and in general, food is less tempting when your mouth feels clean. You'll wonder where the cravings went when you brush your teeth with Pepsodent!

Dioscorides, a Greek physician in the first century AD, recorded several medicinal uses of onions. After that, the Greeks heralded the onion so much that they used the distinctly flavored vegetable to fortify their athletes for the Olympic Games. Before competition, athletes would consume many pounds of onions, drink onion juice, and rub onions on their bodies—forcing their opponents to compete while holding their noses and crying (just kidding!). Kinda makes you wonder: Was the famous symbol of the Olympic Games inspired by someone playing with their onion rings?

The Chicken Coup

Chicken salad with pecans and cranberries in a creamy orange dressing

It's the best plan we've ever *hatched*: Design a chicken salad so extraordinary, it'll cause a revolution! Strategically replace high-fat ingredients with healthier, flavor-packed options in a culinary manoeuvre that'll trigger a taste-bud takeover! The plot thickens, and so does our salad dressing! Brilliant!

Dressing
¼ cup light mayonnaise
¼ cup light sour cream
1 tbsp honey mustard
1 tbsp white vinegar
1 tbsp frozen orange juice concentrate
¼ tsp each salt and freshly ground black pepper

Salad
4 cups chopped cooked chicken (or turkey) breast
1 cup diced celery
1 large apple (your favorite kind), unpeeled, cored, and chopped
⅓ cup dried cranberries
⅓ cup chopped green onions (with white parts)
⅓ cup toasted, chopped pecans
¼ cup chopped fresh parsley

- Combine all dressing ingredients in a small bowl. Cover and refrigerate until ready to use.

- Toss together all salad ingredients in a large bowl. Add dressing and mix well. Cover and refrigerate for 2 hours before serving.

Makes 6 servings

PER SERVING

calories	total fat	saturated fat	protein	carbohydrate	fiber	cholesterol	sodium
274	10 g	1.7 g	28 g	18 g	2.5 g	74 mg	284 mg

An empty belly is the best cook.

Estonian Proverb

Mind Your Peas and Cous

Chickpea and couscous salad with colorful vegetables and sun-dried-tomato dressing

High fiber, high protein, and high flavor make this a high-demand salad at potlucks, buffets, and bridal showers. Better mind your manners and use proper *eatiquette* when asking for seconds: "Peas, sir, I want some more."

Dressing

- **½ cup bottled low-fat Italian dressing**
- **2 tbsp sun-dried-tomato pesto (see tip below)**
- **1 tbsp balsamic vinegar**
- **1 tbsp freshly squeezed lemon juice**
- **2 tsp grated lemon zest**
- **1 tsp granulated sugar**

Salad

- **1⅔ cups uncooked whole wheat couscous (see tip below)**
- **1 can (15.5 oz) chickpeas, drained and rinsed**
- **1 cup peeled, diced English cucumber**
- **1 cup diced orange or yellow bell pepper**
- **1 cup quartered cherry tomatoes**
- **¾ cup chopped green onions (with white parts)**
- **½ cup crumbled light feta cheese (2 oz)**
- **¼ cup chopped fresh dill**
- **¼ cup chopped fresh parsley**
- **¼ cup chopped black olives (optional)**
- **Freshly ground black pepper to taste**

- Whisk together all dressing ingredients in a small bowl and refrigerate until ready to use.

- Prepare couscous according to package directions, omitting salt and butter. Let cool.

- In a large bowl, toss together cooked couscous and remaining ingredients. Add salad dressing and mix well. Cover and refrigerate for at least 2 hours. Toss before serving.

Tip: Look for Classico brand sun-dried-tomato pesto in a small jar where pasta sauces are sold. You can usually find whole wheat couscous in the health-food aisle of your grocery store. If you can't find it, substitute regular couscous.

The Intensive Carrot Unit

Carrots need a better PR agent! They've been getting a bad rap for their high score on the Glycemic Index, and as a result have been snubbed by low-carb fanatics who fear the starchy vegetable will cause crazy blood-sugar spikes, increased hunger, and weight gain. Carrots at the root of weight gain? What's up with *that*, doc? Unless they're chocolate-covered, the chances that carrots will make you fat are pretty slim. Let's set the record straight: Carrots actually have a minimal effect on blood sugar in the amounts normally eaten. When laboratory researchers compare the Glycemic Index of foods, they do so based on portions that deliver 50 grams of carbohydrates. That's a lot! You'd have to eat about one-and-a-half pounds of carrots (about 10 medium carrots) to consume this many carbohydrates—an amount that even Bugs Bunny would be hard-pressed to chomp down in one sitting. So, put in perspective, nibbling on a carrot or two only has a mild effect on blood sugar. And don't forget that carrots are loaded with vitamins, minerals, plant chemicals, and antioxidants like beta-carotene that are potent protectors against cancer and promoters of healthy skin, hair, bones, and teeth—plenty of good reasons to start digging carrots!

In the late 1800s, Chicago-native Nancy Green was better known as...

a) Betty Crocker
b) Aunt Jemima
c) Susie Homemaker
d) Mrs. Butterworth

Answer: (b) Green was signed to a lifetime contract by the R.T. Davis Milling Company to play the role of Aunt Jemima and to promote the Aunt Jemima Pancake Mix. She died in September 1923.

Makes 10 servings

PER SERVING

calories	total fat	saturated fat	protein	carbohydrate	fiber	cholesterol	sodium
196	3.5 g	1.2 g	7 g	35 g	6.2 g	5 mg	197 mg

When you do a good deed for another and gain their approval, you're said to have earned "brownie points." Some experts insist this expression originated with the young girls' club of the same name, since Brownies are awarded points for good behavior and achievements. However, others believe the phrase stems from Scottish superstition. "Brownie" was a house spirit who preferred hanging out at farms. At night, he'd busy himself doing little jobs for the family he presided over, and although he was never seen, the grateful family would sometimes leave offerings to show their thanks for Brownie's good deeds.

Please Don't Overfeed the Animals!

As if the obesity epidemic among children isn't bad enough, now it appears we're responsible for fattening up our pets, too. A full 25% of dogs and cats in North America and Europe are overweight. Who's to blame? Well, no matter how smart you think your little pooch may be, he doesn't have opposable thumbs, so he can't sneak seconds by opening the ziplock on his bag of Dog Chow or turn on the ignition of the family SUV and navigate to the nearest Pizza Mutt. Plus, a recent survey found that as people get fatter, so do their pets. So, if you can't stand seeing Fifi, your formerly svelte feline, with burgeoning midriff rolls, it's up to you to be a positive *roll* model. Only you can stop the bingeing and *purring*.

Chop 'Til You Drop

Oriental chopped chicken salad with peanut dressing

Attention all *choppers!* *Hack* now! Don't delay! Slice and dice your way to an Oriental salad masterpiece! Slash the fat! Cut to the chase! Chop to it!

Dressing

⅓ cup bottled light peanut sauce
¼ cup hoisin sauce
1 tbsp red wine vinegar
1 tbsp toasted sesame oil
1 tsp grated gingerroot

Salad

3 cups chopped cooked chicken breast (see tip below)
2 cups packed chopped napa cabbage (see tip below)
2 cups packed chopped romaine hearts
1 cup shredded carrots
1 cup diced red bell pepper
1 cup bean sprouts
½ cup chopped green onions
2 tbsp chopped fresh cilantro
2 tbsp toasted sesame seeds (optional)

- Whisk together all dressing ingredients in a small bowl. Cover and refrigerate until ready to use.

- Toss together all salad ingredients in a large serving bowl. Add half the dressing and toss again. This may be enough dressing for your taste. If not, add more by the tablespoonful until you're happy with the flavor. Serve immediately.

Tip: The ideal chicken for this recipe is grilled teriyaki chicken (see recipe, page 91), but you can always buy a large rotisserie chicken and use the breast meat to keep things simple. At the grocery store, napa cabbage is often labeled Chinese cabbage.

Makes 6 servings

		PER SERVING					
calories	total fat	saturated fat	protein	carbohydrate	fiber	cholesterol	sodium
190	6.2 g	1.2 g	21 g	13 g	2.4 g	50 mg	385 mg

Did you hear about the restaurant that served submarine sandwiches? It went under.

Kernel Austin

Texas-style smoky corn and black bean salad

This incredible, zesty corn salad with big Texas flavor and tons of nutrients will give you the bionic, super-human strength and energy you'll need to fight crime and conquer evil. (And in case you were wondering, we watched every single episode of *The Six Million Dollar Man* and *The Bionic Woman* when we were little girls.)

1 tbsp olive oil
4 cups whole-kernel corn,
  canned or frozen (thaw first if using frozen)
½ cup minced red onions
1 jalapeño pepper, seeded and minced (optional)
1 tsp minced garlic
¼ tsp each ground cumin and chili powder
1 cup quartered grape tomatoes or
  1 cup diced red bell pepper
1 cup canned black beans, drained and rinsed
2 tbsp freshly squeezed lime juice
2 tbsp minced fresh cilantro
1 tbsp hickory-flavored barbecue sauce
1 tsp granulated sugar
Salt and freshly ground black pepper to taste

- Heat olive oil in a large, non-stick skillet over medium-high heat. Add corn. Cook and stir until corn just begins to char (don't burn it!), about 8 minutes or so. Add onions, jalapeño (if using), garlic, cumin, and chili powder. Cook and stir 1 more minute. Remove from heat.

- Transfer corn mixture to a large bowl and add remaining ingredients. Mix well. Cover and refrigerate for at least 2 hours before serving.

Makes 8 servings

PER SERVING							
calories	total fat	saturated fat	protein	carbohydrate	fiber	cholesterol	sodium
99	2.6 g	0.2 g	3 g	17 g	3.5 g	0 mg	94 mg

All the fuss over fiber's role in weight loss is just a bunch of hot air.

Fat or Fiction?

You can flush that statement down the toilet! A high-fiber diet not only helps ward off cancer and other diseases, but also is a fantastic fat fighter. Studies show that if you give people virtually the same diet—same calories, similar foods—except that one diet is high in fiber (for example, whole-grain bread versus white bread) and the other is low in fiber, those on the high-fiber diet will lose more weight. No wonder so many nutrition experts consider fiber the ticket to weight control. How does fiber work its magic? Well, it's like a natural appetite suppressant. Besides keeping you feeling fuller longer on fewer calories, fiber slows the entry of sugar into the bloodstream, minimizing the highs and lows that make you crave sweets. Lower blood sugar means you'll have lower insulin levels too, and that means you're likely to burn fat rather than store it. Like a personal scouring pad for internal use only, fiber (or "roughage," as Grandma called it) mops up suspicious, disease-promoting substances so they don't spend time loitering in your system. And while it's quickly transporting wastes out of your body, fiber also takes some unabsorbed fat (and calories) along for the ride. So, if you eat your beans, fat will be gone with the wind!

'96 was a fine year for bacteria

YOGURT

People who eat yogurt are well-cultured.

Cooking TIP

To make this salad in advance, combine all ingredients except the tomatoes and dressing and refrigerate until serving time. Add the tomatoes and dressing just before serving. Never refrigerate tomatoes—they'll lose their flavor! If you can find a beautiful yellow or orange tomato, add it to the mix for extra color.

"SAY IT AIN'T SO!"

Gummy bears, jujubes, licorice, wine gums. Sure seems impossible to walk past those enticing, colorful candy bins at movie theaters without scooping up a yummy snack. Oh, what the heck! A couple of handfuls are a harmless, fat-free alternative to popcorn, right? Sure, if you stop at a couple of handfuls, but most candy grab-bags contain four to five servings and more than 500 sugar-filled calories! And those mammoth bags of licorice? More than 800 calories! Yes, movie fans, you've made it a blockbuster night...for your fat cells! "Harmless" snacks like these help explain why they're making movie theater seats a lot wider these days.

Funky Factoid

You may be surprised to know that chefs in Greece never include lettuce in a traditional Greek salad. Apparently, mythology is to blame for *leafing* the lettuce out. The story goes something like this: When beautiful Adonis tried to steal Zeus's wife, Hera, the angry father of the gods turned the would-be lover boy into a wilting head of lettuce. And no one wants a wilting lover *or* a wilted salad!

It's All Greek to Me

Traditional Greek salad with fresh oregano, mint, and a light vinaigrette dressing

Do you pour over ingredient lists and recipe instructions, scratching your head and muttering, *"Graecum est; non potest legi"*?* We sure do. That's why we created this uncomplicated but delicious Greek salad that's so basic, even Janet can make it.

4 large ripe tomatoes (about 2 lbs), cut into 1-inch chunks
1 English cucumber, peeled, halved lengthwise, and cut into 1-inch chunks
1 large green bell pepper, seeded and cut into 1-inch chunks
1 small red onion, halved and very thinly sliced
½ cup Kalamata olives or other black olives
1 cup crumbled light feta cheese (4 oz)
2 tbsp minced fresh oregano leaves
2 tbsp minced fresh mint leaves
3 tbsp red wine vinegar or balsamic vinegar
2 tbsp olive oil
Salt and freshly ground black pepper to taste

- Combine tomatoes, cucumber, green pepper, red onion, olives, feta cheese, oregano, and mint in a large decorative serving bowl.

- Just before serving, add vinegar, olive oil, salt, and pepper and toss gently. To make salad in advance, see tip in margin.

* The phrase, "It's all Greek to me," although attributed to Shakespeare, actually comes from a medieval Latin proverb, Graecum est; non potest legi— meaning "It is Greek; it cannot be read"—and refers to something that is unintelligible.

Makes 8 servings

			PER SERVING				
calories	total fat	saturated fat	protein	carbohydrate	fiber	cholesterol	sodium
132	8.8 g	2.7 g	4 g	12 g	2.5 g	13 mg	271 mg

I am pushing sixty.
That is enough exercise for me.

Mark Twain

Thai One On

Exotic sweet potato and coconut soup with shrimp

Loaded with shrimp, *half-cut* veggies, and an *intoxicating* blend of spices, this savory, Thai-inspired soup will have you seeing double helpings!

Gee Honey, you've really come out of your shell tonight!

2 tsp butter or olive oil

1 cup each chopped onions and chopped red bell pepper

3/4 cup chopped celery

2 tsp minced garlic

4 cups peeled, cubed sweet potatoes (about 2 large)

1 tbsp grated gingerroot

3/4 tsp each ground cumin, ground coriander, and curry powder

1/4 tsp ground cinnamon

2 cups chicken broth

1 can (14 oz) light coconut milk

1/2 tsp salt

1/4 tsp freshly ground black pepper

3 tbsp each chopped fresh cilantro and chopped fresh basil leaves

2 tbsp light peanut butter

1 tbsp brown sugar

1 tbsp freshly squeezed lime juice

1 lb cooked medium shrimp, tails removed (thaw first if using frozen)

- Heat butter in a large, non-stick soup pot over medium heat. Add onions, red pepper, celery, and garlic. Cook and stir until vegetables begin to soften, about 4 minutes.

- Stir in sweet potatoes, gingerroot, cumin, coriander, curry powder, and cinnamon. Cook and stir for 30 more seconds. Add broth, coconut milk, salt, and pepper. Bring soup to a boil. Reduce heat to low, cover, and simmer for 10 minutes, just until sweet potatoes are tender.

- Transfer half the soup to a blender and purée until smooth. Return puréed soup to pot with remaining soup. Stir in cilantro, basil, peanut butter, brown sugar, and lime juice. Mix well. Add shrimp and heat for about 2 more minutes, just until shrimp is hot.

Makes 6 servings

PER SERVING

calories	total fat	saturated fat	protein	carbohydrate	fiber	cholesterol	sodium
239	8.2 g	4.6 g	19 g	24 g	3 g	120 mg	501 mg

SEE YA LADLE

52

Funky Factoid

Enjoying those *I Dream of Jeannie* reruns? Well, if you care about stimulating your brain, you're better off actually *dreaming* of Jeannie than you are watching the old sitcom. Believe it or not, your brain is more active while you're sleeping than it is while you're watching TV. Just one more reason to get off the couch, potato.

"SAY IT AIN'T SO!"

While we've been busy blaming our ballooning bellies on carbs, fat, and sugar, there's another very nasty villain lurking in the shadows, and the scary thing is you may never have heard of it. Who's the dirty rotten scoundrel that's helping to make us fat? It's high-fructose corn syrup (a.k.a. HFCS), the sweetener used to replace sugar in many processed foods. Manufacturers love it because it's cheap and doubly sweet. Problem is our fat cells love it, too! Research shows that it's more easily turned into fat than any other carbohydrate, and it also shuts off the switches that control appetite. Plus, in high levels, HFCS boosts triglycerides (fatty compounds that circulate in the bloodstream and are stored in fat tissue) by as much as 32%. That's a heart attack waiting to happen! And you'll find it just about everywhere: soft drinks, juice, candy, barbecue sauce, fruit-flavored yogurt, even some breakfast cereals. Over the past 15 years, North American consumption has increased by a girth-shattering 250%. The only way to avoid the evil wrath of HFCS is by reading labels carefully. If high-fructose corn syrup, fructose, or glucose/fructose appears near the top of the ingredient lists, you can bet you're getting a hefty dose of trouble.

To retain respect for sausages and laws, one must not watch them in the making.

Otto von Bismarck

Which form of exercise is best: weights or cardio?

Ideally, you need both: a little hustle and a little muscle! Exercise should be as much a part of your daily life as brushing your teeth, and the only way that'll happen is if you make it fun. Choose activities that best suit your personality and lifestyle, and chances are, you'll stick with them. Are you a loner? Then don't sign up for a softball team. Take a hike or ride a bike! Love the outdoors? Forget the gym. Run for the hills or get some rollerblading thrills! Almost any activity that makes you breathe heavily and gets your muscles working will help keep you fit as a fiddle. Aerobic exercise not only burns fat, but also strengthens the heart and lungs. Weight training sculpts your body and boosts your metabolism by building fat-burning muscle. But what's truly most important is that you don't let a day go by without doing at least 30 minutes of *some* kind of physical activity. Cutting the grass counts! So does shoveling snow! *Running* up your phone bill or *climbing* the corporate ladder doesn't! Find something you love to do and just do it. Ten minutes here, ten minutes there. It all adds up to a stronger, healthier you. When you think about it, weights and cardio really aren't meant to be pitted against each other, but should be viewed as complementary components of an overall fitness program. Whichever form of exercise you choose, focus on becoming a real-life *action* figure, starring in your own *motion* picture!

Looks like you got some vinegar in your ear. You're suffering from Pickled Hearing!

The Three Mushketeers

Aromatic, rich-tasting, three-mushroom soup

All for yum and yum for all!

Ordinary mushroom soup is *sworda* boring, but our version's a taste adventure—a *novel* idea that'll make you a cooking *hero*! Three types of mushrooms are simmered with smoky bacon and herbs to produce a beautiful bowl of soup that's worth fighting for!

- **4 slices bacon, chopped**
- **1 1/2 cups sliced leeks (white part only)**
- **2 tsp minced garlic**
- **1 1/2 lbs sliced portobello, shiitake, and button mushrooms (8 oz each)**
- **1 tsp dried thyme**
- **1/2 tsp dried rosemary**
- **4 cups beef broth**
- **1/2 tsp each salt and black pepper**
- **1/2 cup light (5%) cream or light sour cream or evaporated 2% milk**
- **1/4 cup chopped fresh parsley**
- **2 tbsp balsamic vinegar**

- Cook bacon in a large, non-stick soup pot over medium-high heat until lightly browned but not crisp. Add leeks and garlic. Cook and stir until leeks begin to soften, about 3 minutes.

- Stir in mushrooms. Cook and stir until mushrooms are tender, about 5 more minutes. Add thyme and rosemary. Cook 30 more seconds. Add broth, salt, and pepper, and bring soup to a boil. Reduce heat to low, cover, and simmer for 10 minutes.

- Transfer half the soup to a blender and purée until smooth. Return puréed soup to pot with remaining soup and mix well. Add cream, parsley, and balsamic vinegar. Taste soup and add more salt and pepper, if desired.

Makes 6 servings

PER SERVING							
calories	total fat	saturated fat	protein	carbohydrate	fiber	cholesterol	sodium
131	6.6 g	2.7 g	8 g	12 g	1.9 g	19 mg	575 mg

The Squash Court

Butternut squash soup with orange and ginger

When it comes to what to make your family for dinner, the ball's in your court. Why not *serve* up this spectacular butternut squash soup and score some big points? So healthy and flavorful, it's sure to create a *racquet* at the dinner table.

2 tsp olive oil
1 cup chopped onions
1 tsp minced garlic
1 tbsp grated gingerroot
1/2 tsp ground cumin
6 cups peeled, cubed
   butternut squash
2 cups chicken broth
1 1/2 cups unsweetened
   carrot juice
1/4 cup frozen pineapple juice concentrate
1 tsp grated orange zest
1/2 tsp salt
1/4 tsp freshly ground black pepper
Light sour cream (optional)

- Heat olive oil in a large, non-stick soup pot over medium heat. Add onions and garlic. Cook and stir until onions begin to soften, about 3 minutes.

- Stir in gingerroot and cumin, and cook for 30 more seconds. Add squash and remaining ingredients, except sour cream. Mix well. Bring soup to a boil. Reduce heat to low, cover, and simmer for 12 to 14 minutes, or until squash is tender.

- Working in batches, transfer soup to a blender or food processor and purée until smooth. Return puréed soup to pot. Serve hot soup with a dollop of light sour cream in the center, if desired.

Makes 6 servings

PER SERVING							
calories	total fat	saturated fat	protein	carbohydrate	fiber	cholesterol	sodium
102	1.9 g	0.3 g	3 g	20 g	2.4 g	2 mg	372 mg

A man's health can be judged by which he takes two at a time—pills or stairs.

Joan Welsh

THE E FILES

Attention busy moms with no time for exercise! Here's a great way to multitask your way to fitness: Play with your kids! If you want to keep Buffy and Jody entertained while buffing and toning your physique, then kidding around is the ticket. Have you played a game of tag lately? Talk about a humbling cardiovascular experience! But it's also fun, and with all the stop-and-go moves, it's a super interval workout. That's a good thing, because researchers say that short bursts of intense activity give you the most metabolic bang for your buck. Even simple games like Duck Duck Goose, Red Light/Green Light, Hide 'n' Seek, and Dodge Ball can get your heart racing and your metabolism humming. Then it's on to strength training. You and the kiddies can stage your own mini-Olympics by seeing who can traverse the monkey bars the fastest or hold a chin-up the longest. Who needs a personal trainer when you've got Jungle Gym showing you the ropes? (By the way, playing video games doesn't count as exercise!)

Funky Factoid

When Napoleon was attacking Russia, he offered a handsome cash prize to anyone who could develop a reliable method of preserving food for his troops. In the early 1800s, Nicolas Appert, a Parisian candy maker, won the competition (and 12,000 francs!) with his system of packing foods into airtight glass jars and then sufficiently heating them. The use of metal containers for canning was patented in 1810, and troops that fought in The Battle of Waterloo ate canned rations. Unfortunately, the can opener hadn't yet been invented! By relying on knives and bayonets to pierce the thick metal cans, many soldiers ended up wounding themselves, some even cutting off a finger. Needless to say, they lost the *opening* battle!

Melts in Your Mouth, and in Your Hands!

Even though it's been a healthy staple food throughout history, butter has been getting a bad rap for the last decade or so. And that's a shame—it's actually a good fat! If you use it sparingly, it won't make you fat, and it won't clog your arteries, either. Butter's saturated fat molecules are short, making them easy for the body to digest and burn for fuel. In fact, the human body can digest butter more easily than other saturated fats. To illustrate this point, try holding butter in your hand—it'll quickly melt. When you eat butter, it will similarly dissolve because your body temperature on the inside is the same as on the skin (98.6°F), and that's much warmer than butter's melting point. Try the same experiment with shortening, beef fat, or other animal fats. You'll notice they won't dissolve quickly in your hand. Likewise, they won't dissolve as easily in your body and they'll become difficult to digest, clogging your arteries, causing blood platelets to stick together, and potentially causing heart problems and high blood pressure. And scientists are churning out more positive news for butter lovers: They've discovered that one-third of butter's fat is a health-promoting type called conjugated linoleic acid (CLA). Plus, butter has properties that help protect us from viruses, yeasts, and harmful bacteria that live in our gut. Butter is also a good choice for cooking because it's very stable—heat doesn't drastically alter butter's chemical structure (as it does with vegetable oils). Basically, that means it won't do weird things in your body after it's heated. So if you like butter, *stick* with it! Just don't go slathering it on everything. Here a pat, there a pat, little bits won't make you fat.

Shanks for the Memories

Old-fashioned, smoky ham and split-pea soup with lentils

And you thought *slicing* was a bad thing! *Putter* around in the kitchen, slicing, dicing, and spicing, and you'll end up with a memorable soup that's on *par* with the best.

Hope you like it!

2 tsp olive oil
1 ½ cups chopped onions
1 cup each chopped
    celery and chopped carrots
2 tsp minced garlic
1 tbsp minced fresh thyme, or 1 tsp dried
½ tsp dried oregano
7 cups chicken broth
1 whole meaty smoked ham shank or ham hock (about 2 lbs)
1 cup dry lentils, rinsed
1 cup dry green split peas, rinsed
2 bay leaves
½ tsp freshly ground black pepper
¼ cup chopped fresh parsley
1 tbsp balsamic vinegar
Salt to taste

- Heat olive oil in a large, non-stick soup pot over medium heat. Add onions, celery, carrots, and garlic. Cook and stir until vegetables begin to soften, about 6 minutes. Add thyme and oregano and cook 1 more minute.

- Add remaining ingredients, except parsley, vinegar, and salt. Bring soup to a boil. Reduce heat to low. Cover and simmer for 1 hour.

- Remove ham shank from soup. Purée half the soup in a blender or food processor and return to pot with remaining soup. Cover to keep hot. Cut meat from ham shank (this part's a little fussy) and return meat to pot. Discard bone. Stir in parsley and vinegar. Taste soup and add more pepper and a bit of salt, if desired.

Why are you eating lunch sitting on the sidewalk?

My doctor told me to curb my appetite!

Makes 8 servings

PER SERVING

calories	total fat	saturated fat	protein	carbohydrate	fiber	cholesterol	sodium
192	4 g	1 g	17 g	22 g	7.8 g	30 mg	394 mg

Melancauli Baby

Curried cauliflower soup with
Swiss cheese and wild rice

When you're feeling
down in the dumps,
raise your spirits with this
outstanding combination of
ingredients that's so tasty,
it'll bring tears of joy to
your eyes!

1 tbsp butter or olive oil
2 cups thinly sliced leeks
   (about 2 large)
2 tsp minced garlic
4 cups small
   cauliflower florets
1 1/2 cups peeled, cubed sweet potato
1 1/2 tsp curry powder
1 tsp ground cumin
4 cups chicken or vegetable broth
1/2 tsp salt
1/4 tsp freshly ground black pepper
1 cup cooked brown and wild rice blend (see tip in margin)
1 cup evaporated 2% milk
1/2 cup packed shredded light Swiss cheese (2 oz)

- Heat butter in a large, non-stick soup pot over medium heat.
  Add leeks and garlic. Cook and stir until leeks begin to soften,
  about 3 minutes.

- Stir in cauliflower, sweet potato, curry, and cumin. Cook and stir
  for 1 more minute. Add broth, salt, and pepper. Bring mixture to
  a boil. Reduce heat to low, cover, and simmer for 12 to 15
  minutes, until vegetables are tender.

- Transfer half the soup to a blender and purée until smooth.
  Return puréed soup to pot with remaining soup and mix well.
  Stir in cooked rice, milk, and Swiss cheese. Heat soup for 1
  more minute. Serve hot.

Makes 8 servings

PER SERVING

calories	total fat	saturated fat	protein	carbohydrate	fiber	cholesterol	sodium
142	3.7 g	1.7 g	8 g	20 g	3 g	16 mg	448 mg

On organic farms, they till it like it is.

Cooking TIP

Rather than using
plain ol' (boring!)
long-grain white rice
in this recipe, you
can bump up the
nutritional value and flavor by
using an interesting variety of
brown and wild rices. Look for a blend made
up of brown, wild, and red rices if you can
find it. It looks and tastes great. Or, you can
make your own blend by combining brown
basmati rice with wild rice in a 2:1 ratio,
respectively. Make this soup a complete meal
by stirring in some chopped, cooked
chicken breast or turkey breast in the final
step. Like most soups, this one tastes even
better the next day!

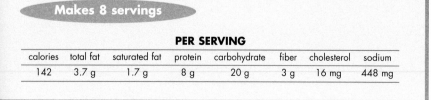

RETURN TO SLENDER

"I'm so stuffed! I ate way too much!" Sound
familiar? One reason we stuff ourselves silly
is because we're experiencing portion
distortion. Food has undergone some serious
sprawl lately, and those ballooning,
industrial-sized portions encourage people to
eat whether they're hungry or not. To prevent
love handles, you've got to get a handle on
portion sizes. Always read labels and check
both the calories and the servings per
package. You might think you're eating a
200-calorie snack, but, unbeknownst to you,
each bag contains two servings. Ouch!
When cooking at home, use measuring cups
at first, until you get the hang of what's
"normal." One cup of cooked pasta has 200
calories, making the typical three-cup serving
worth a whopping 600! For a perfect
spaghetti portion, keep a quarter near your
stovetop. The diameter of a quarter is exactly
the size of a two-ounce stack (about 200
calories), enough to serve one person. And
when it comes to fast food, super size isn't
super wise. Is an extra 250 calories, even
for a mere 39 cents, really a smart
expenditure? Those are the differences, in
calories and cost, between a small order of
fries and a large one. Remember: Sometimes
less is more!

Oinkers Away!

Navy bean and turkey bacon soup

All right, all right. We admit this recipe title's a bit of a stretch, since we use turkey bacon, and not pork, in our delectable bean soup. *Navy* mind our little fib— when you're *hanchorin'* for a bowl of hearty, *gobble-de-goodness*, it's hard not to *oink* out on this one.

6 slices turkey bacon, chopped
1 cup each chopped onions, chopped celery, and chopped carrots
2 tsp minced garlic
4 cups chicken broth, divided
1 tsp dried thyme
3/4 tsp dried marjoram
3 tbsp all-purpose flour
1 can (15.5 oz) navy beans, drained and rinsed
1/4 cup chopped fresh parsley
2 bay leaves
1/2 tsp each salt and freshly ground black pepper

- Cook bacon in a large, non-stick soup pot over medium heat for about 4 minutes, stirring often. Be careful not to burn it. Stir in onions, celery, carrots, garlic, and 1/2 cup chicken broth. Cook and stir for 5 more minutes, until vegetables begin to soften.

- Add thyme and marjoram and cook 1 more minute. Stir in flour and mix well. Add remaining chicken broth and bring mixture to a boil. It will thicken slightly.

- Stir in beans, parsley, bay leaves, salt, and pepper. Reduce heat to low, cover, and simmer for 30 minutes.

- Remove bay leaves. Transfer half the soup to a blender and purée until smooth. Return puréed soup to pot with remaining soup and mix well. Serve hot.

Makes 6 servings

PER SERVING

calories	total fat	saturated fat	protein	carbohydrate	fiber	cholesterol	sodium
144	3 g	0.5 g	8 g	21 g	5.8 g	13 mg	680 mg

Fat or Fiction?

Beverage calories don't count.

Better think before you drink. North Americans are guzzling more fruity, juicy concoctions, designer coffees, and sugary sports drinks than ever before. But have you ever stopped to consider how many empty calories you're sucking up through that straw? Two hundred? Three hundred? Maybe even four hundred? And those calories are just "add-ons"—meaning you don't consume them in place of food calories, you have them *in addition* to food. To be blunt, if you don't cut back on what you eat to make up for what you drink, you'll end up with huge liquid *assets*. Another problem is that fluids don't help our brains register that same "full" feeling we get when we eat solids, so we consume more. When you swig back that frothy cappuccino before lunch or suck back that strawberry daiquiri after work, they don't feel like a rich, creamy slab of cheesecake, but to your fat cells, there's no difference. Chug it or chew it, a calorie is a calorie. Plus, when a drink has 10 teaspoons of sugar, like most soft drinks and fruity beverages do, you can pretty much guarantee your blood sugar's going to Mars and back. That'll make you ravenous later, and it'll also send your hormones into a fat-storing frenzy. The final straw: Many experts believe that high-fructose corn syrup, the inexpensive sweetener found in many sodas, fruit drinks, and alcohol coolers, ranks right up there with trans fats as one of the most health-defeating substances you can put in your body. Wouldn't you rather *Eat, Shrink & Be Merry* than *Eat, Drink & Be Huge*?

A cluster of bananas is officially called...

a) a pack
b) a bunch
c) a band
d) a hand

answer: (d) And a single banana is called a finger, to make another point.

Cooking TIP

To drain tomatoes, empty the canned tomatoes into a sieve and press down on them to remove as much liquid as possible. You want the chunks of tomato, but not their juice, which would make this soup a little bitter. To make this soup a snap to prepare, buy a rotisserie chicken at the take-out counter of your grocery store. Remove the skin and use the breast meat for this recipe (it's the perfect amount!). Save the legs for tomorrow's lunch.

THE E FILES

If you can put one foot in front of the other, you can exercise. Burning fat, firming your muscles, and flooding your cells with health-promoting oxygen is as easy as a walk in the park. Walking is cheap, it's enjoyable, it relieves stress, it's easy on the joints, and it's something you can do for the rest of your life. In fact, it's probably the greatest form of exercise ever invented (not that walking was *invented*, but you know what we mean). Too boring? Grab some headphones and listen to your favorite tunes, a book on tape, or the ball game. Grab a friend so you can gab and burn flab at the same time. No matter where you walk, take in the beauty of nature, whether it's your neighbor's prized daisies or Daisy, the prized cow. Stride, strut, stroll—move your body any way you like and you'll start reaping the health benefits. And the more you walk, the more you'll love walking! Don't believe us? Then take it from The Rolling Stones: "It's only walk 'n' stroll, but I like it, like it, yes I do!"

Chowdy Doody

Smoky roasted chicken and corn chowder

It's Chowdy Doody time! It's Chowdy Doody time! This creamy, dreamy chicken soup is sure to satisfy everyone in your peanut gallery.

4 slices bacon, chopped
1 cup diced onions
1/2 cup each diced celery and
    diced red bell pepper
2 tsp minced garlic
1 1/2 tbsp minced fresh thyme,
    or 1 tsp dried
2 tbsp all-purpose flour
1 1/2 cups chicken broth
1 can (12 oz) fat-free evaporated milk
1 can (14.5 oz) diced tomatoes,
    well drained (see tip in margin)
1 can (14.75 oz) cream-style corn
2 cups chopped roasted chicken breast (see tip in margin)
1 tbsp hickory-flavored barbecue sauce
1/2 tsp freshly ground black pepper
1/4 tsp salt (or to taste)

- Cook chopped bacon in a large, non-stick soup pot over medium-high heat until lightly browned but not crisp. Stir in onions, celery, red pepper, and garlic. Cook and stir until vegetables begin to soften, about 5 minutes.

- Add thyme and flour. Mix well. Stir in broth and evaporated milk. Bring mixture to a gentle boil and stir continuously until soup thickens slightly.

- Reduce heat to medium-low. Stir in remaining ingredients. Cover and let simmer for 10 minutes, stirring occasionally. Serve hot.

Makes 6 servings

PER SERVING

calories	total fat	saturated fat	protein	carbohydrate	fiber	cholesterol	sodium
270	7.1 g	2.6 g	24 g	30 g	3 g	53 mg	619 mg

He's such a hypochondriac, he puts cough syrup on his pancakes.

Beef Noodle Doodle

Asian beef-noodle soup with spinach, mint, and basil

We doodled over noodles, scribbling while nibbling, to get this *souper*-duper recipe just right. Finding a better-tasting Asian beef soup would be like searching for a *noodle* in a haystack!

4 oz uncooked soba noodles, whole wheat spaghetti, or rice vermicelli

6 cups beef broth

3 tbsp hoisin sauce (see tip in margin)

1 tbsp each reduced-sodium soy sauce, grated gingerroot, toasted sesame oil, and freshly squeezed lime juice

12 oz beef tenderloin, thinly sliced (see tip in margin)

3 cups chopped fresh spinach leaves or thinly sliced bok choy

⅓ cup chopped green onions

¼ cup each chopped fresh mint leaves and chopped fresh basil leaves

Salt and pepper to taste

1 cup bean sprouts

- Cook noodles according to package directions. Drain well, rinse with cold water, and drain again. Set aside until soup is ready to serve.

- In a large soup pot, combine beef broth, hoisin sauce, soy sauce, gingerroot, sesame oil, and lime juice. Bring to a boil. Reduce heat to low and simmer for 3 minutes.

- Add beef, spinach, green onions, mint, and basil. Simmer for 5 more minutes, just until beef is cooked through. Taste soup and add salt and pepper, if desired.

- To serve soup, place some cooked noodles in the bottom of a soup bowl. (You can chop the noodles into shorter pieces if you prefer.) Top with a few bean sprouts and ladle soup over top. Serve hot.

Makes 6 servings

PER SERVING

calories	total fat	saturated fat	protein	carbohydrate	fiber	cholesterol	sodium
220	7 g	2 g	18 g	22 g	2.3 g	40 mg	656 mg

Cooking is like love. It should be entered into with abandon or not at all.

Harriet Van Horne

Hoisin sauce, a sweet and spicy Chinese sauce made from soybeans, garlic, chili peppers, and various spices, can be found near the soy sauce in the Asian cooking aisle of your grocery store. That's also where you'll find soba noodles—Japanese buckwheat noodles that resemble spaghetti. For a more economical soup, substitute flank steak for beef tenderloin. (By the way, it's easier to slice beef thinly if it's partially frozen.)

Radical Thinking

Are you unstable and unbalanced? Well, if it makes you feel any better, so are we! Every minute of every day, *everyone's* cells are being ravaged by chemically unstable and unbalanced molecules called free radicals. They may be free, but they're no bargain. They can critically damage cells, and contribute to heart disease, cancer, arthritis, and other illnesses. Wondering what's causing those new wrinkles and gray hairs? Blame it on the rads. Free radicals cause *youth* decay, accelerating the aging process by making us rust from the inside out. How dare they! And how'd they get inside us in the first place? Well, they're formed naturally when our cells use oxygen to produce energy. Our bodies can handle a certain amount, but excess free radicals are created as a result of everyday modern life: poor diet, stress, smoking, alcohol, trans fats, food additives, chlorinated water, pollution, and force fields generated by TVs, computers, and power lines. Too much exercise can also pump up the free radical damage, which explains why some marathoners and triathletes look older than their years. The only way to battle the radicals is with cellular superheroes (no, not Nokia picture phones) called antioxidants. Consuming plenty of antioxidant-rich fruits and vegetables is the surest way to remain stable and well-balanced without an expensive visit to the shrink.

Pop Quizine

In Germany, they swear that eating a bowl of oatmeal with cooked onions is a surefire cure for...

a) insomnia
b) a hangover
c) heart disease
d) hemorrhoids

Answer: (b) Nein, danke! We'd rather have a headache!

RETURN TO SLENDER

The average person fuels his body the same way he gases up his vehicle—when it's running on fumes! The red warning light comes on, triggering an emergency pit stop for large fries and a chocolate shake. To avoid crazy blood-sugar spikes and uncontrollable urges to binge, never (ever!) let your tank run dry. Instead, go *grazey*! Eating smaller meals more often keeps your hunger in check, your metabolism revved, your energy levels stoked, and your mind sharp all day long. Gas up every three hours and make it a high-octane, balanced blend of lean protein (such as turkey or chicken breast), good carbohydrates (such as veggies, fruit, and whole grains), and healthy fats (such as olive oil or some nuts). Warning: Do not overfill the tank! According to researchers, your body can efficiently handle up to 500 calories in one sitting. Any more than that tends to shift your fat-storing engine into overdrive. If you eat small, eat often, and eat smart, you won't end up with a wider chassis!

Gourdian Angel

Silky pumpkin soup with apples and ginger

When you're too busy flying around and don't have time to fuss over dinner, just *wing* it with this *heavenly* pumpkin soup. It's quick, easy, and simply *gourdious*!

- **2 tsp olive oil or butter**
- **1 cup chopped onions**
- **1 tsp minced garlic**
- **1 tbsp grated gingerroot**
- **1 tsp curry powder**
- **1/2 tsp ground cumin**
- **4 cups chicken broth**
- **2 cups peeled, chopped Granny Smith apples**
- **2 cups canned pure pumpkin (not pumpkin pie filling)**
- **1 cup chopped carrots**
- **1/2 tsp salt**
- **1/4 tsp freshly ground black pepper (or to taste)**
- **3/4 cup evaporated 2% milk or light (5%) cream**

It's heavenly!

- Heat olive oil in a large, non-stick soup pot over medium heat. Add onions and garlic. Cook and stir until onions begin to soften, about 3 minutes. Add gingerroot, curry powder, and ground cumin. Mix well and cook for 30 more seconds.

- Add broth, apples, pumpkin, carrots, salt, and pepper. Bring mixture to a boil. Reduce heat to low and simmer, covered, for 12 to 15 minutes, or until carrots are tender. Stir occasionally.

- Working in two batches, transfer soup to a blender and purée until smooth. Soup will be very thick. Return puréed soup to pot and stir in evaporated milk. Serve hot.

Makes 6 servings

		PER SERVING					
calories	total fat	saturated fat	protein	carbohydrate	fiber	cholesterol	sodium
142	3 g	0.4 g	7 g	23 g	4.4 g	13 mg	533 mg

I've milked those dudes for all they're worth!

Invest in a dairy farm. You'll have lots of liquid assets.

Salmon and Garfunkel

Creamy salmon and corn chowder with dill

Are you going to Scarborough Fair? Don't pick up parsley, sage, or rosemary— just thyme (plus tarragon, dill, and a bottle of wine!). Then you might want to invite Cecilia and Mrs. Robinson over to taste your *dillicious* salmon chowder. You'll all be feelin' groovy!

BRIDGE OVER TROUBLED WATER

- **1 tbsp olive oil or butter**
- **1 cup sliced leeks (white part only) or chopped onions**
- **³/4 cup each chopped celery and diced red bell pepper**
- **1 tsp minced garlic**
- **1 tsp each dried thyme and dried tarragon**
- **3 tbsp all-purpose flour**
- **3 cups chicken broth**
- **1 can (14.75 oz) cream-style corn**
- **¹/2 cup light (5%) cream**
- **12 oz boneless, skinless salmon fillet, cut into bite-sized pieces**
- **¹/2 tsp each salt and freshly ground black pepper**
- **2 tbsp minced fresh dill**
- **1 tbsp freshly squeezed lemon juice**
- **1 tsp each grated lemon zest and Dijon mustard**

- Heat olive oil in a large, non-stick soup pot over medium heat. Add leeks, celery, red pepper, and garlic. Cook and stir until vegetables begin to soften, about 3 minutes.

- Add thyme and tarragon. Cook and stir for 30 more seconds. Add flour and mix well, until vegetables are completely coated. Add chicken broth. Bring mixture to a boil, stirring constantly. Soup will thicken slightly. Stir in corn and cream. Reduce heat to medium-low and stir in salmon, salt, and pepper. Cover and simmer until salmon is cooked through, about 5 to 6 minutes, depending on size of salmon pieces.

- Remove soup from heat and stir in dill, lemon juice, lemon zest, and mustard. Serve immediately.

Makes 6 servings

PER SERVING

calories	total fat	saturated fat	protein	carbohydrate	fiber	cholesterol	sodium
206	7.6 g	1.6 g	16 g	20 g	1.9 g	40 mg	617 mg

"SAY IT AIN'T SO!"

I left my heart…in a vat of Crisco! It's no secret that deep-fried foods like potato chips, French fries, and fried chicken go straight from your lips to your hips. But that's not the main reason health experts beg us not to overindulge. Research consistently shows that deep-fried foods contribute to cancer and hardening of the arteries. Why? Well, when any kind of oil (even heart-healthy olive oil) is heated to the extremely high temperatures used in deep-frying, the chemistry of the oil molecules changes. These chemically altered molecules don't fit into the very precise architecture of the human body. Our bodies don't know how to deal with these "mystery molecules" and they interfere with how our cells function. That's when health problems start creeping up. To make matters worse, many restaurants re-use the oil to fry other foods, causing a doubly disastrous oil spoil. Yes, you may love your potato chips, fries, and donuts, but it's time to face reality: They don't love you back. If you resist their seductive advances more often, you can avoid the inevitable heartbreak.

Funky Factoid

Before starring on *Bonanza* and *Little House on the Prairie*, Michael Landon was a machine operator, sealing hot cans of Campbell's Tomato Soup for a living. He traded tin for Tinseltown in a *mmm mmm good* career move!

AEROBICS CLASS
Please wear loose fitting clothing

If I had any loose fitting clothing, I wouldn't have joined up in the first place!

Now that's Italian!

Rome on the Range

Roasted tomato and red pepper soup with mini meatballs

Seldom is heard, a discouraging word about our tantalizing roasted tomato and meatball soup. There's a little Italy and a lotta flavor packed into this one.

Soup

**8 large plum or Roma tomatoes
(about 2 lbs)**

**2 large red bell peppers, seeded and
coarsely chopped**

1 large red onion, coarsely chopped

1 tbsp minced garlic

1 tbsp olive oil

**2 tbsp each minced fresh thyme
and fresh rosemary
(or 2 tsp dried Italian seasoning)**

2 cups beef broth, divided

1 cup V8 juice

**¼ cup chopped fresh basil leaves,
or 2 tsp dried**

1 tbsp balsamic vinegar

1 tsp granulated sugar

**½ tsp each salt, freshly ground
black pepper, and crushed red
pepper flakes**

Meatballs

12 oz extra-lean ground beef

¼ cup minced shallots or onions

¼ cup unseasoned dry bread crumbs

2 tbsp grated Parmesan cheese

1 egg

½ tsp dried Italian seasoning

**¼ tsp each salt and freshly ground
black pepper**

- Preheat oven to 450°F. Coarsely chop tomatoes and combine with red peppers, onion, garlic, olive oil, thyme, and rosemary in a very large roasting pan or on a very large rimmed baking sheet. It's best if vegetables are in a single layer.

- Place roasting pan in oven on middle rack and roast vegetables for 15 minutes. Remove vegetables from oven and give them a quick stir. Return pan to oven on middle rack and turn on the broiler. Broil vegetables for 10 minutes.

- Meanwhile, prepare meatballs. Combine all meatball ingredients in a medium bowl and mix well. Using your hands works best! Form 48 mini meatballs using 1 tsp or so of meat mixture per ball. Set aside.

- Remove vegetables from oven. Transfer half the vegetables to a blender or food processor, along with 1 cup beef broth, and purée until smooth. Transfer puréed vegetables to a large soup pot. Chop remaining vegetables into bite-sized pieces (if any tomato or pepper skins come loose, discard them) and add to pot, along with remaining beef broth, V8 juice, basil, balsamic vinegar, sugar, salt, black pepper, and crushed red pepper flakes. Bring soup to a boil. Add meatballs. Reduce heat to low, cover, and simmer for 5 to 6 minutes, until meatballs are cooked through. Taste soup and add more salt and pepper, if desired.

Tip: This soup looks nice and tastes great when you sprinkle some freshly grated Parmesan cheese on top of individual servings.

Makes 8 servings

PER SERVING

calories	total fat	saturated fat	protein	carbohydrate	fiber	cholesterol	sodium
184	7.8 g	3.3 g	15 g	16 g	2.9 g	64 mg	440 mg

Cooking TIP

Try to use fresh herbs for this recipe if you can—they make a big difference to the flavor of the soup. Also, if you don't feel like making your own meatballs, buy some pre-made, frozen, lean meatballs, cook them according to package directions, then stir them into the soup before serving. They'll be a bit bigger than our homemade meatballs, so use only about 24 of them.

Chicken Soup with Humpty Dumplings

Old-fashioned chicken soup with mini dumplings

All the king's horses, and all the king's men, couldn't eat soup without dumplings again! Our Polish mother, Alfreda, used to make this soup for us when we were little, and it was one of our favorites. It was only recently that she divulged the secret ingredient in her mini dumplings: Cream of Wheat!

Soup

2 tsp olive oil

1 cup each chopped onions, chopped celery, and chopped carrots

1 tsp minced garlic

1½ tsp dried thyme

1 tsp dried marjoram

6 cups chicken broth

2 plum tomatoes, chopped

¼ cup chopped celery leaves

2 bay leaves

½ tsp each salt and freshly ground black pepper

6 bone-in, skinless chicken thighs (about 1½ lbs)

Dumplings

1 cup 1% or 2% milk

1 tbsp butter

¼ tsp salt

⅓ cup Cream of Wheat cereal (not instant)

- Heat olive oil in a large, non-stick soup pot over medium-high heat. Add onions, celery, carrots, and garlic. Cook and stir until vegetables begin to soften, about 5 minutes. Stir in thyme and marjoram and cook 30 more seconds. Add broth, tomatoes, celery leaves, bay leaves, salt, and pepper. Bring soup to a boil. Add chicken thighs. Reduce heat to low and simmer, covered, for 30 minutes.

- While soup is simmering, make dumplings. Combine milk, butter, and salt in a medium, non-stick pot and bring to a gentle boil. Reduce heat to low. Stir in Cream of Wheat. Continue to cook, stirring constantly, until mixture is very thick, about 2 minutes. Remove from heat and let cool for 10 minutes.

- Using 1 tsp or so of "dough" for each dumpling, form 24 1-inch dumplings, using your hands to roll dumplings into little balls, as if you were making meatballs. (Put a drop of olive oil on your hands so the dough doesn't stick.) Place dumplings on a plate and cover with plastic wrap until soup is ready to serve.

- When soup is ready, remove chicken thighs from pot, cut meat from bone, and chop into bite-sized pieces. Discard bones and return meat to pot. Remove bay leaves. Place 4 dumplings in each serving bowl and ladle hot soup over top.

Tip: If you prefer pasta or don't feel like making dumplings, you can serve the soup over cooked egg noodles or rotini.

Makes 6 servings

PER SERVING

calories	total fat	saturated fat	protein	carbohydrate	fiber	cholesterol	sodium
223	8.8 g	3 g	17 g	17 g	2.3 g	54 mg	804 mg

A silly *soup*erstition? In the court of French King Louis XI, ladies of the upper class dined primarily on soup, believing that excess chewing would cause them to develop premature wrinkles. This practice, of course, led to the creation of the well-known *soup* opera, The *Bowled* and the Beautiful.

Shroom With Ado

Marinated, grilled portobello mushroom fajitas

There's much ado about mushrooms thanks to these *flab-u-less* fajitas. Why all the fuss? Well, with red meat out, the fat's way down. And spiced-up, grilled portobellos have the taste and texture of a thick, juicy steak, so you better leave *shroom* for seconds.

Feast your eyes on me!

PORTABELLADONNA

½ cup light balsamic vinaigrette dressing
2 tbsp steak spice rub (see tip in margin)
½ tsp each ground cumin, chili powder, and dried oregano
4 large portobello mushrooms (about 6-inch diameter)
1 tbsp olive oil
1 large red onion, sliced
1 large red bell pepper, seeded and cut into strips
1 large green bell pepper, seeded and cut into strips
1 tbsp each freshly squeezed lime juice and minced fresh cilantro
8 small whole wheat flour tortillas
Fajita fixin's: light sour cream, salsa, chopped lettuce, shredded light cheddar cheese, guacamole

- To make marinade, combine dressing, steak rub, cumin, chili powder, and oregano in a small bowl. Using a pastry brush, brush marinade over both sides of mushrooms. Let stand at room temperature for 1 hour.

- Preheat grill to high setting. Spray grill rack with cooking spray or brush lightly with oil. Grill mushrooms for about 3 minutes per side, until tender with nice grill marks. Remove from heat. Cut each mushroom into 6 slices. Cover with foil and keep warm.

- Heat olive oil in a large, non-stick wok or skillet over medium-high heat. Add onion slices and peppers. Cook and stir until vegetables are tender crisp, about 5 minutes. Add lime juice, cilantro, and reserved mushrooms. Stir gently and cook just until mushrooms are hot.

- To prepare fajitas, 10 minutes before serving time, wrap tortillas in foil and heat in a 350°F oven to warm (or wrap in a damp tea towel and heat in microwave). To serve, layer your favorite fajita fixin's on warm tortilla, followed by cooked vegetables. Wrap up and enjoy!

Makes 4 servings

PER SERVING

calories	total fat	saturated fat	protein	carbohydrate	fiber	cholesterol	sodium
353	10.6 g	0.6 g	12 g	56 g	8.4 g	0 mg	651 mg

Cooking TIP

The steak spice rub helps give the mushrooms a meaty, steak-like flavor. Our favorite is Club House La Grille Montreal Steak Rub Marinade. It's a thick paste sold in a small jar in the spice aisle. It keeps for months in the refrigerator and, needless to say, it's great on steak, too!

The Blame Game

There's no doubt that marketing campaigns for gut-busting, artery-clogging fast foods are everywhere, and they're really persuasive, too. But before you launch a lawsuit alleging that The Hamburglar stole your waistline and left behind an unidentifiable mass of flesh, ask yourself this: Who's really to blame? Sure, the fast-food giants haven't done us too many favors, but remember, we're the ones who keep buying their gargantuan combos and eating them. Every last morsel. Can't we take more personal responsibility for our own health? Do we need lawsuits or even laws to protect us from junk food? A Twinkie tax? Certainly consumers have responsibilities, too. If restaurants are willing to serve food that's better for us, we have to order the healthy stuff, not the Godzilla burger and super-size fries. Across North America, there's a trend toward innovative menus that dish up plenty of tasty, nutritious, balanced meals. Restaurants will take bigger strides toward healthier fast food as long as we keep beating a path to their doors. If we want them to deliver the goods, we've gotta say no to the bads!

That new Food Pyramid Diet is really working!

You can say that again

Fat or Fiction?

Eating pasta will make me fat.

Despite finger-pointing and blacklisting by high-protein, low-carb fanatics, there's really no need to place pasta on your list of banned substances. Nope, you don't have to resort to *pastacide* if you just use your noodle. First, drill into your noggin the notion that a serving of pasta is one cup—not four! The typical restaurant portion is enough to feed Tony Soprano and his entire family. Second, realize that pasta, especially cooked firm (al dente), is actually low to moderate on the Glycemic Index. That means it won't cause wild blood-sugar fluctuations and stimulate insulin, the fat-storage hormone—unless, of course, you eat too much. Overeating even a low-glycemic food can send blood sugar and insulin into a frenzy. Third, think balance. When you combine fiber (say, from vegetables), protein (how 'bout some chicken?), and good fat (maybe some olive oil) with pasta (try whole wheat), this slows the release of sugar into the bloodstream and dampens the insulin response. No harm done. Those who blame pasta for their weight gain most likely indulge in plain ol' noodles 'n' sauce, and they probably eat too much, too often. So when ya hasta have pasta, remember that naked noodles are naughty. Cover 'em up. Accessorize. And don't forget to downsize.

Pop Quizine

For hundreds of years, the Scots refused to eat potatoes because...

a) they had to be imported from England

b) they were too high on the Glasgow Glycemic Index

c) they weren't mentioned in the Bible

d) they caused severe gas when eaten with haggis

Answer: (c) Guess they missed the part about "Thou shalt not cover thy neighbors' tatties."

Touched by an Angel Hair Pasta

Angel hair pasta with roasted bell peppers and basil pesto

Say *halo* to a divine creation of delicate angel hair pasta tossed with heavenly roasted sweet peppers and saintly, slimmed-down basil pesto. It's so light and fresh tasting, you'll be floating on cloud nine.

2 large red bell peppers
1 large yellow bell pepper
1 large orange bell pepper
1 1/2 cups packed fresh basil leaves
2 tbsp olive oil
2 tsp minced garlic
1/2 tsp salt
8 oz uncooked angel hair pasta (capelli d'angelo)
1/4 cup freshly grated Parmesan cheese
Freshly ground black pepper (optional)

- Preheat broiler. Halve red, yellow, and orange peppers. Remove stems and seeds. Place peppers cut-side down on non-stick baking sheet. Broil until blistered and charred. Transfer to a large bowl, cover with plastic wrap, and let stand for 15 minutes. Peel off skins. Set 1 red pepper half aside. Cut remaining peppers into thin strips. Set aside.

- In food processor, purée reserved red pepper half, basil, olive oil, garlic, and salt until smooth.

- Cook pasta according to package directions until tender but firm. Drain and return to pot. Add pepper strips and basil purée. Toss to combine. Serve sprinkled with Parmesan cheese and freshly ground black pepper, if desired.

Makes 4 servings

PER SERVING

calories	total fat	saturated fat	protein	carbohydrate	fiber	cholesterol	sodium
346	10 g	2.2 g	11 g	53 g	5.4 g	5 mg	411 mg

Sealed With a Quiche

Broccoli and roasted red pepper quiche with a brown rice crust

It's a lip-smacking quiche that's much healthier than its kissing cousin.
More fiber, healthier carbs,
and less fat make it a real beauty.
You can kiss any hope
of leftovers goodbye!

1 tsp olive oil
¹/₂ cup minced onions
1 tsp minced garlic
1¹/₂ cups cooked
    brown rice
    (see tip below)
5 tbsp grated
    Parmesan cheese, divided
2 tbsp + 1¹/₂ cups fat-free egg substitute, divided (see tip below)
1 cup chopped broccoli florets (see tip below)
¹/₂ cup chopped bottled roasted red peppers
¹/₂ cup packed shredded light Swiss cheese (2 oz)
¹/₂ tsp salt
¹/₄ tsp dried basil or dried dill
¹/₄ tsp freshly ground black pepper
1 plum tomato, thinly sliced

- Preheat oven to 350°F. Spray an 8-inch round cake pan or casserole dish with cooking spray and set aside.

- Heat olive oil in a small skillet over medium heat. Add onions and garlic. Cook and stir until onions are tender, about 2 minutes. Transfer onion mixture to a medium bowl. Add cooked rice, 3 tbsp Parmesan cheese, and 2 tbsp egg substitute. Mix well. Spread mixture evenly over bottom of prepared pan and press down with the back of a spoon to make a crust.

- Top crust with broccoli florets, roasted red peppers, and shredded cheese, in that order. In another medium bowl, whisk together remaining egg substitute, salt, basil, and pepper. Pour over vegetables and cheese. Top with tomato slices and sprinkle with remaining 2 tbsp Parmesan cheese.

- Bake quiche for 45 minutes, or until it's puffed up and golden, and eggs are set. Let stand for at least 5 minutes before slicing.

Tip: Try using brown basmati rice in this recipe. If you like asparagus, you can substitute 3/4-inch pieces for the broccoli. If you prefer, use 7 whole, beaten eggs instead of the egg substitute.

Makes 6 servings

PER SERVING

calories	total fat	saturated fat	protein	carbohydrate	fiber	cholesterol	sodium
155	4.8 g	2.1 g	13 g	16 g	1.7 g	10 mg	430 mg

Funky Factoid

Talk about putting your foot in your mouth! Did you know that if you rub garlic on the heel of your foot, it will be absorbed by the pores and eventually show up on your breath? We've all heard that garlic has *heeling* qualities, though we couldn't help but wonder: If you eat garlic, does the smell show up on your feet?

RETURN TO SLENDER

In many households, there's a frequent guest at dinnertime: the television! When TV and eating go hand in hand, overconsumption of both is often the result. That's because neither is your real focus. Mindless TV watching promotes mindless munching, and that makes it easy to forget about the quality and quantity of your food. When you dine in the company of the television, you'll eat almost anything, and often too much of the worst things—hot dogs, take-out pizza, chicken wings, cookies, chips, crackers, ice cream, and so on. To avoid the need for a wider-framed La-Z-Boy, switch off the TV and switch your focus to the food you're eating. That way, you'll have a better chance of receiving the satellite signal from your brain that shouts "I'm satisfied! Enough already!" Now *that's* a channel worth tuning in to!

I can't remember the name of the pill, but it's on the tip of my tongue.

Cooking TIP

You know those cheap little packs of instant soup noodles that you survived on during your college days? That's what you'll need for this recipe. They come in all sorts of flavors, but it doesn't matter which type you buy, because you'll be throwing away the little seasoning packs anyway. If you prefer, you can cook some whole wheat spaghetti and substitute about 3 cups for the ramen noodles.

Grapefruit the Greatfruit

Seems like just about every diet plan begins the day with half a grapefruit. At a measly 40 calories, it's been a mainstay of waist-watchers for decades. But it's not just the low-calorie status that makes grapefruit an ideal diet food. Lately, scientists have revisited the grapefruit-weight-loss link, and you'll be tickled pink to know that consuming grapefruit does, indeed, seem to have a positive effect on metabolism. Weight-loss benefits aside, slice up a grapefruit for its immense stash of nutritional goodies: antioxidants (such as vitamins A and C), fiber, and potassium. This juicy fruit not only protects your heart and arteries, but also may help prevent cancer, too. In Japanese studies, grapefruit extract injected under the skin of mice stopped tumor growth dead in its tracks. No wonder grapefruit has such ap*peel*! By the way, the name "grapefruit" stems from the arrangement of the fruit as it grows: hanging in clusters just like grapes. (Note: If you're taking medication, you might want to check with your doctor or pharmacist before gorging on grapefruit. Special substances in the fruit affect the way some drugs, such as those for high blood pressure, high cholesterol, and anxiety, are metabolized in your liver, and this can dangerously boost or suppress the drug's effect.)

A good laugh and a long sleep are the best cures in the doctor's book.

Irish Proverb

The Soy in the Plastic Bubble

Quick and colorful tofu stir-fry with hoisin-peanut sauce

Sick and tired of the same old chicken stir-fry? Our scrumptious rendition with marinated tofu may be just what the doctor ordered. Contagious flavor!

2/3 cup bottled light peanut sauce
2 tbsp hoisin sauce
1 tsp toasted sesame oil
2 pkgs (3 oz each) instant ramen noodles (see tip in margin)
12 oz teriyaki- or Szechuan-flavored firm tofu, cubed
1 medium red onion, sliced
2 cups broccoli florets
1 cup baby corncobs, halved crosswise
1 cup sliced red bell pepper
1 cup snow peas or sugar snap peas
1/3 cup chopped green onions
1/4 cup coarsely chopped fresh basil leaves or 2 tbsp minced fresh cilantro (or a bit of both)
1/4 cup chopped peanuts for garnish (optional)

This recipe's a real ~~germ~~ gem!

- Before making this recipe, gather all of the ingredients. The stir-fry comes together very quickly once you start.

- Whisk together peanut sauce, hoisin sauce, and sesame oil in a small bowl. Set aside.

- Place noodles in a glass bowl (discard seasoning packets) and pour boiling water over top to cover. Let soak 1 minute, then drain in a colander. Using kitchen scissors, snip the noodles a bit so they aren't in 10-mile-long wavy pieces. Set aside.

- Spray a large, non-stick wok with cooking spray and heat over medium-high heat. Add tofu. Cook and stir until tofu begins to brown, about 2 minutes. Remove tofu from wok and set aside. Add red onion and 1/4 cup water. Cook and stir until onion begins to soften, about 2 minutes. Add broccoli, corncobs, red pepper, and snow peas. Cook and stir for 3 to 4 more minutes, until vegetables are tender crisp. If vegetables begin to stick, add a little more water. Add green onions and cook 1 more minute. Add sauce and tofu. Mix well. Stir in noodles and basil. Cook 1 more minute. Remove from heat. Sprinkle individual servings with chopped peanuts, if desired.

Makes 4 servings

PER SERVING

calories	total fat	saturated fat	protein	carbohydrate	fiber	cholesterol	sodium
303	7.5 g	1 g	14 g	49 g	6.6 g	0 mg	576 mg

Pizza for the Upper Crust

Grilled Margherita pizza: Tomatoes, basil, and fresh mozzarella on a crispy, thin crust

It's the crown jewel of thin-crust pizzas— in an upper class by itself! One taste of our exquisite tomato and mozzarella pizza and you'll be *waisting* away in Margheritaville!

1 can (14.5 oz) tomatoes with Italian herbs
⅓ cup pizza sauce
1 12-inch, prebaked, thin-crust pizza shell
¼ cup freshly grated Romano, Parmesan, or Asiago cheese
3 oz fresh mozzarella cheese (see tip in margin)
¼ cup chopped fresh basil leaves
Freshly ground black pepper

Fit for a Queen!

- Preheat grill to medium setting and leave lid closed to keep hot. (Or, preheat oven to 425°F.)

- Drain tomatoes in a sieve, pressing down on them to remove as much liquid as possible. Break up any large chunks using your fingers.

- Spread pizza sauce over crust, leaving a ¼-inch border. Top with drained tomatoes. Sprinkle tomatoes evenly with Romano cheese.

- Using a small, sharp knife, cut the mozzarella cheese into thin slices. Distribute the mozzarella evenly over pizza. Sprinkle with basil and some freshly ground black pepper.

- Place pizza directly onto grill or middle oven rack. If grilling, close lid and cook for 4 minutes, checking pizza halfway through cooking time to make sure crust isn't burning (every grill is different!). After 4 minutes, turn grill off, but keep lid down. Cook another 3 minutes or so, until toppings are hot and cheese is melted. If using oven, bake pizza for about 10 minutes, until cheese is melted and edges are lightly browned.

Makes 1 pizza, 8 slices

PER SLICE

calories	total fat	saturated fat	protein	carbohydrate	fiber	cholesterol	sodium
129	4.5 g	2.2 g	6 g	15 g	0.9 g	11 mg	286 mg

Cooking TIP

Fresh mozzarella cheese is milder, softer, and whiter than regular mozzarella, which tends to be drier and has an elastic texture. Look for fresh mozzarella at the deli-cheese counter of your supermarket or in small containers where the specialty cheeses are sold.

THE E FILES

Want to burn fat like there's no tomorrow? Then tomorrow, wake up and smell your running shoes! Studies show that exercising first thing in the morning before breakfast for a mere 20 minutes is more effective in melting fat than a full hour of aerobic exercise performed later in the day after you've eaten. When you first wake up, your blood sugar and carbohydrate reserves are at their lowest levels. So, if you exercise before eating your Wheaties, you force your body to look elsewhere for energy to fuel your rude awakening. That "elsewhere" is stored fat. Need another incentive to rise and shine your sneakers? Exercising in the morning kick-starts your metabolism when it's naturally the slowest. Normally, your metabolism doesn't peak until the afternoon, but now you've ignited a fat-burning fire that'll blaze all day long. Simply put, the early bird gets the *burn*!

We can thank Don Raffaele Esposito of Naples, Italy, for the creation of the Margheri pizza back in 1889. The restaurant owner wa asked to prepare a special dish in honor of Queen Margherita Teresa Giovanni's visit to Naples, so he developed a pizza featuring tomatoes, mozzarella cheese, and basil— ingredients bearing the three colors of the Italian flag: red, white, and green. He named his masterpiece after his royal guest of honor.

Livin' on **the** Vedge

Roasted vegetables with
lemon couscous

Looking for more
excitement when it
comes to roasted
vegetables? We've
gone over the edge
and pushed the flavor limit by
adding lemon-scented couscous,
sweet potatoes, and aromatic herbs.
The taste will knock your Birkenstocks off!

> It's okay, Honey. Just makin' the garden a little bigger.

2 cups vegetable broth
1½ cups uncooked whole wheat couscous
Grated zest of 1 lemon
1 large sweet potato, peeled and diced
1 large red bell pepper, seeded and chopped
1 large yellow bell pepper, seeded and chopped
1 medium red onion, chopped
1 medium zucchini, chopped
1 large portobello mushroom, chopped
1 cup canned chickpeas, drained and rinsed
2 tbsp olive oil
1 tbsp balsamic vinegar
2 tsp minced garlic
1 tsp dried rosemary
¼ tsp each salt and freshly ground black pepper
½ cup crumbled light feta cheese (2 oz) or
⅓ cup freshly grated Parmesan cheese
¼ cup chopped fresh basil leaves or fresh mint leaves

- Preheat oven to 450°F.

- Bring vegetable broth to a boil in a medium saucepan. Stir in couscous and lemon zest. Remove from heat. Cover and let stand until ready to use.

- In a large bowl, toss together all vegetables, chickpeas, olive oil, balsamic vinegar, garlic, rosemary, salt, and pepper. Spread vegetable mixture in a large roasting pan that has been sprayed with cooking spray. Roast for about 25 minutes, stirring once or twice, until vegetables are tender.

- To serve, combine hot vegetables, cooked couscous, feta cheese, and fresh basil in a large serving bowl and toss well. Add a bit more freshly ground black pepper to taste, if desired.

Makes 6 main-dish or 8 side-dish servings

PER SERVING (BASED ON 8 SERVINGS)

calories	total fat	saturated fat	protein	carbohydrate	fiber	cholesterol	sodium
253	6.2 g	1.7 g	8 g	42 g	7.6 g	6 mg	322 mg

My LDL cholesterol is too high. My HDL cholesterol is too low. What the H_LL is my doctor talking about?

Ask Greta

Rather than obsess over the ABCs of HDLs, let's get to the heart of the matter where cholesterol's concerned. The majority of cholesterol in your bloodstream is manufactured by your liver and actually doesn't come from cholesterol-containing foods such as cheese, eggs, and red meat. According to the latest research, the real culprits in the cholesterol caper may be cookies, crackers, chips, white bread, French fries, and sweets! That's right! A diet high in processed, refined carbohydrates (read: white flour and sugar) and low in fiber seems to send your liver into a cholesterol-manufacturing frenzy. Now remember, cholesterol's a sticky subject, and there are lots of other complicated factors that affect it, such as a sedentary lifestyle, low thyroid function, alcohol, smoking, and just plain ol' bad genes. If you have high cholesterol (and even if you don't!), you need to watch your intake of saturated fat from animal products, and even more important, steer clear of trans fats. On a more positive note, there are plenty of healthy *additions* you can make to your diet and lifestyle to help keep cholesterol in check. Some proven cholesterol-lowering foods include apples, pears, grapefruit, berries, oatmeal and oat bran, whole grains, beans, nuts, seeds, ground flaxseed, green tea, garlic, onions, artichokes, ginger, cayenne pepper, and cold-water fish (like salmon). Exercise and relaxation (managing stress) can lower LDL cholesterol (the lousy kind) and raise HDL cholesterol (the healthy kind). And it appears that how often you eat is just as important as what you eat. Studies show that people who eat five or six small meals per day have lower LDL cholesterol than those who eat two large meals.

The trouble with eating Italian food is that five or six days later, you're hungry again.

George Miller

Cooking TIP

Use an egg substitute such as Egg Beaters for this recipe. Don't use liquid egg whites— the frittata won't be nearly as tasty. If you prefer, you can use 8 whole eggs instead. We recommend using eggs that are high in omega-3 fatty acids (see page 83). They cost a bit more but they're worth every penny. Also, you can substitute fresh dill for oregano for a different (and delicious!) flavor. Finally, you really need to use a good non-stick skillet to make any frittata. An old skillet with scratch marks and chipped non-stick coating makes removing the frittata a pain in the butt.

Pop Quizine

Before Popeye wooed Olive Oyl, she had a boyfriend named:

a) Crisco
b) Ham Gravy
c) Balsamic Sam
d) Castor

Answer: (b) Ham Gravy. We can attribute the relationship break-up to bad food combining! By the way, Castor was Olive Oyl's brother.

If at first you don't succeed, fry, fry again!!

Hakuna Frittata

Simple and delicious vegetable and herb frittata with feta cheese

You'll be singing the praises of this *king* of frittatas! *Kenya* imagine waking up to an eggstra-nutritious breakfast that's also eggstra quick and easy to make? Of *chorus*, you could also serve it for lunch or dinner. It's our problem-free recipe...no worries for the rest of your day!

2 tsp olive oil
1/2 cup diced red onions
1 tsp minced garlic
1/2 cup each diced red bell pepper, thinly sliced zucchini, and chopped mushrooms
1 tbsp minced fresh oregano leaves, or 1 tsp dried
1 1/2 tsp minced fresh thyme, or 1/2 tsp dried
2 cartons (8 oz each) fat-free egg substitute (see tip in margin) or 8 whole eggs, lightly beaten
Salt and freshly ground black pepper to taste
1/2 cup crumbled light feta cheese (2 oz)

- Heat olive oil over medium heat in a 10-inch, non-stick skillet. Add onions and garlic. Cook and stir until onions begin to soften, about 2 minutes. Add red pepper, zucchini, and mushrooms. Cook and stir until vegetables are tender, about 5 more minutes. Stir in oregano and thyme. Cook for 30 more seconds.

- Reduce heat to low. Pour egg substitute over vegetables, making sure that vegetables are evenly distributed in skillet. Sprinkle with salt and pepper. Sprinkle feta cheese evenly over egg mixture.

- Cover skillet with a tight-fitting lid and let cook until eggs are completely set, about 12 minutes. Slice into 4 servings and serve hot.

Makes 4 servings

PER SERVING

calories	total fat	saturated fat	protein	carbohydrate	fiber	cholesterol	sodium
141	6.2 g	2.5 g	16 g	7 g	1.3 g	13 mg	529 mg

Did you hear about the valedictorian of the cooking class? She passed her exams with frying colors.

Greek With Envy

Greek tortellini salad with vegetables and a light vinaigrette dressing

Turn yourself into a Greek goddess and become the envy of all your friends by whipping up this sensational, substantial tortellini salad that's loaded with tomatoes, cucumbers, feta cheese, oregano, and an irresistible balsamic dressing. You'll covet every last morsel!

What? This old rag?

She's always the best dressed tortellini

Dressing

⅓ cup fat-free Italian salad dressing
1 tbsp each balsamic vinegar and
**   freshly squeezed lemon juice**
1 tsp each Dijon mustard and liquid honey

1 lb cheese-filled tortellini
1½ cups peeled, diced English cucumber
10 cherry tomatoes, halved
¾ cup chopped bottled roasted red peppers
¾ cup crumbled light feta cheese (3 oz)
½ cup chopped green onions
⅓ cup minced red onions
2 tbsp minced fresh oregano leaves
¼ tsp freshly ground black pepper

- To make dressing, whisk together all dressing ingredients in a small bowl. Refrigerate until ready to use.

- Cook tortellini according to package directions until tender but firm. Drain and rinse under cold running water. Drain again. Transfer tortellini to a large bowl.

- Add cucumber, tomatoes, red peppers, feta cheese, green and red onions, oregano, and pepper. Mix well. Add dressing and toss again. Cover and refrigerate for 1 hour before serving.

THE E FILES

With plenty of heavy breathing and half-naked bodies all around you, what's not to like about yoga? If you've never tried it, you don't know what you're missing. Close your eyes and visualize the following: You're sitting there in blissful silence…ohm…in a warm, serene environment…ohm…you've managed to get all your chakras aligned…ohm…and you're thinking that the last time your legs, torso, and arms were so curiously contorted and flexed, you were swimming in amniotic fluid. Seriously, yoga has become one of the most popular paths to good health for good reason: Besides calming your mind and opening up your creative and spiritual potential, yoga increases your heart rate, getting blood pumping and oxygen flowing to all your body's cells. (You might notice how great your skin looks and feels!) It boosts your metabolism and helps you burn fat. It also helps your lymphatic system (your body's sewer) dispose of waste, and gives your liver and kidneys a hand in their detoxifying efforts. Plus, yoga improves your posture, flexibility, and range of motion, keeping your joints limber and lubed up. It can even help lower your stress hormone levels. In short, yoga might get you all bent out of shape, but you'll be in much better shape as a result!

If you think you're a set of curtains, either see a psychiatrist or pull yourself together!

Makes 4 servings

PER SERVING

calories	total fat	saturated fat	protein	carbohydrate	fiber	cholesterol	sodium
433	12 g	7 g	19 g	62 g	4 g	94 mg	867 mg

I'm having a grate time!

It's a meat market out there! Why not stay home and experience this luscious, meatless, three-cheese lasagna with a friend or two? No (cheese) strings attached.

Tomato Sauce

½ cup sun-dried tomatoes
   (not oil-packed)
1½ cups chopped red onions
2 tsp minced garlic
3 cups sliced mushrooms
1 cup each diced zucchini and
   diced red or yellow bell pepper
1 tbsp dried Italian seasoning
1 jar (26 oz) your favorite tomato
   pasta sauce
1 can (14.5 oz) tomatoes with
   Italian herbs, undrained, cut up
⅓ cup chopped fresh basil leaves
1 tbsp balsamic vinegar
½ tsp freshly ground black pepper

2 cups light ricotta cheese (1 lb)
1 cup crumbled feta cheese with herbs
   (4 oz)
1 pkg (10 oz) frozen spinach, thawed,
   squeezed dry, and chopped
1 egg
12 oven-ready lasagna noodles
   (see tip below)
1½ cups packed shredded light
   mozzarella cheese (6 oz)

Makes 10 servings

Place sun-dried tomatoes in a small bowl and pour 1 cup boiling water over top. Let stand for 20 minutes while you prepare the sauce. Spray a 9 x 13-inch baking dish with cooking spray and set aside.

Spray a large, non-stick pot with cooking spray. Add onions and garlic. Cook and stir over medium-high heat until onions begin to soften, about 3 to 4 minutes. Add mushrooms, zucchini, and bell pepper. Cook and stir until vegetables are tender, about 7 more minutes. Stir in Italian seasoning. Cook 1 more minute. Add pasta sauce, undrained tomatoes, basil, balsamic vinegar, and pepper. Bring mixture to a boil. Reduce heat to low and simmer, covered, for 20 minutes. When sun-dried tomatoes have softened, chop and add, along with their soaking liquid, to the sauce.

While sauce is simmering, mix together ricotta cheese, feta cheese, spinach, and egg in a medium bowl. Refrigerate until ready to use.

Preheat oven to 375°F. To assemble lasagna, spread 1½ cups vegetable sauce over bottom of baking dish. Top with 4 lasagna noodles. It's okay to have space between the noodles—they'll expand as they cook. Spread ⅓ of the remaining sauce over noodles, followed by ½ the ricotta mixture. (Use a teaspoon to drop the ricotta in small mounds all over the noodles.) Top with ⅓ mozzarella. Repeat layer: 4 noodles, ⅓ sauce, remaining ricotta, ⅓ mozzarella. For top layer: 4 noodles, ⅓ sauce, ⅓ mozzarella. Cover lasagna with foil. If your baking dish is full, place it on a cookie sheet in case the sauce bubbles over.

Bake lasagna for 35 minutes. Uncover and bake an additional 15 minutes. Remove lasagna from oven and let stand, uncovered, for 15 minutes before serving.

PER SERVING

calories	total fat	saturated fat	protein	carbohydrate	fiber	cholesterol	sodium
305	8.6 g	5.3 g	19 g	39 g	4.6 g	52 mg	672 mg

Cooking TIP

Oven-ready lasagna noodles are the type you don't need to boil before using—a brilliant, time-saving culinary invention! During baking, the moisture from the sauce softens, or rehydrates, the noodles, especially when the pan is covered as the lasagna bakes. If you'd prefer to precook your lasagna noodles (try whole wheat noodles!) instead of using oven-ready noodles, you won't need as much sauce. Therefore, don't add the soaking liquid from the sun-dried tomatoes to the sauce, or your lasagna will be too runny.

Born to be Wild Mushroom Pizza

Herbed wild mushroom pizza with hummus

Like a true nature's child, we were born, born to eat wild... mushrooms, that is! (As long as they've been declared safe by a mushroom expert, of course!)

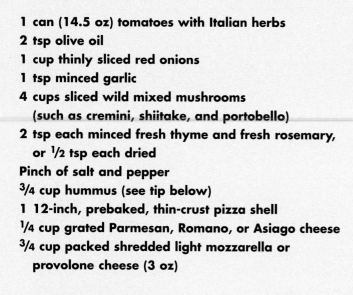

1 can (14.5 oz) tomatoes with Italian herbs
2 tsp olive oil
1 cup thinly sliced red onions
1 tsp minced garlic
4 cups sliced wild mixed mushrooms
  (such as cremini, shiitake, and portobello)
2 tsp each minced fresh thyme and fresh rosemary,
  or 1/2 tsp each dried
Pinch of salt and pepper
3/4 cup hummus (see tip below)
1 12-inch, prebaked, thin-crust pizza shell
1/4 cup grated Parmesan, Romano, or Asiago cheese
3/4 cup packed shredded light mozzarella or
  provolone cheese (3 oz)

- Preheat oven to 425°F.

- Drain tomatoes in a sieve, pressing down on them to remove as much liquid as possible. Set aside. They won't look pretty at this point, but that's okay.

- Heat olive oil in a large, non-stick skillet over medium heat. Add onions and garlic. Cook and stir until onions have softened, 3 to 4 minutes. Add mushrooms and cook until mushrooms are tender, about 5 more minutes. Stir in thyme, rosemary, salt, and pepper. Cook 1 more minute. Remove from heat.

- To assemble pizza, spread hummus over pizza crust, leaving a 1/2-inch border. Top hummus with drained tomatoes. Sprinkle Parmesan cheese over tomatoes. Spread mushroom mixture evenly over top, followed by mozzarella.

- Place pizza directly on middle oven rack and bake for 10 to 12 minutes, until cheese is completely melted and edges are lightly browned. Remove from oven to cutting board and let cool 1 minute before slicing.

Tip: For this recipe, try our hummus on page 22 or use store-bought hummus. This pizza makes a great appetizer when sliced into thin wedges.

Makes 1 pizza, 8 slices

PER SLICE

calories	total fat	saturated fat	protein	carbohydrate	fiber	cholesterol	sodium
190	7.3 g	2.5 g	9 g	22 g	2.6 g	8 mg	410 mg

You're Darn Tootin'!

When grandma nagged you to eat your beans, she wasn't just being an old fart. No, she obviously had the inside scoop: Beans are on the Dean's list of super foods! They're packed with folate, which helps prevent birth defects and cuts your risk of heart disease. Plus, they're also a good source of potassium and magnesium, so they can help stabilize high blood pressure. Some beans, like black, for instance, have levels of disease-fighting antioxidants that are equal to those found in oranges, grapes, and cranberries. But it's their mega dose of fiber that gives us real reason to *toot* and holler. The soluble fiber in beans is like an internal Swiffer mop, picking up toxic goop that might otherwise linger in your darkest regions and contribute to cancer, high cholesterol, and diabetes. The most exciting news? Beans can be a lethal weight-loss weapon. How's that? Well, beans have both fiber and protein, a dynamic duo that'll keep your blood-sugar levels even Steven, and help you to feel full longer, so you're less likely to overeat. Plenty of reasons to jump on the *bean* wagon!

DON'T HAVE A COW, MAN!

Cooking TIP

Boca Ground Burger is precooked, simulated ground beef made from soy. It's a good source of protein, it's cholesterol free and low in fat, and it's pretty darn tasty when used in chili and spaghetti sauce. Since it's precooked, you just add it frozen to your simmering sauce until it's heated through. Look for Boca Ground Burger in a red box where frozen hamburgers are sold at your grocery store.

RETURN TO SLENDER

Dining out again? If restaurants are where you get your daily bread, you might need to pull up a larger chair for your blossoming buns. Did you know that many restaurant entrées have 1,000 to 1,500 calories, and that's not even counting the bread, appetizer, beverage, or dessert? Creamy sauces, gratuitous use of oil, gargantuan portions—your fat cells are salivating just thinking about it! If you're a frequent diner, try sharing your meal, ordering an appetizer as the main course, or asking for a doggie bag that you can take to work for lunch. Can't resist dessert? *Halve* your cake and eat it, too! And here's a waist-trimming tip: Once in a while, stay home and cook. That way you control what goes on your plate. Plus, cooking from scratch is fun, fun, fun! (What do you expect cookbook authors to say?)

Pop Quizine

Beany Baby

Spicy vegetarian chili with two kinds of beans

Yeah, baby! If you're keen about beans, you'll want to stuff yourself silly with this high-protein, meatless, fiber-filled meal. Tastes *toy*riffic with a *doll*op of low-fat sour cream.

- **1 tbsp olive oil**
- **1 1/2 cups chopped red onions**
- **1 cup each chopped green bell pepper and chopped celery**
- **2 tsp minced garlic**
- **1 pkg (12 oz) frozen Boca Ground Burger (see tip in margin)**
- **1 1/2 tbsp chili powder**
- **2 tsp each ground cumin and dried oregano**
- **1 tsp ground coriander**
- **1/2 tsp crushed red pepper flakes**
- **1/4 tsp ground cinnamon**
- **1 can (28 oz) diced tomatoes, undrained**
- **2 cans (15.5 oz each) beans, drained and rinsed (see tip below)**
- **1 can (14 oz) tomato sauce**
- **1 cup vegetable or chicken broth**
- **1 tbsp brown sugar**
- **1/2 tsp salt**
- **1/4 tsp freshly ground black pepper**
- **1/4 cup chopped fresh cilantro (optional)**

- Heat olive oil in a large, non-stick pot over medium-high heat. Add onions, green pepper, celery, and garlic. Cook and stir until vegetables begin to soften, about 5 minutes.

- Add frozen ground burger, chili powder, cumin, oregano, coriander, red pepper flakes, and cinnamon. Mix well and cook for 1 more minute. Add undrained tomatoes, beans, tomato sauce, broth, brown sugar, salt, and pepper. Bring mixture to a boil. Reduce heat to low and simmer, covered, for 20 minutes. Remove from heat and stir in cilantro (if using). Serve hot.

Tip: When selecting canned beans for this recipe, choose from red kidney beans, black beans, chickpeas, navy beans, cannellini beans, or even lentils. We like the combination of red kidney beans and navy beans, but you should pick your favorites.

Makes 6 to 8 servings

PER SERVING (BASED ON 8 SERVINGS)

calories	total fat	saturated fat	protein	carbohydrate	fiber	cholesterol	sodium
223	2.8 g	0.3 g	18 g	36 g	12 g	1 mg	634 mg

Parma Chameleon

Tofu Parmesan: A healthy alternative to the
traditional eggplant favorite

Boy George, I think we've got it:
A creative way to prepare tofu
and actually *like* it!

Olive oil cooking spray
1 lb firm tofu
(see tip in margin)
1 cup fresh whole wheat
bread crumbs (see tip in margin)
¼ cup + 2 tbsp grated Parmesan cheese, divided
½ tsp each dried basil and dried oregano
¼ tsp each salt and freshly ground black pepper
1 egg
1½ cups your favorite tomato pasta sauce, divided
½ cup packed shredded light mozzarella cheese (2 oz)
1 tbsp chopped fresh parsley

- Please read tips in margin before starting! Preheat oven to 400°F.
  Spray a non-stick baking sheet with olive oil spray and set aside.

- Drain liquid from tofu and blot dry with paper towels. Slice block
  into 6 to 8 equal slices, about ½-inch thick. Lay slices on paper
  towels and blot dry again.

- Combine bread crumbs, ¼ cup Parmesan cheese, basil,
  oregano, salt, and pepper in a shallow bowl. Place egg in
  another shallow bowl and beat lightly with a fork.

- Working one piece at a time, dip tofu in egg and then in crumb
  mixture. Make sure both sides are well coated with crumb
  mixture. Place on cookie sheet. Repeat with remaining tofu
  pieces. (Don't worry if you have some crumbs left over—you'll use
  them later.) Spray tops of tofu with olive oil spray. Bake for 8
  minutes. Using a spatula, gently turn pieces over. Bake an
  additional 8 minutes. Remove tofu from oven but leave oven on.

- Spray a medium casserole dish with cooking spray. Spread ½
  cup pasta sauce over bottom of dish. Lay browned tofu pieces in
  dish close together and in a single layer if possible. Top with
  remaining pasta sauce, followed by mozzarella, remaining
  Parmesan cheese, and parsley. If you have any crumbs left over,
  sprinkle them over the entire dish. Bake, uncovered, for 15
  minutes. Turn broiler on and broil about 4 inches from heat
  source for 2 minutes, or until cheese is golden brown. Let stand 5
  minutes before serving.

Makes 4 servings

	PER SERVING						
calories	total fat	saturated fat	protein	carbohydrate	fiber	cholesterol	sodium
247	9.8 g	3.9 g	22 g	19 g	4.5 g	68 mg	895 mg

Most ordinary tofu
has a bland,
slightly nutty flavor
and a chameleon-
like ability to
absorb the flavor of the food
with which it's cooked. Make
sure you buy plain tofu for this recipe, not
the flavored kind, such as Szechuan or
teriyaki. You'll need the firm or extra-firm
variety, too. Silken or soft tofu will fall apart
and make a big mess! It's best to store tofu
in water in the refrigerator and to change
the water daily, if possible. It'll keep for
about a week. To make fresh bread
crumbs, place a couple slices of whole
wheat bread in a food processor or mini
chopper and pulse on and off until soft
crumbs are formed. And lastly, for a tastier
dish, try grating or shredding your own
Parmesan cheese instead of using pre-
shredded cheese or the powdery stuff sold
in the pasta aisle.

"SAY IT AIN'T SO!"

No one would argue that baling hay,
plowing fields, and milking cows isn't tough
physical work that requires ample energy,
but if you choose the following breakfast as
your fuel, you might just buy the farm! A
"Farmer's Slam" breakfast platter at a
popular family restaurant (we don't like to
name names, but we can't *Denny* you the
truth) has three scrambled eggs mixed with
scrambled sausage, shredded potatoes,
peppers, and onions, topped with gravy and
cheddar, plus two hotcakes with margarine
and syrup, two bacon strips, two sausage
links, and a side of hash browns. That's not
breakfast, it's a shopping list! At 1,430
calories, 90 grams of fat, and 3,350 mg of
sodium, you'll be the broad size of a barn if
this is your regular chow. Mind over platter
or your body's getting fatter!

*I was a vegetarian until I started
leaning toward the sunlight.*

Rita Rudner

Poultry in Motion

Chicken recipes that'll really move you

Caribbean jerk chicken • Indian coconut-curry chicken • Lemon-dill chicken breasts • Orange-teriyaki chicken breasts • Chicken and wild rice skillet • Greek chicken skewers • Orange-ginger chicken stir-fry • Spicy peanut chicken • Thai coconut chicken • Tuscan chicken • Baked chicken • Barbecue sauce • Indian butter chicken • Roasted whole chicken • Honey mustard and herb drumsticks • Oven "fried" chicken

Tuskinny Chicken

A hearty, one-pot Italian dinner that is sure to become a family favorite

This delectable chicken dinner is a *leaning* tower of goodness and contains everything under the Tuscan sun: tender chicken, colorful vegetables, nutritious chickpeas, and a hint of white wine. *Italeave* you satisfied!

1 tbsp olive oil
12 boneless, skinless chicken thighs (about 2¼ lbs)
1½ cups coarsely chopped red onions
2 tsp minced garlic
3 cups sliced mushrooms
1 medium zucchini, sliced
1 large yellow bell pepper, sliced
2 tbsp each minced fresh basil leaves, fresh oregano leaves, and fresh rosemary, or 1½ tsp each dried
1 jar (26 oz) your favorite tomato pasta sauce
½ cup dry white wine
1 cup canned chickpeas or white kidney beans, drained and rinsed
¼ tsp freshly ground black pepper
¼ cup grated Romano or Parmesan cheese

- Heat olive oil in a large (14-inch), deep, non-stick skillet over medium-high heat. Add chicken thighs. Cook until chicken is lightly browned, 2 to 3 minutes on each side. Remove chicken from skillet and keep warm.

- Add onions and garlic to the same skillet. Cook and stir until onions begin to soften, about 3 minutes. Be careful not to burn them. Add mushrooms, zucchini, and yellow pepper. Cook and stir until vegetables are tender-crisp, about 6 more minutes. Stir in chopped herbs and cook for 1 more minute.

- Add pasta sauce, wine, chickpeas, and black pepper. Bring mixture to a boil. Reduce heat to medium-low. Return chicken pieces to skillet. Cover and simmer for 20 minutes. Uncover and cook an additional 10 minutes (this will help sauce to thicken). Remove from heat and, if you have the patience, let dish stand, uncovered, for another 5 minutes to cool slightly.

- Serve in shallow bowls, topped with a sprinkling of grated Romano cheese.

Makes 6 servings

PER SERVING

calories	total fat	saturated fat	protein	carbohydrate	fiber	cholesterol	sodium
377	10.8 g	2.9 g	41 g	26 g	6 g	142 mg	660 mg

Cooking TIP

If you prefer, you can substitute 6 boneless, skinless chicken breasts for the thighs. Cut them in half so they're about the same size as thighs. If you're making this meal for a special dinner, it's worth the effort to buy fresh herbs instead of using the dried variety.

THE E FILES

Instead of jumping on the latest fad-diet bandwagon, just start jumping! Many experts think we'd all be slimmer—and healthier—if we focused more on exercise than on diet. That's because weight maintenance is where most people fail, and the best tool for successfully keeping off the pounds is good ol' physical activity. And you don't have to run marathons or sweat buckets at butt-blaster class, either. Any kind of movement counts and every little bit helps. Just move your extremities in a simultaneous fashion any chance you get. Every time you take the stairs instead of the elevator, use a shovel rather than a snowblower, walk on your lunch break instead of snoozing at your desk, or play with your kids instead of saying, "I'm too tired," you've marched one step closer to victory in the war against fat.

Pop Quizine

The only "real" man to be immortalized by having his head on a PEZ candy dispenser was...

a) American pioneer Daniel Boone
b) first *Pezident* of the United States George Washington
c) basketball superstar Michael Jordan
d) king of rock 'n' roll Elvis Presley

Answer: (a) The only real woman to share the same honor was seamstress Betsy Ross, the sewer of the first American flag. Incidentally, the name PEZ was derived from the German word for "peppermint"—**PfefferminZ.**

Ask Greta

If I do 3,000 sit-ups, will I have a washboard stomach?

Think super-human crunch sessions will give you fab abs? Well, you've got another thing comin'—and it's most likely a stiff neck! Sure, sit-ups strengthen your abs and help lighten the load on your back, but they do not—even if you do a hundred every day—make stomach fat disappear. You can't spot-reduce fat. If you want the sculpted-stomach look, you need to shed overall body fat so you can actually see the result of those sit-ups, and that means eating less and moving your muscles more. Remember, muscle is your blubber-burning furnace. The more muscle you have, the more powerful your furnace, and the more fat you'll incinerate 24 hours a day—all over your body, including those nasty trouble spots. Think of it this way: If you upgraded the furnace in your home, it wouldn't be just the kitchen that received more heat. There'd be more heat in the bedroom and bathrooms, too! Believe it or not, building muscle all over your body, even in your arms, actually helps flatten your belly. By all means keep doing sit-ups—any calorie-burning, strengthening exercise is a boon to your physique. But if you're a *Belly* Idol wannabe, make sure you're doing push-ups, pull-ups, stand-ups, and jump-ups, too!

In olden times, saloons offered free lunches, most of which were overly salted, forcing the diner to buy a drink. Hence the origin of the phrase, "There's no such thing as a free lunch."

Sticky Chicky

Baked chicken thighs in a sticky-sweet barbecue sauce

Even if your kids are picky, there's no way they'll call these "icky." Instead of saying "phooey," they'll shout, "Yahooey! These are gooey!"

16 boneless, skinless chicken thighs (about 3 lbs)

Sauce
½ cup barbecue sauce (hickory flavored is nice!)
¼ cup reduced-sodium soy sauce
¼ cup red wine vinegar
¼ cup liquid honey or maple syrup
1 tbsp chili powder
1 tbsp Dijon mustard
1 tbsp grated gingerroot
2 tsp minced garlic
1 tsp ground cumin

1 tbsp cornstarch

- Preheat oven to 400°F. Spray a 9 x 13-inch baking pan with cooking spray. Arrange chicken thighs in pan in a single layer.

- Whisk together all sauce ingredients in a medium bowl. Pour evenly over chicken. Turn pieces to coat both sides with sauce. Bake, uncovered, for about 40 minutes, or until chicken is no longer pink in the center.

- Remove chicken from pan and keep warm. Carefully pour sauce from pan into a small pot. Bring to a boil over medium-high heat. Combine cornstarch with an equal amount of water and mix until smooth. Add to sauce. Cook until sauce is bubbly and thickened, about 1 minute. Serve hot chicken with extra sauce on top.

Makes 8 servings

PER SERVING

calories	total fat	saturated fat	protein	carbohydrate	fiber	cholesterol	sodium
287	7.1 g	1.7 g	32 g	19 g	0.5 g	141 mg	590 mg

Did you hear about the dog that ate a pound of garlic? His bark was worse than his bite.

The Better Butter Chicken

Fragrant Indian butter chicken

It's the star of India! A real jewel. A gem of a recipe. Our healthier rendition of this popular ethnic dish doesn't use gobs of butter and tons of heavy cream, so you can save those precious calories for dessert.

2 tbsp butter
1 ½ cups chopped onions
2 tsp minced garlic
1 tbsp grated gingerroot
1 ½ tsp chili powder
¾ tsp each ground coriander and ground turmeric (see tip in margin)
½ tsp each ground cinnamon and ground cumin
1 can (28 oz) diced tomatoes, drained
1 ½ cups reduced-sodium chicken broth
1 tbsp brown sugar
¼ tsp each salt and freshly ground black pepper
1 whole cooked rotisserie chicken, skin removed and meat cut up (see tip in margin)
⅓ cup light sour cream (not fat free)
1 tbsp minced fresh cilantro
Hot cooked basmati rice (optional)

- Melt butter in a deep, 10-inch skillet or soup pot over medium heat. Add onions and garlic. Cook slowly, stirring often, until onions are tender, about 5 minutes. Add gingerroot, chili powder, coriander, turmeric, cinnamon, and cumin. Cook 1 more minute. Add drained tomatoes, broth, brown sugar, salt, and pepper. Reduce heat to low. Cover and simmer for 10 minutes, stirring occasionally. Remove from heat.

- Transfer half the sauce to a blender and purée until smooth. Return puréed sauce to pot with remaining sauce. Mix well and return to heat. Stir in cut-up chicken. Cook until chicken is heated through. Remove from heat and stir in sour cream and cilantro. Serve over hot basmati rice, if desired.

Makes 5 servings

PER SERVING

calories	total fat	saturated fat	protein	carbohydrate	fiber	cholesterol	sodium
297	10.5 g	4.5 g	33 g	18 g	4 g	102 mg	395 mg

Cooking TIP

Turmeric is a vibrant orangey-yellow spice that comes from the root of a tropical plant. It's used to add both flavor and color to food, and you'll almost always find it in East Indian curry recipes. Ground or powdered turmeric is widely available in the spice aisle of most grocery stores. Using a store-bought, rotisserie chicken makes this recipe much tastier than using plain, cooked chicken breast. The combination of dark meat and light meat makes it absolutely scrumptious! Remove all of the skin from the chicken, discard the wings, and cut the meat from the thighs and breasts into large chunks. Don't shred or cut the meat too small, or the finished dish won't look very appealing.

Fat or Fiction?

A high-fiber diet helps reduce cholesterol.

Got high cholesterol? How 'bout constipation? Both? Actually, that's not surprising. High cholesterol and constipation often go hand in hand. Think of your body as a magnificently engineered waste-management facility. Normally, nasty LDL cholesterol, harmful fats, and other debris are whooshed quickly out of your body via the colon. But if you become constipated as a result of eating too much junk food, the sludge just kinda sits there. And sits there. After a while, some of the toxic guck (including bad cholesterol) gets *reabsorbed* through the lining of your intestine and ends up back in your bloodstream where it started. Yikes! Avoiding a backlog is as easy as one, two, three: First, get yourself the best "Colon Hoover" money can buy—otherwise known as soluble fiber. That's the kind of fiber found in oat bran, beans, flaxseed, fruit (especially apples and pears), and veggies. Second, get your bowels moving by getting your butt moving. Literally! Exercise is like a "kick in the pants" to your intestinal tract and can be your bowel's best buddy. The more regularly you exercise, the more regular you'll become. Finally, don't treat your body like a dump. For successful waste (and waist) management, stop eating so much garbage!

Sellers of dried grapes are always raisin awareness.

Great Eggspectations

Like the ad says, it really is "the incredible, edible egg." Eggs are the perfect protein. You might even call eggs the mother of all protein, because they're the standard against which all proteins are compared. Not only that, they're packed with some of nature's most synergistic nutrients: For a mere 75 calories and five grams of fat, you get six grams of protein, vitamins A and D, B-12, folate, and just about every other important vitamin and mineral there is. Nowadays, you can even buy omega-3 eggs, laid by sorority-pledging chickens. Truthfully, omega-3 eggs come from chickens that are fed flaxseed, one of the richest sources of omega-3 fatty acids. These essential fatty acids are good for your heart, brain, nervous system, immune system, joints, and just about everything in between. So, if you love to eat eggs at the crack of dawn, it's worth shelling out a few *eggstra* cents to buy the omega-3 variety.

"SAY IT AIN'T SO!"

Yee-ha! Chicken fingers! No doubt, your kids will be high-fiving (in more ways than one) when you let them order those tasty strips from the restaurant menu. A typical five-finger order will hand them more than 600 fried, trans-fat-laden calories! Want some fries to go with those fingers? Say "yes" and count on an additional 400 artery-clogging calories. To get the upper hand where your children's health is concerned, forget the fingers and point to the baked chicken or grilled chicken sandwich more often.

Chick Flick

The Roastess with the Mostest

Lemon and herb roasted whole chicken

You'll be the hostess with the mostest when you serve this tantalizing roasted whole chicken to your dinner guests. They're sure to appreciate the carefully plucked, organic, grain-fed chicken that you raised in your backyard coop, infused with freshly snipped, homegrown rosemary and thyme from your greenhouse herb garden, and lovingly presented on the decorative platter that you handcrafted in your very own pottery barn. It's a good thing!

1 whole roasting chicken (about 4 lbs)
1 tbsp Dijon mustard
1 tbsp brown sugar
1 tbsp minced fresh rosemary
1 tbsp minced fresh thyme
1 tsp minced garlic
1 tsp olive oil
½ tsp each salt and freshly ground black pepper
Grated zest and juice of half a lemon

- Move oven rack to bottom third of oven. Preheat oven to 425°F. Place a small rack inside a roasting pan. Pour 1 cup water in pan. Rinse chicken inside and out, and pat dry with paper towels.

- In a small bowl, mix together mustard, brown sugar, rosemary, thyme, garlic, oil, salt, and pepper to make a paste. Add lemon zest and mix again. Set aside.

- Squeeze juice from lemon inside cavity of chicken, then tuck the used lemon half right inside it. Tie legs together with kitchen string. Rub reserved paste over surface of chicken and, using your fingers, carefully rub paste between skin and meat on breast and thighs.

- Place chicken on rack breast-side down. Roast, uncovered, for 30 minutes. Remove chicken from oven and flip over. Add a bit more water to pan if it has evaporated. Return to oven and roast for 35 to 40 more minutes, depending on size of bird. If chicken browns too quickly, cover it loosely with foil. When cooked, legs should move easily in sockets and thigh juices should be clear (not pink) when pierced with a small knife. A meat thermometer inserted in thigh (away from bone) should read 170°F.

- Remove chicken from oven and let rest for 10 minutes before carving.

Makes 4 servings

PER SERVING (LIGHT AND DARK MEAT)

calories	total fat	saturated fat	protein	carbohydrate	fiber	cholesterol	sodium
222	7.3 g	2 g	33 g	5 g	0.4 g	108 mg	417 mg

Not Humdrumsticks

Baked honey mustard and herb chicken drumsticks

Bored to tears with your usual weekday fare? Our simple, succulent, finger-lickin' baked chicken will have your family dancing to the beat of a different drumstick!

Ho hum. He's not humdrum!

12 skinless chicken drumsticks (about 2½ lbs)

¼ cup liquid honey

2 tbsp cider vinegar

2 tbsp grainy Dijon mustard

1 tsp minced garlic

1 tsp dried Herbs de Provence (see tip below)

¼ tsp each salt and freshly ground black pepper

- Preheat oven to 400°F. Spray a 9 x 13-inch baking pan with cooking spray. Arrange drumsticks in pan in a single layer.

- Whisk together remaining ingredients in a small bowl. Spoon sauce evenly over chicken pieces. Bake for 20 minutes. Remove pan from oven and baste chicken with sauce. (Tilting the pan to one side helps!) Return chicken to oven and bake an additional 20 to 25 minutes, until chicken is no longer pink in the center.

- Arrange chicken on a serving platter and pour sauce from pan over chicken. Serve hot.

Tip: Herbs de Provence is an herb blend that you'll likely find right beside all the other dried herbs you buy at the grocery store. It's simply a combination of herbs commonly used in southern French cooking: basil, marjoram, rosemary, sage, thyme, savory, and lavender.

Makes 6 servings

PER SERVING

calories	total fat	saturated fat	protein	carbohydrate	fiber	cholesterol	sodium
201	5.4 g	1.3 g	25 g	12 g	0.2 g	82 mg	209 mg

*I got food poisoning today.
But I don't know when I'm going to use it.*

Steven Wright

Don't eat this. Avoid that. This'll make you fat. That raises cholesterol. Ugh! What's a guy or gal to do? Like real estate's mantra for success, "location, location, location," the sane way to navigate the murky waters of today's nutritional landscape is to think "moderation, moderation, moderation." Most foods in moderation are okay. Most foods in excess—even some healthy foods—are *not* okay. It's our excesses that can lead to problems. Obesity, cancer, diabetes, and heart disease are not the result of eating "unhealthy" or "taboo" foods every once in a while. They're usually the result of regular consumption of unhealthy foods—day in and day out, year after year. A helpful and realistic healthy-eating guideline is the 80/20 rule: 80% of the time, try choosing foods that are nutritious, high in fiber, and low in bad fats. Twenty percent of the time, eat what you want and let yourself have an indulgence. Craving chocolate ice cream? Scoop up a small serving and savor every spoonful. Then, get back on the healthy eating track for the rest of the day. It's not every morsel of food you eat that's important—it's what you do consistently, over the long haul, that really counts.

In the early 1950s, Swanson executive Gerry Thomas invented the world's first frozen dinner. He desperately needed to get rid of 520,000 pounds of the company's excess turkey, so he sketched a drawing of a three-compartment aluminum tray, presented it to the Swansons—his bosses—and came up with the name "TV dinner." The first TV dinner meal consisted of turkey and corn bread dressing with gravy, buttered peas, and sweet potatoes. It sold for 98 cents (or about $6 in today's money) and came in a box that looked like a TV set. Initially, the company timidly ordered only 5,000 TV dinners, but consumers gobbled up 10 million of them within the first year!

Cooking TIP

Look for barbecue chicken seasoning in the spice aisle near the steak seasonings and rubs. It may be called "rotisserie chicken seasoning" or something similar. Make sure it's a dry powder, not a wet, marinade-type seasoning, and avoid brands that list MSG in the ingredients. For a flavor variation, add 1/2 cup low-fat ranch salad dressing to the egg mixture (omit water if using real egg).

THE E FILES

Tap your fingers, twirl your hair, bounce your leg, shift here and there. No, we're not callin' a square dance. We're callin' on you to take up fidgeting! Researchers at the Mayo Clinic in Rochester, Minnesota, found that small, habitual movements like tapping your feet, adjusting your posture, and pacing back and forth can burn hundreds of calories per day. Golleeee! You'd have to do an awful lot of doe-see-doeing to burn off that many calories! In the study, a group of volunteers aged 20 to 35 were asked to eat 1,000 extra calories per day for eight weeks. As a result, some subjects gained as much as 16 pounds, whereas others gained as little as two pounds. The people who gained the least amount of weight were "the young and the restless." The toe-tappin', knee-bobbin', chair-shiftin', ear-scratchin' crowd may not have made any new friends in the study group, but they didn't make much new fat, either. Looks like any little movement is better than no movement at all!

Kentucky Freud Chicken

Oven "fried" chicken with a spicy herb coating

Wanna boost your ego? Whip up our scrumptious, crispy-coated chicken and get everyone *psyched* about dinner! We don't mean to play mind games, but our chicken isn't exactly fried—it's baked! (But not half-baked, if you know what we mean.)

- **3 slices 100% whole wheat bread**
- **2 tbsp barbecue chicken seasoning, divided (see tip in margin)**
- **2 tbsp grated Parmesan cheese**
- **1/2 tsp dried thyme**
- **1/2 cup whole wheat flour**
- **1/3 cup fat-free egg substitute or 1 large egg beaten with 1 tbsp water**
- **6 bone-in, skinless chicken thighs (about 1 1/2 lbs)**
- **6 skinless chicken drumsticks (about 1 1/2 lbs)**
- **Olive or canola oil cooking spray**

- Preheat oven to 400°F. Spray a baking sheet with cooking spray and set aside. Move oven rack to bottom third of oven.

- Tear bread into chunks and place in the bowl of a food processor or mini chopper. Pulse on and off until bread is reduced to fluffy crumbs. You should have about 1 1/2 cups bread crumbs.

- Transfer bread crumbs to a shallow bowl and add 1 tbsp barbecue chicken seasoning, Parmesan cheese, and thyme. Mix well and set aside.

- In another shallow bowl, mix together flour and remaining barbecue chicken seasoning and set aside.

- Pour egg substitute into another shallow bowl. Working one chicken piece at a time, roll it first in flour mixture, then dip it in beaten egg. Shake off excess egg, then coat chicken in seasoned crumbs. Place on baking sheet. Repeat with remaining chicken pieces. (It can get messy, so hang in there.)

- Spray chicken pieces with a light coating of cooking spray. Bake for 40 minutes, until crumbs are lightly browned and chicken is no longer pink in the center.

Makes 6 servings

PER SERVING (1 THIGH, 1 DRUMSTICK)

calories	total fat	saturated fat	protein	carbohydrate	fiber	cholesterol	sodium
250	7 g	2 g	32 g	11 g	1.4 g	113 mg	776 mg

Jamaican Me Hungry!

Caribbean jerk-style chicken

What *Jamaican* for dinner tonight? If you love bold flavors and a little adventure in the kitchen, quit *jerkin'* around and try our spiced-up grilled chicken recipe.

Ya Mon! I hear ya!

GROWL RUMBLE

Marinade

1/3 cup chopped green onions (with white parts)
1/4 cup freshly squeezed lime juice
2 tbsp olive oil
2 tbsp reduced-sodium soy sauce
2 tbsp liquid honey
1 tbsp grated gingerroot
2 tsp minced garlic
2 jalapeño peppers, seeded and minced (wear gloves!)
2 tsp ground allspice
1 tsp each dried thyme, salt, and freshly ground black pepper
1/2 tsp each ground cinnamon and ground nutmeg

12 boneless, skinless chicken thighs (about 2 1/4 lbs)

- Whisk together all marinade ingredients in a medium bowl. Place chicken thighs in a large, heavy-duty, resealable plastic bag. Add marinade and seal bag. Turn bag several times to coat chicken with marinade. Marinate in the refrigerator overnight.

- Preheat grill to medium setting. Remove chicken from marinade (discard marinade) and place on a grill rack that has been coated with cooking spray or lightly brushed with oil. Grill for about 15 minutes, turning occasionally, until chicken is no longer pink in the center. Be careful not to burn the chicken.

- Serve hot chicken with Tropical Fruit Salsa on page 99.

Makes 6 servings

PER SERVING (WITHOUT SALSA)

calories	total fat	saturated fat	protein	carbohydrate	fiber	cholesterol	sodium
242	9 g	2 g	31 g	5 g	0.5 g	141 mg	431 mg

The Battle of the Bulge

Stand at attention, girls! We have the right to bare flabby arms! When it comes to the war on fat, we're sorely lacking men's arsenal, and that means there's a fat chance we'll beat them in *this* battle of the sexes. Since fat is essential for childbearing, women have more fat cells than men and our fat cells are up to five times larger. Go figure! Stacking the odds against us even further, women have, on average, 40 pounds less muscle than men. And the more muscle you have, the more fat you burn! To add insult to injury, during premenopause, when the ovaries slow down estrogen production, fat cells take up the slack. That's right—fat becomes an estrogen-producing factory! Holy hot flashes, Batman! Because estrogen is so important, women's bodies devise sneaky ways to protect and add to their fat stores so they can keep churning out the hormone. One way is by sacrificing fat-burning muscle. It's not unusual for a half pound of muscle to be lost each year during premenopause, and be replaced with one-and-a-half pounds of fat. Over 20 years, that's 30 additional pounds of blubber! With more weapons of body-mass destruction, men will usually beat us in the war against fat. Oh well, we can't have the brains and the brawn!

From tool time to teatime! Researchers have discovered that scattering tea bags throughout a newly remodeled room can reduce the toxicity level of chemicals in the air by up to 90 percent. The porous, dry tea bags apparently soak up what's around them, including fumes from paint, polyurethane, and glue. Maybe it's time to stop and smell the *Red Rose*!

Pessimist's blood type: B negative

Indian Appleous 500

Indian coconut-curry chicken with chopped apples

Ladies and gentlemen, start your engines! This ultra-healthy Indian curry dish is the perfect vehicle for injecting some high-performance fuel into your system. You'll lap up every last morsel!

12 boneless, skinless chicken thighs (about 2¼ lbs), each thigh cut in half
1 cup chopped onions
1 cup chopped red bell pepper
2 tsp minced garlic
1½ tbsp grated gingerroot
1½ tsp each curry powder and chili powder
½ tsp each ground turmeric and ground cinnamon
1 can (14 oz) light coconut milk
¼ cup mango chutney
Grated zest of 1 lemon
½ tsp salt
1 cup peeled, cored, and chopped Golden Delicious apples (see tip below)
½ cup frozen green peas
2 tbsp minced fresh cilantro

- You'll need a large, deep, non-stick skillet with a lid. Spray skillet with cooking spray and place over medium-high heat. Add chicken pieces and cook until both sides are lightly browned, about 2 minutes per side. Remove chicken and keep warm.

- Add onions, red pepper, and garlic to the same skillet. Cook and stir until vegetables begin to soften, about 3 minutes. Add gingerroot, curry powder, chili powder, turmeric, and cinnamon. Cook and stir for 1 more minute. Add coconut milk, mango chutney, lemon zest, and salt. Mix well. Stir in chicken pieces and apples. Cover and simmer over low heat for 15 minutes. Add peas and cilantro. Simmer, uncovered, for 5 more minutes.

- Serve hot. Tastes great on a bed of basmati rice.

Tip: Don't cut the apple pieces too small, or they'll turn to mush. Aim for 1-inch pieces. For a different flavor, substitute fresh mango for the apple.

Makes 6 servings

PER SERVING

calories	total fat	saturated fat	protein	carbohydrate	fiber	cholesterol	sodium
297	10.4 g	4.9 g	33 g	16 g	2.6 g	141 mg	378 mg

Funky Factoid

Everyone always asks us, "What's your secret formula for dreaming up those ridiculous, super-corny recipe titles?" After much introspection and a little brain-cell dissection (which got kinda messy!), we thought we'd provide some insight into our complex methodology. For instance, here's the brilliant thought process that led to the extremely clever title on this page: Indian flavor + chopped apples + fewer than 500 calories per serving = Indian Appleous 500! Are we *driving* you nuts or are you *lapping* it up?

Ongoing stress can lead to a flabby abdomen— a flabdomen!

Fat or Fiction?

The car won't start. Bills are piling up. Your boss is a jerk. Your daughter got a tattoo to complement her navel piercing. "Ahhhh! Someone pass the cookies!" Wonder why you crave sweets when you're stressed out? Well, when you're under stress, the hormones cortisol and adrenaline rise. These stress hormones take sugar out of your liver and rush it into your blood, making energy readily available for fight or flight. In prehistoric days Mr. and Mrs. Neanderthal needed that extra burst of energy to fend off hostile beasts or to migrate across rough terrain. Nowadays, most of us experience mental rather than physical stress, but our bodies don't know the difference. Once the stress is gone, our bodies insist on replacing the sugar stolen from our livers. To do that, stress hormones make us hungry, especially for sweets. No wonder "stressed" spelled backwards is "desserts!" Over long periods of time, too much cortisol wreaks havoc on your system, disturbing your sleep, lowering your immunity, and eating away at the muscle you need to burn fat. It also encourages the body to store abdominal fat for easy burning during stressful times. Since the body's stress reaction doesn't have an automatic "off" switch, it's up to you to find a way—mental or physical—to shut it down. Basically, you gotta chill out or you're gonna fill out! Massage, deep breathing, yoga, a hot bath, listening to music, and even laughing are effective ways to turn off the cortisol tap.

"SAY IT AIN'T SO!"

Say it ain't soda! No doubt you've heard that soft drinks have about 10 cubes of sugar per can. And you've probably glanced at those scary posters in the dentist's office showing how pop decays, corrodes, and discolors our teeth. If the prospect of rotting teeth doesn't stop you (or more importantly, your kids) from guzzling gallons of the carbonated, sweet stuff, maybe rotting bones will: Did you know that something called phosphoric acid in soft drinks causes calcium to be leached from our bones? Can you say osteoporosis? Remember: Soft drinks = soft bones.

Sometimes You Feel Like a Nut

Nuts may have recently shed their unhealthy reputation, but that's still no reason to...well...go nuts! Almonds, pistachios, walnuts, and their nutty relatives are good sources of protein, calcium, magnesium, and potassium, not to mention healthy, unsaturated fats. But that doesn't mean you should squirrel away bowlfuls like you're eating popcorn. Remember that nuts are packed with calories—shelling out roughly 800 calories per cup! To keep their high-calorie content from going straight to your butt, use nuts sparingly as a condiment, garnish, or a light snack. For instance, add a tablespoon of slivered almonds to cereal, oatmeal, salads, or steamed vegetables, or throw a few cashews or peanuts into a stir-fry. Store nuts in the fridge or freezer to prevent them from going rancid, and follow this rule of thumb to prevent over-consumption: You can open the fridge and take out a small handful, but never take the bag or container out of the fridge. An ounce a day is a good target, and since nuts are a satisfying snack, you'll still get your *fil, bert*.

Fake 'n' Bake Chicken

Baked chicken breasts with a lip-smacking barbecue sauce

It's the *breast*-kept secret! Just slap on some fake grill marks and no one will know this spicy-sweet chicken came out of the oven. Not trying these would be such a *sham*!

4 large boneless, skinless chicken breasts (about 1½ lbs)
⅓ cup hoisin sauce
⅓ cup hickory-flavored barbecue sauce
1 tbsp freshly squeezed lemon juice
2 tsp grated gingerroot
½ tsp chili powder

- Preheat oven to 400°F. Spray a medium casserole dish with cooking spray, or line with foil for easy cleanup. (The dish should be just large enough to hold the chicken breasts in a single layer.) Arrange chicken in dish.

- Whisk together remaining ingredients in a small bowl. Spoon sauce over chicken. Turn pieces to coat both sides with sauce. Bake, uncovered, for about 30 minutes, or until chicken is no longer pink in the center. Spoon sauce from bottom of pan over chicken and serve immediately.

Tip: You can substitute 12 boneless, skinless chicken thighs for the chicken breasts (add 10 minutes to the cooking time).

Makes 4 servings

			PER SERVING				
calories	total fat	saturated fat	protein	carbohydrate	fiber	cholesterol	sodium
252	3.3 g	0.7 g	40 g	13 g	1 g	99 mg	628 mg

People who transport salt are movers and shakers.

Dilly Beloved

Baked chicken breasts with maple, mustard, lemon, and dill

It's the wedding of the *scentury*! One bite of these happily marinated chicken breasts and your dinner guests will be exchanging *wows*. Easy enough for every day... fancy enough for company.

Marinade
¼ cup pure maple syrup
3 tbsp grainy Dijon mustard
2 tbsp minced fresh dill
2 tbsp freshly squeezed lemon juice
1 tbsp olive oil
1 tbsp balsamic vinegar
2 tsp grated lemon zest
1 tsp minced garlic
¼ tsp each salt and freshly ground black pepper

4 large boneless, skinless chicken breasts (about 1½ lbs)

- Whisk together all marinade ingredients in a small bowl. Arrange chicken breasts in a glass or ceramic baking dish that's just large enough to hold the chicken breasts in a single layer. Pour marinade over chicken. Turn pieces to coat both sides with marinade. Cover with plastic wrap and refrigerate for at least 1 hour or up to 1 day.

- Preheat oven to 350°F. Remove plastic wrap and transfer casserole dish to middle oven rack. Bake, uncovered, for about 35 minutes, or until chicken is no longer pink in the center.

- Spoon sauce from bottom of pan over chicken and serve immediately.

Tip: Do not use a large casserole dish, such as a lasagna pan, for this recipe. It's too big and will cause the marinade to spread too thinly and likely burn while the chicken is baking. The marinade also makes a great salad dressing when you add an extra tablespoon of balsamic vinegar and olive oil.

Makes 4 servings

			PER SERVING				
calories	total fat	saturated fat	protein	carbohydrate	fiber	cholesterol	sodium
289	6.4 g	1.1 g	40 g	16 g	0.4 g	99 mg	322 mg

Juicy Gossip About Lemons

Like other vitamin C-rich fruits, the lemon was highly prized by miners during the California Gold Rush in the mid-19th century, since it helped protect against scurvy. Almost as good as gold, people rushed to pay up to $1 per lemon, a price that would be considered high today, never mind in 1849! Making lemons your main squeeze will help boost your immune system and protect your body from disease and the effects of aging, since lemon juice is an effective antioxidant. Consumed before or with a meal, it's also a helpful digestive aid, as it gets the stomach's digestive acids flowing. That's one reason why it appears as a garnish with so many foods. Interestingly, the custom of serving a slice of lemon with fish dates back to the Middle Ages. It was believed that if a person accidentally swallowed a fish bone, the lemon juice would dissolve it. And if you're a follower of the Glycemic Index, you'll be pleased to know that adding a few tablespoons of lemon juice to a meal can lower its glycemic value by about 30%, making lemons a powerful aid in controlling blood-sugar levels. By the way, warmer lemons yield more juice. Leave them at room temperature for at least 30 minutes before juicing, or soak them in hot water for 15 minutes. Roll lemons back and forth on the counter a few times for the juiciest results.

"SAY IT AIN'T SO!"

Feeling a little weak in the bean after your third cup of coffee? No wonder. In nature, caffeine is designed to cause confusion in the brain. It's true about the brew! Caffeine is actually used by the coffee plant as a pesticide—a nerve-warfare chemical that wards off predators. Caffeine inhibits the nervous system and the memory of the coffee plant's enemies (insects) so they lose their art of camouflage, become less alert, and less able to protect themselves against their own predators (animals). We humans harvest the same caffeine-containing coffee beans, brew them, and drink them *for pleasure*. Are we stunned?

Pop Quizine

Which of the following is an actual name for a Chinese dish?

a) Drunken Chicken
b) Saddened Cow
c) Peeking Duck
d) Disheveled Pig

Answer: (a) The chicken is boiled and then marinated in a rice-wine mixture. If you answered (c), the proper spelling is Peking Duck! Fooled ya!

"Take two dumbbells and call me in the morning." That's what doctors should be prescribing for optimum health. And speaking of prescriptions, if exercise were a pill, the following "warnings" just might appear on the label: May experience dramatically increased muscle tone, significant fat loss, surging energy levels, stronger heart, lungs, and bones, lower cholesterol levels, increased immune function, and improved sleep. Other side effects may include stress relief, increased confidence and self-esteem, and dizzying spells of overall well-being. Take daily with plenty of water and do not skip dosages. In rare case of overdose, get plenty of rest and soak in a bath with Epsom salts. Oh! And please keep within reach of children!

Oh dear! you're starting to peel.

Chicken Teriwacky
Marinated, grilled, orange-teriyaki chicken

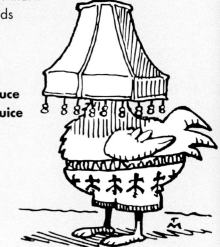

What's so wacky about our teriyaki? We added a hint of orange flavor that'll make you cuckoo! Great for salads or grilled chicken sandwiches.

Marinade
- **2 tbsp reduced-sodium soy sauce**
- **2 tbsp freshly squeezed lime juice**
- **2 tbsp liquid honey**
- **2 tbsp ketchup**
- **2 tbsp minced green onions (with white parts)**
- **1 tbsp grated gingerroot**
- **1 tsp grated orange zest**
- **1 tsp minced garlic**

4 large boneless, skinless chicken breasts (about 1½ lbs)

- Whisk together all marinade ingredients in a small bowl. Place chicken breasts in a large, heavy-duty, resealable plastic bag. Add marinade and seal bag. Turn bag several times to coat chicken with marinade. Marinate in refrigerator for at least 4 hours, or overnight if possible.

- Preheat grill to medium setting. Remove chicken from marinade and place on a grill rack that has been coated with cooking spray or lightly brushed with oil. Discard marinade (see tip below). Grill for about 15 minutes, turning occasionally, until chicken is no longer pink in the center. Be careful not to burn the chicken.

Tip: If you want to baste the chicken with the used marinade, boil it first to kill any bacteria that may be present.

Makes 4 servings

PER SERVING
calories	total fat	saturated fat	protein	carbohydrate	fiber	cholesterol	sodium
214	2.1 g	0.6 g	40 g	7 g	0.2 g	99 mg	300 mg

Chicken Pandemoniyum

Chicken and wild-rice skillet meal with grated Parmesan

This wildly delicious, one-pot wonderful creation is sure to cause an uproar! Your friends will think you're a gourmet, but it really takes no *skillet* all.

- **3 large boneless, skinless chicken breasts (about 1 1/4 lbs)**
- **2 tsp olive oil**
- **3 cups sliced mushrooms (see tip below)**
- **3/4 cup chopped onions**
- **1 tsp minced garlic**
- **1 pkg (6 oz) Uncle Ben's Long Grain & Wild Rice original recipe**
- **1 1/4 cups chicken broth**
- **1/2 cup dry white wine**
- **1/2 cup freshly grated Parmesan cheese**

- Cut chicken breasts into large chunks (about 6 pieces per breast). Heat oil in a 10-inch, non-stick skillet with a tight-fitting lid. Add chicken pieces and cook over medium-high heat for about 4 minutes, stirring often, until chicken is lightly browned all over. Remove chicken from skillet and set aside.

- Add mushrooms, onions, and garlic to the same skillet. Cook and stir until vegetables begin to soften, about 3 minutes. If vegetables start to stick, add a little water or broth.

- Add rice and seasoning pouch. Mix well and cook for 30 seconds. Stir in broth and wine. Return chicken to skillet. Bring mixture to a boil. Reduce heat to medium-low, cover, and simmer for about 20 minutes, until rice is tender and liquid is absorbed. Remove from heat. Let stand, covered, for 10 minutes. Stir in Parmesan cheese and serve immediately.

Tip: To save some time, buy an 8-oz package of pre-sliced mushrooms. For a fancier dish, use a blend of sliced wild mushrooms, such as portobello, shiitake, and cremini.

Makes 4 servings

PER SERVING

calories	total fat	saturated fat	protein	carbohydrate	fiber	cholesterol	sodium
404	6.1 g	2 g	42 g	37 g	1.8 g	89 mg	760 mg

The Joy of Not Cooking

Let's hear it for the joy of not cooking! Raw! Raw! Raw! Throwing some raw food into your daily menu is crucial to good health. And we're not talking about sushi, egg yolk shakes, or steak tartars, either. Raw, uncooked foods like fruits, vegetables, nuts, seeds, and sprouts are "live" foods. They're full of living enzymes that are like spark plugs for our cells, providing boundless energy and vitality. In fact, our organs and glands depend on enzymatic activity and can't function properly without it. Problem is, when food is heated above 118°F, enzymes start to break down, just like our bodies would if we had a fever that high. Fortunately, your body can manufacture missing enzymes, but over time, digesting cooked foods overworks the glands, wears out the body, and sets the stage for chronic disease. That's why people who live on a diet of cooked protein and starches (the ol' meat and potatoes diet) and very little enzyme-rich fruits and vegetables, are often tired and have little pep in their step. And if we don't get sufficient enzymes, we age faster! That's because our body's own enzyme production slows. Now, don't get us wrong—we're not bad-mouthing cooking! How stupid would that be? Why, we'd be out of jobs! Everyone knows that cooking improves the flavor of food, plus it also enhances the digestibility of many foods, and in some cases, makes them safer to eat. But every once in a while, for optimum health and longevity, go ahead and get eatin' alive!

Wool Sweaters

Bird on a Wire

Greek chicken skewers with cucumber-dill sauce

Don't be a *slowpoke*! The quicker you thread these zesty, marinated chicken pieces onto the wire, the faster your taste buds will be knocked *askewer*. These are kebobs with ke-pow!

Marinade

¼ cup freshly squeezed lemon juice

1 tbsp liquid honey

1 tbsp olive oil

1 tbsp each minced fresh oregano leaves and minced fresh mint leaves

2 tsp balsamic vinegar

2 tsp minced garlic

½ tsp salt

¼ tsp freshly ground black pepper

4 large boneless, skinless chicken breasts (about 1½ lbs), cut into 1-inch chunks

Cucumber-Dill Sauce

1 cup low-fat, plain yogurt

1 cup peeled, seeded, and diced English cucumber

1 tbsp minced fresh dill or minced fresh mint leaves

1 tsp minced garlic

¼ tsp each salt and freshly ground black pepper

4 12-inch metal skewers

Makes 4 servings

- Combine all marinade ingredients in a small bowl. Place chicken in a large, heavy-duty, resealable plastic bag. Add marinade and seal bag. Turn bag several times to coat chicken with marinade. Marinate in the refrigerator for at least 1 hour (6 hours is perfect).

- While chicken is marinating, prepare Cucumber-Dill Sauce. Combine all sauce ingredients in a medium bowl and mix well. Cover and refrigerate until ready to use. (Make sure you refrigerate the sauce for at least 1 hour.)

- Preheat grill to high setting. Thread chicken pieces onto metal skewers and discard marinade. Coat grill with cooking spray or brush lightly with oil. Grill chicken for 8 to 10 minutes, turning occasionally, until no longer pink in the center. Do not overcook chicken, or it will be dry.

- Serve hot chicken with cool Cucumber-Dill Sauce. Tastes great with Greek salad (page 49) and hummus (page 22) with warm pita wedges.

PER SERVING

calories	total fat	saturated fat	protein	carbohydrate	fiber	cholesterol	sodium
258	4.8 g	1.3 g	43 g	9 g	0.4 g	104 mg	450 mg

To make a grilled salad using the above recipe, alternately thread marinated chicken pieces and chunks of green bell pepper and red onions onto six metal skewers. Then, thread only cherry tomatoes onto two more metal skewers. Cook as directed in recipe, but remove the tomato skewers halfway through cooking time (they don't take long to heat up). To serve, remove chicken, vegetables, and tomatoes from skewers and place in a serving bowl. Top with crumbled, light feta cheese, freshly ground black pepper, and a dollop of Cucumber-Dill Sauce for a delicious, hot Greek salad! Yum!

Whistle While You Wok

Family-pleasing chicken stir-fry with vegetables and rotini

Other chicken stir-fries *dwarf* in comparison. Ours is the fairest of them all! Don't be *Grumpy* when you can't figure out what to make for dinner. Just whip up this magical recipe and make 'em all *Happy*.

8 oz uncooked whole wheat rotini pasta (about 3 cups—see tip below)

Sauce
½ cup orange juice
⅓ cup hoisin sauce
2 tbsp reduced-sodium soy sauce
1½ tbsp cornstarch
1 tbsp each grated gingerroot and toasted sesame oil
1 tsp minced garlic
¼ tsp crushed red pepper flakes

4 large boneless, skinless chicken breasts (about 1½ lbs), cut into strips or cubes
2 cups broccoli florets
2 cups halved medium-sized mushrooms
1 large red bell pepper, cut into strips
½ cup frozen green peas
⅓ cup coarsely chopped green onions
10 fresh basil leaves, coarsely chopped

- Cook pasta according to package directions. Drain. Rinse with cold water and drain again. Set aside.

- Whisk together all sauce ingredients in a medium bowl. Set aside.

- Spray a large, non-stick wok with cooking spray and place over high heat. Add chicken and cook, stirring often, until chicken is lightly browned on the outside but still pink in the center. Add broccoli, mushrooms, and red pepper. Cook and stir until vegetables are tender-crisp, about 6 minutes. Add ¼ cup water to prevent sticking, if necessary. Add peas and onions. Cook 1 more minute. Add sauce and basil. Continue cooking until sauce is bubbly and has thickened, about 1 minute. Add rotini and cook 1 more minute, just until rotini is heated through. Serve hot.

Tip: You can substitute whole wheat spaghetti for the rotini.

Makes 6 servings

PER SERVING

calories	total fat	saturated fat	protein	carbohydrate	fiber	cholesterol	sodium
372	5.5 g	0.8 g	35 g	46 g	5.3 g	66 mg	509 mg

94

RETURN TO SLENDER

If you're trying to lose fat, then plan for a *whiteout*! Despite their saintly color, refined sugar and flour can be dietary devils that encourage overeating and weight gain. These highly processed foods cause a quick rise in blood sugar, followed by a rise in blood insulin levels. Insulin is a hormone that leads to weight gain, either by making the body store fat or by lowering blood-sugar levels so much that it causes intense hunger later on. The result: "I want a Hostess Ding Dong and want it NOW!" Plus, sugar and white flour provide only "empty" calories, and usually lots of them. Now, we're not loony enough to suggest you never eat cake again. Heaven knows, we love our desserts! Moderation is the key. However, to jump-start your fat-loss efforts, try avoiding refined sugar and white flour for at least two weeks. Instead, choose whole, unprocessed, nutritious foods, including veggies, fruit, whole grains, beans, nuts, and lean meats. With only high-quality fuel in your tank, you should see quick results, especially around your midsection. You know what they say: "We all have a washboard stomach. It's just that some of us have a little extra laundry on top." Well, time to hang your whites out to dry!

The phrase "with a grain of salt" dates back thousands of years, and is a translation of the Latin *cum grano salis*. Initially, the expression was thought to have a positive and literal meaning. Roman historian Pliny the Elder wrote that General Pompey had discovered an antidote for poison and believed it was only effective if it was taken with a grain of salt. Over the centuries, historians decided that Pliny was iffy on the antidote's efficacy and took *cum grano salis* to mean "with a dose of skepticism." That, of course, is the meaning of the expression today. "With a grain of pepper" (*cum grano pepis*), on the other hand, is a much less famous saying and means just the opposite: Believe everything you've just read! (But take it with a grain of salt.)

Cooking TIP

Nowadays, it's pretty easy to buy a tasty, low-fat peanut sauce. Bottles of peanut sauce are usually sold near the salad dressings or barbecue sauces at the grocery store. Some are very spicy; others are milder. Same goes for salsa. You can control the heat factor and the flavor of this recipe by choosing sauces that suit your taste buds and your heat-tolerance level.

Solid as a Brocc

When it comes to cancer-fighting super foods, broccoli's definitely at the head of its class. Study after study shows that people who eat their broccoli have fewer cancers of the colon, breast, cervix, lungs, prostate, esophagus, larynx, and bladder. Broccoli's power lies in its abundance of powerful disease-fighting compounds called phytochemicals, including beta-carotene, indoles, and isothiocyanates. What a mouthful! A crunchy, delicious mouthful! And, as if that's not enough, a half cup of cooked broccoli provides more than 100% of your daily vitamin C needs, a hefty dose of calcium, plenty of folate to prevent heart disease, more fiber than a slice of whole wheat bread, and nearly two-thirds of a banana's potassium—all for just 23 calories! Who needs a multivitamin? Those superpowers seem to run in the family, by the way. All the cruciferous vegetables (cabbage, cauliflower, kale, brussels sprouts, and bok choy) are blessed with these enormous cancer-fighting abilities. Eat 'em to your health's content!

Kickin' Chicken

Spicy baked chicken in a super-simple and extra-flavorful peanut sauce

If you can't take the heat, get outta the *chicken*! This sizzling, super-spicy creation will leave you hot, but not bothered, since it's so easy to make. It's the perfect choice when you want to kick things up a notch.

12 boneless, skinless chicken thighs or
6 boneless, skinless chicken breasts (about 2¼ lbs)
¾ cup bottled light peanut sauce (see tip in margin)
½ cup medium or hot salsa
¼ cup chopped fresh basil leaves

- Preheat oven to 400°F. Spray a 9 x 13-inch baking pan with cooking spray. Arrange chicken thighs in pan in a single layer. If you're using chicken breasts, cut them in half to make them fit in pan if necessary.

- Combine peanut sauce, salsa, and basil in a medium bowl. Pour sauce evenly over chicken and make sure all pieces are well-coated with sauce. Bake, uncovered, for 40 to 45 minutes for thighs and 35 to 40 minutes for breasts, or until chicken is no longer pink in the center and sauce is bubbly.

- To serve, arrange chicken on a serving platter and pour extra sauce from pan over top.

Makes 6 servings

PER SERVING (2 THIGHS PLUS SAUCE)

calories	total fat	saturated fat	protein	carbohydrate	fiber	cholesterol	sodium
234	8.8 g	2 g	29 g	5 g	0.4 g	126 mg	546 mg

PER SERVING (1 BREAST PLUS SAUCE)

calories	total fat	saturated fat	protein	carbohydrate	fiber	cholesterol	sodium
241	5 g	1 g	41 g	5 g	0.4 g	99 mg	526 mg

Manure, Compost, Peat Moss. Don'tcha like it when I talk dirty?

Obscene Fern Calls

Thai Beau

Thai coconut chicken with mango and basil

This colorful, Thai coconut chicken packs a lot of kick and a lot of punch. A real knockout!

1¼ cups light coconut milk
1 tbsp grated gingerroot
1 tbsp reduced-sodium soy sauce
1 tbsp brown sugar
1 tbsp Asian fish sauce (see tip, page 179)
1 tbsp cornstarch
Juice of 1 lime
1 tsp minced garlic
Pinch crushed red pepper flakes (optional)
2 tsp peanut oil or safflower oil
4 large boneless, skinless chicken breasts
   (about 1½ lbs), cut into strips
1 large red bell pepper, seeded and cut into strips
4 green onions (with white parts), coarsely chopped
½ cup frozen green peas
½ cup coarsely chopped fresh basil leaves
3 tbsp minced fresh cilantro
1 ripe medium-sized mango, peeled and sliced
Hot, cooked basmati or jasmine rice (optional)

- To make sauce, whisk together coconut milk, gingerroot, soy sauce, brown sugar, fish sauce, cornstarch, lime juice, garlic, and crushed red pepper flakes (if using) in a medium bowl. Set aside until ready to use.

- Heat oil in a large, non-stick wok over high heat. Add chicken pieces. Cook and stir until chicken is lightly browned, about 4 minutes. Remove chicken from wok and keep warm.

- Reduce heat to medium-high. Add red pepper and onions to the same wok. Cook and stir for 3 minutes, until red pepper begins to soften. Return chicken to wok. Add sauce, peas, basil, and cilantro. Continue cooking and stirring until sauce is bubbly and has thickened. Reduce heat to medium-low. Simmer for 5 to 6 minutes, or until chicken is cooked through. Stir in mango and cook 1 more minute.

- Serve over hot basmati or jasmine rice, if desired.

Tip: If you like your food really spicy, replace the crushed red pepper flakes with 1 tsp Thai green curry paste, available in the Asian food section of your grocery store.

Makes 4 servings

			PER SERVING				
calories	total fat	saturated fat	protein	carbohydrate	fiber	cholesterol	sodium
336	8.7 g	4.6 g	43 g	23 g	2.8 g	99 mg	638 mg

The Soaperb Herb

Cilantro, also called Chinese parsley or coriander, is an herb commonly used to add flavor to chili, salsa, and other highly spiced Mexican, Asian, and Caribbean dishes. It's one of those tastes you either love or hate—some people describe cilantro's distinctive, pungent odor and taste as "soapy." (For the record, we love it!) Regardless, you'll probably *want* to wash your mouth out with cilantro when you find out how it cleanses your insides. The leaves are rich in calcium, iron, carotenes, and vitamin C, and studies have shown that cilantro is one of the few substances that can help remove toxic heavy metals, such as mercury, lead, and aluminum, from the central nervous system. That's great news for those with Alzheimer's disease, depression, and other neurological disorders worsened by toxic overload, but it's also useful for the rest of us who are constantly exposed to harmful heavy metals from environmental pollution, certain foods, and even cosmetics and other consumer products. Still feelin' wishy-washy about cilantro?

Mageirocophobia is the persistent, abnormal, and irrational fear of...

a) having dinner conversations
b) expelling gas in public
c) cooking
d) peanut butter sticking to the roof of your mouth

Answer: (c) When you fear peanut butter thicking to the roov uf your mouth, ith called arachibutyrophobia. Honest! For more unusual phobias, check out www.phobialist.com.

With everything you read about spray cans and the ozone layer, it's enough to scareosol to death.

Stick 'em Up!

Lemon and basil marinated, grilled shrimp skewers

Freeze! Caught ya pink-handed! You're guilty of robbing the taste bank and *shellfishly* hoarding the grilled goods for yourself! Though you'll be tempted to eat these lip-smacking shrimp skewers in solitary confinement, not sharing their *arresting* flavor with friends would be a crime.

Marinade

⅓ cup chopped fresh basil leaves
2 tbsp freshly squeezed lemon juice
1 tbsp each olive oil, melted butter, Dijon mustard, and liquid honey
2 tsp each minced garlic, grated gingerroot, and grated lemon zest
1 tsp balsamic vinegar
½ tsp salt
¼ tsp freshly ground black pepper

2 lbs uncooked large or jumbo shrimp, peeled and deveined (leave tails intact)
8 12-inch metal skewers

- Combine all marinade ingredients in a small bowl. Place shrimp in a large, heavy-duty, resealable plastic bag. Pour marinade over shrimp and seal bag. Turn bag several times to coat shrimp with marinade. Marinate in refrigerator for 1 hour.

- Preheat grill to high setting. Thread shrimp onto skewers (5 or 6 shrimp per skewer, depending on size of shrimp). Discard marinade. Spray grill rack with cooking spray or brush lightly with oil. Grill shrimp for about 2 minutes per side, just until shrimp turns pink and no gray remains. Be careful not to overcook shrimp or they will be rubbery.

- Serve skewers hot or cold, on a salad, or with a hot rice side dish, with grilled vegetables, or as an appetizer.

When people ask us, "What's the one relatively simple thing I can do to help me lose weight?" our answer is always the same: Cut back on nighttime snacking! Yes, we believe in exercise. Yes, we want you to embrace fruits and vegetables and eat less sugar. And yes, we'd love you to drink more water. But if you're looking for one small tip that can help you drop clothing sizes faster than a Survivor finalist, then put a "closed" sign on the refrigerator door at about 7:30 p.m. Not only will this kitchen curfew give your liver a much-deserved break from digestion duties, freeing it to concentrate on its lengthy "to-do" list while you're sleeping, but you'll also cut out a ton of calories. Let's face it: If you actually wrote down everything you unconsciously nibble on or absentmindedly swig back after dinner while puttering around the house, watching TV, surfing the Net, or helping kids with homework, you might be shocked to see how it all adds up—literally and *figure*atively!

Funky Factoid

Salmonella, the bacteria in contaminated food that causes intestinal infections, actually has nothing to do with fish. It was named after U.S. veterinary pathologist Daniel E. Salmon, who, in 1885, discovered the first strain in a pig's intestine.

Waiter, do you have any lobster tails?

Certainly, sir. Once upon a time there was a little lobster...

Makes 8 servings

		PER SERVING					
calories	total fat	saturated fat	protein	carbohydrate	fiber	cholesterol	sodium
161	5.3 g	1.5 g	23 g	4 g	0.2 g	176 mg	324 mg

THE E FILES

Losing your flex appeal? Too bad. If you want to stay trim and slim without depriving yourself on the latest fad diet, flexing some muscle is the *weigh* to go. Muscle is a calorie-zapping machine. It's your fat-burning furnace. For each pound of muscle you gain, you'll burn an extra 50 calories per day just to maintain it. So, if you start working out with weights and add five pounds of lean muscle to your body, you'll burn an additional 250 calories per day! Burn, baby, burn. Blubber inferno! The more muscle you have, the more fat you'll incinerate 24 hours a day, while exercising and at rest. You'll even burn more calories while catching some zzz's (giving new meaning to the term "you snooze, you lose!"). See! Strength training's definitely worth the *weight*!

Keep Them Guessing with Oil of EFA

The orthopedic specialist keeps telling you to bone up on salmon to ease your arthritis, the cardiologist has been carping on you to eat more fish to help your heart, and the immunologist keeps bugging you to take cod liver oil to prevent flu and colds. Still not taking the bait? Well, maybe we should appeal to your vanity. Did you know that fish oil each day keeps the dermatologist away? It's true. You don't need the Ponds, just the fish! Essential Fatty Acids (or EFAs, for short) found in fish promote beautiful, youthful, glowing skin. Instead of just slathering on the Wrinkle Obliterating Muck Mask and praying for an overnight miracle, treat your body's cells to nutrients that'll help strengthen them, repair damage, and create a more youthful you from the inside out. If you care about your face (and let's face it, who doesn't?), get your wrinkle-fighting, age-defying EFAs from fish (or fish oils), flaxseed oil, nuts, omega-3 enriched eggs, and green, leafy vegetables. Why raise eyebrows with a visit to a plastic surgeon when you can get a natural face-lift at home?

Buoy Meets Grill

Grilled tuna steaks with tropical fruit salsa

Light the barbecue with a match made in heaven and watch the sparks fly! When you grill up these mouthwatering tuna steaks and couple them with a fresh-tasting, tropical fruit salsa, it'll be love at first bite.

Marinade

3 tbsp hoisin sauce
2 tbsp freshly squeezed lemon juice
2 tbsp pure maple syrup
1 tbsp Dijon mustard
1 tbsp grated gingerroot
1 tsp grated lemon zest

4 boneless, skinless tuna steaks (about 5 oz each)

Salsa

1 cup diced fresh pineapple
1 cup diced fresh mango
¼ cup each minced red onions, minced red bell pepper, and minced green bell pepper
1 tbsp minced fresh cilantro
1 tbsp freshly squeezed lime juice
1 tsp granulated sugar
¼ tsp salt

- Whisk together all marinade ingredients in a small bowl. Place tuna steaks in a large, heavy-duty, resealable plastic bag. Add marinade and seal bag. Turn bag several times to coat tuna with marinade. Marinate in refrigerator for 1 hour.

- Meanwhile, combine all salsa ingredients in a medium bowl. Cover and refrigerate until ready to use.

- Preheat grill to high setting. Remove tuna from marinade and reserve marinade. Place tuna steaks on a grill rack that has been coated with cooking spray or lightly brushed with oil. Grill for about 4 minutes per side, basting generously with reserved marinade. Tuna should still be slightly pink in the center. Overcooked tuna is very dry, so keep your eye on it.

- Spoon salsa over hot tuna and serve immediately.

Makes 4 servings

PER SERVING

calories	total fat	saturated fat	protein	carbohydrate	fiber	cholesterol	sodium
263	1.6 g	0.3 g	37 g	29 g	2.3 g	57 mg	491 mg

The Soprawnos

Scrumptious Italian shrimp dish with tomatoes, zucchini, and feta cheese

When you make this delectable shrimp recipe for the family, it'll be a *hit, man!* And you won't get *whacked* with a ton of fat and calories, either.

They mobbed me for the recipe.

2 tsp olive oil
1 cup chopped red onions
1 medium zucchini, chopped
2 tsp minced garlic
½ tsp dried oregano
½ cup dry white wine
3 cups chopped plum tomatoes
1 tbsp balsamic vinegar
¼ tsp each salt and freshly ground black pepper
¼ cup chopped fresh basil leaves
1 lb uncooked large shrimp, peeled and deveined
½ cup crumbled feta cheese with herbs (2 oz—see tip below)
1 tbsp chopped fresh parsley

- Heat olive oil over medium-high heat in a 10-inch, non-stick skillet. Add onions, zucchini, and garlic. Cook and stir until vegetables are softened, about 5 minutes. Add oregano and cook 30 more seconds. Add wine, tomatoes, vinegar, salt, and pepper. Mix well. Reduce heat to medium and simmer, uncovered, for about 8 minutes, until most of the wine has evaporated and the tomatoes are broken up.

- Stir in basil and shrimp. Cook and stir until shrimp turns pink and is cooked through, about 4 minutes. Be careful not to overcook shrimp or it will be rubbery. Remove from heat and sprinkle with feta cheese and parsley. Serve hot.

Tip: Look for feta cheese flavored with sun-dried tomatoes and basil. If you prefer, you can use plain feta cheese instead.

"SAY IT AIN'T SO!"

When you think of comfort food, chicken potpie probably comes to mind. Wanna know what's in store when it comes to store-bought chicken pies (especially those convenient little frozen ones that you can microwave)? Well, we've dissected a few in our day (don't ask) and this is what we found: Fat and calories. Lots of 'em. Some puny potpies have more than 700 calories and almost 50 grams of fat! There's nothing comforting about that! Hiding under all that pastry and gravy are a few peas, a couple specks of carrot, 1/48th of a potato, and if it's your lucky day, about four mini-cubelets of chicken. If you're craving potpie, forgo convenience and get out a cookbook. The good, old-fashioned kind like Ma used to make will stick to your ribs—not to your arteries!

Funky Factoid

Coming soon to your local grocer: *Ants Jemima?* Did you know that there are more than 1,450 recorded species of edible insects? (Who are the lucky folks on *that* taste panel?) Entomophagy is the scientific name for insect eating, and it's a diet plan we don't expect will create a huge *buzz* across the nation anytime soon. But Atkins followers take note: Ounce for ounce, many species of insects are lower in fat and higher in protein than beef, lamb, pork, or chicken. Talk about guilt-free *grub*!

The Italian Scallion

Makes 4 servings

PER SERVING

calories	total fat	saturated fat	protein	carbohydrate	fiber	cholesterol	sodium
253	7.8 g	2.9 g	27 g	14 g	2.9 g	185 mg	488 mg

Ask Greta

One minute, salmon is a healthy eater's best friend. The next, it's contaminated with toxins. What's the *reel* deal?

Don't toss the salmon back! Low in fat, high in protein, and one of the best sources of heart-healthy, brain-boosting, omega-3 fatty acids, salmon is a total catch. And when you buy it canned, you get extra calcium, too, because the canning process makes the bones soft enough to eat. The dark cloud hanging over salmon's head is a result of a well-publicized, 2004 study that revealed higher levels of PCBs in farmed salmon versus wild salmon. PCBs are industrial chemicals banned nearly 30 years ago that are still lingering in the environment and that have been linked to cancer. Despite the findings, the U.S. Food and Drug Administration and the World Health Organization insist that PCB levels present in salmon don't pose a risk to humans. Still, limiting your consumption of farm-raised salmon to one serving per month may be a good idea. Experts agree that wild salmon contains fewer toxins and is safe to eat four to eight times per month. Since most contaminants are found in the skin and in the fat just beneath it, you can reduce your exposure to PCBs by removing the skin, trimming any fat, and letting the juices drip away while cooking. The bottom line is that we don't eat enough fish to begin with, and the health benefits far outweigh the negatives. Don't forget that red meat, poultry, and full-fat dairy products also harbor environmental toxins—even the fillings in your teeth are a source of potentially harmful mercury. It's just that we haven't heard much about it in the news, so we don't freak out. Constantly worrying and neurotically obsessing over possible dangers lurking in our food could be more damaging to our health than the stuff we're fretting about. So relax. Don't fear the fish. The experts who've studied its merits and pitfalls are telling us it's healthy. Let's give them the benefit of the *trout*.

If they like it, it serves four; otherwise, six.

Elsie Zussman

Salmon Cowell

Grilled salmon in an orange-ginger marinade

It's absolutely pathetic. Utterly ghastly, if you want our honest opinion. But Paula loves it. Go ahead, you be the judge. You just might *idolize* it.

Marinade
¼ cup frozen orange juice concentrate
¼ cup hoisin sauce
1 tbsp reduced-sodium soy sauce
1 tbsp grated gingerroot
1 tsp grated orange zest
Pinch crushed red pepper flakes (optional)

4 boneless, skinless salmon fillets (about 5 oz each)

- Whisk together all marinade ingredients in a small bowl. Place salmon in a large, heavy-duty, resealable plastic bag. Add marinade and seal bag. Turn bag several times to coat salmon with marinade. Marinate in refrigerator for 30 minutes.

- Preheat grill to medium setting. Remove salmon from marinade (reserve marinade) and place on a grill rack that has been coated with cooking spray or lightly brushed with oil. Grill for 3 to 4 minutes per side, until done (salmon should be slightly pink in the center). Do not overcook salmon or it will be dry. Baste salmon with reserved marinade during last minute of cooking time, if desired.

Tip: If you can't grill the salmon, broil it. Place fish on a baking sheet that has been sprayed with cooking spray. Broil 4 inches from heat source for about 8 minutes, turning salmon once, halfway through cooking time. Salmon should flake easily when tested with a fork.

Makes 4 servings

			PER SERVING				
calories	total fat	saturated fat	protein	carbohydrate	fiber	cholesterol	sodium
253	9.4 g	1.5 g	29 g	11 g	0.5 g	78 mg	358 mg

In Cod We Trust

Oven "fried" Cajun cod fillets

Cod almighty! It's a miracle! If you've secretly wished your family would eat more fish, these yummy baked cod fillets with a crumb coating are the answer to your prayers.

**6 large cod fillets
(about 5 oz each)**
2/3 cup buttermilk
Grated zest of 1 lemon
3 cups Special K cereal, ground into crumbs (see tip below)
1/4 cup freshly grated Parmesan cheese
1 tbsp chopped fresh parsley
1 1/2 tsp Cajun seasoning
Canola oil cooking spray

- Preheat oven to 450°F. Spray a baking sheet with cooking spray and set aside.

- Pat cod fillets dry with paper towels. Whisk together buttermilk and lemon zest in a shallow bowl or casserole dish. Add cod fillets and turn to coat both sides with buttermilk mixture. Let stand for 10 minutes.

- In another shallow bowl, combine Special K crumbs, Parmesan cheese, parsley, and Cajun seasoning.

- Working one piece at a time, remove cod from buttermilk mixture and shake off excess liquid. Press one side of fish into crumb mixture, making sure it's well-coated with crumbs. Place fish, crumb-side up, on prepared pan. Repeat with remaining cod pieces and crumb mixture. Lightly spray tops of fish with cooking spray (or drizzle with a bit of melted butter).

- Bake for 10 to 15 minutes, until fish flakes easily with a fork. Cooking time will depend on thickness of fish. Serve hot. Tastes great with light tartar sauce on top.

Tip: To make fine crumbs, process Special K cereal in your food processor using the pulse feature. Otherwise, you can put the cereal in a heavy-duty, resealable plastic bag and crush it with a rolling pin (your crumbs won't be as fine this way, but they'll be good enough).

Oils Well That Ends Well

According to Penn State chemical engineers, cooking oils and salad oils could lubricate machinery, such as cars and boats. Tests found that when blended with an additive developed at Penn State, some vegetable oils performed as well or better than commercial motor oils (though very few motor oils tasted good on a garden salad!). These polyunsaturated oils might be beneficial for your car's valves, but as far as your heart's valves are concerned, it's a slippery situation. Unfortunately, most commercial cooking oils in grocery stores today (such as vegetable, corn, sunflower, and safflower) are not as healthy as they could be, thanks to the tinkering and tampering of manufacturers. In order to extend shelf life, cooking oils are often overly refined and processed, subjected to intense heat, bleached, and deodorized during the manufacturing process. In short, they've been put through the ringer! That changes the oil's chemical structure, making it tough for your body to handle. But not to worry! A basic oil change is all that's required to keep your pipes clear. Check your oil and make sure the label says "expeller-pressed" or "cold-pressed"—a process that doesn't damage the oil's structure. The healthiest choice is extra virgin olive oil because it's not subjected to harsh refining processes. Look for expeller-pressed (even better, organic) versions of canola, safflower, and sunflower oils at health-food stores and well-stocked grocery stores. Your heart's valves are worth the extra expense, don'tcha think?

Created in 1898 by a North Carolina pharmacist, the original name of Pepsi-Cola was...

a) Dispepsia
b) Peppy Pop
c) Brad's drink
d) Dr. Popper

Answer: (c) Caleb Bradham served his homemade beverage to drug-store customers. The drink was later renamed Pepsi-Cola after the pepsin and cola nuts in the recipe.

Makes 6 servings

PER SERVING

calories	total fat	saturated fat	protein	carbohydrate	fiber	cholesterol	sodium
206	2.7 g	1.2 g	31 g	13 g	0.8 g	65 mg	314 mg

When making wraps or fajitas, your tortillas must be very fresh, or they'll crack and break when you roll them up. To soften slightly stale tortillas, just wrap them in a lightly dampened, clean tea towel and microwave them for 15 to 20 seconds (adjust time according to your microwave and the number of tortillas you're using). Now they're as fresh as the day you bought them!

RETURN TO SLENDER

Losing weight is a lot like driving a car. In order to get results, you need to concentrate on where you want to go. Focusing on what you *don't* want—"I don't want to be fat"—isn't going to work. That's like staring intently at the curb and saying, "I don't want to drive there." Next thing you know, your fender's wrapped around a light post. To get what you want, focus on what you want! Picture it vividly, as if you've already achieved it. Say it out loud. Write it down. Be positive, be specific, and speak in terms of "now," not in terms of some vague hope for the future. "I'm too fat. I need to lose weight," isn't nearly as effective as saying, "I'm in the process of losing five pounds of fat this month. I'm a svelte, sexy, sculpted hottie!" (Well, that's a little over the top, but you get our drift.) This positive affirmation gives your goal clarity, focus, and a deadline—the quickest and surest way to get from point A to point B.

Wrap Star

Zesty tuna roll-ups with whole wheat tortillas

Bling it on! You'll love this wrapper's delight: Tuna with colorful chopped veggies, light feta cheese, and a tangy dressing, all rolled up in a whole wheat tortilla. *Hip hop* hooray!

2 cans (6 oz each) water-packed tuna, drained
1/3 cup diced grape tomatoes
1/3 cup diced celery
1/4 cup minced red onions
1/4 cup crumbled light feta cheese (1 oz)
3 tbsp fat-free or reduced-fat mayonnaise
2 tbsp light sour cream
2 tbsp chopped black olives (optional)
2 tbsp sweet pickle relish
1 tbsp freshly squeezed lemon juice
Salt and freshly ground black pepper to taste
4 small whole wheat flour tortillas (see tip in margin)
4 lettuce leaves (any type)

- Combine all ingredients except tortillas and lettuce in a medium bowl. Mix well.

- Working one tortilla at a time, lay one lettuce leaf on bottom half of each tortilla, followed by 1/4 tuna mixture. Spread tuna to edges. Roll up tortilla as tightly as possible. Cut in half using a sharp knife. Secure with toothpicks, if desired. Proceed with remaining tortillas, lettuce, and filling. Serve immediately or cover with plastic wrap and refrigerate until ready to serve.

Makes 4 servings

PER SERVING

calories	total fat	saturated fat	protein	carbohydrate	fiber	cholesterol	sodium
234	5.9 g	2 g	20 g	25 g	2.4 g	25 mg	549 mg

He used to work at a seafood restaurant, but then he pulled a mussel.

Skewer Always On My Mind

Lime and cilantro marinated salmon skewers

"Maybe I didn't feed you… quite as healthy as I should have. Maybe I didn't serve fish… quite as often as I could have." If you constantly fret over your family's poor eating habits, *skewer* not alone. Make these ultra-nutritious, ultra-delicious salmon kabobs and you'll get one more chance to keep them satisfied…keep them satisfied.

Marinade

¼ cup freshly squeezed
   lime juice
2 tbsp minced fresh cilantro
1 tbsp reduced-sodium soy sauce
1 tbsp honey mustard
1 tbsp barbecue sauce or ketchup
1 tsp grated lime zest
1 tsp minced garlic
¼ tsp each cumin, ground coriander, salt,
   and freshly ground black pepper

1½ lbs boneless, skinless salmon fillets,
   cut into chunks
4 12-inch metal skewers

- Combine all marinade ingredients in a small bowl. Mix well.

- Place salmon chunks in a large, heavy-duty, resealable plastic bag. Add marinade and seal bag. Turn bag several times to coat salmon with marinade. Marinate in refrigerator for 30 minutes.

- Meanwhile, preheat grill or broiler to high setting. Remove salmon from marinade (reserve marinade) and thread pieces onto skewers. Coat grill rack or broiler pan with cooking spray or brush lightly with oil. Grill or broil salmon for 3 to 4 minutes per side, brushing often with reserved marinade. Salmon should be just slightly pink in the center. Be careful not to overcook the salmon or it will be dry. Serve hot.

Makes 4 servings

PER SERVING

calories	total fat	saturated fat	protein	carbohydrate	fiber	cholesterol	sodium
264	10.9 g	1.7 g	34 g	5 g	0.3 g	94 mg	429 mg

Fat or Fiction?

> As long as I drink low-carb beer and don't use sugary mixes with my liquor, I won't get *waisted.*

If you want to win the No-Belly Prize, better banish the bottle. Yes, low-carb beers have fewer calories, but don't be fooled into thinking a low-carb six-pack will help you get six-pack abs. It's not just the empty-calorie wallop from beer that makes your Buttwider, it's the alcohol itself. When you drink, your body's driven to use the calories from alcohol as fuel *first*, leaving fat as the second choice. Researchers found that a mere three ounces of alcohol reduced the body's ability to burn fat by one-third! You booze, you *don't* lose! Even if you're chugging a low-carb beer or using a sugar-free mix with your hard liquor, the alcohol in those drinks still raises blood sugar, stimulating insulin— the powerful fat-storage hormone—spurring our appetites and compelling us to order a large plate of wings to go with our Butt Lite. Drinking beer and liquor also tends to raise levels of cortisol, a nasty, muscle-eating stress hormone that steers fat toward the waistline, hence the dreaded beer-belly syndrome. Finally, alcohol bogs down your liver, and one of the liver's roles in the body involves fat metabolism. So drinking makes your *liverwurst* and your beer belly even *worster!*

It is said that the bubbles in coffee can foretell the day's weather. Supposedly, you need to stare at your coffee before adding milk. If the bubbles float toward the rim of the cup, the pressure is low, and you can expect clouds and stormy weather. However, if the bubbles float to the center, the pressure is high, and fair weather is on its way. Looks like a meteorologist's job has many *perks!*

I never worry about diets. The only carrots that interest me are the kind you get in a diamond.

Mae West

Hook, Line, and Simple

Easy broiled salmon with creamy dill sauce

Waiting with *baited* breath for a *reel* tasty, *reel* simple salmon recipe? Well, you can breathe easy—this dish is the *reel* McCoy! You'll fall for it hook, line, and sinker.

6 boneless, skinless salmon fillets (about 6 oz each)
Salt and freshly ground black pepper to taste, plus ¼ tsp each (for sauce)
⅓ cup light sour cream
1-2 tbsp pure maple syrup
1 tbsp Dijon mustard
1 tbsp freshly squeezed lemon juice
1 tbsp minced fresh dill
1 tsp grated lemon zest

- Preheat broiler. Sprinkle salmon fillets lightly on both sides with salt and pepper.

- Place salmon on a baking sheet that has been sprayed with cooking spray. Broil 4 to 6 inches from heat source for about 4 minutes per side, or until fish flakes easily but is still just slightly pink in the center.

- While fish is cooking, prepare sauce. In a small bowl, whisk together sour cream, maple syrup, mustard, lemon juice, dill, lemon zest, salt, and pepper.

- Remove salmon from oven and drizzle with sauce. Serve immediately.

Makes 6 servings

PER SERVING

calories	total fat	saturated fat	protein	carbohydrate	fiber	cholesterol	sodium
273	11.2 g	1.8 g	35 g	6 g	0.1 g	94 mg	193 mg

Fish, to taste right, must swim three times— in water, in butter, and in wine.

Polish Proverb

THE E FILES

If you think nagging arthritis pain or that old rotator-cuff tear gives you license to retire to the sofa with a remote control, a bottle of pop, and a bag of chips, think again! Twenty years ago doctors said arthritis and other age-related aches and pains were reason enough to donate your sneakers to The Salvation Army. These days, they recommend some form of exercise for almost everyone. Orthopedic specialist Dr. William Raasch put it best: "My older patients who exercise complain they have arthritis pain in their knees for a few hours after exercising. But my patients who don't exercise have arthritis pain 24 hours a day." As you grow older, it's important to find a fitness routine that suits your age. After all, you wouldn't drive a vintage car the same way you would a modern sports car. Let's face it, you have a different body than you had in your 30s. It needs kinder, gentler handling. Trade high-impact sports for lower-impact ones like walking, swimming, and biking. If you want a good "quality-of-life" insurance policy, focus on flexibility and strength. Yoga, Pilates, stretching, and weight training should keep your moving parts lubricated, prevent your spare tire from inflating, and give you unlimited mileage. C'mon! Shift out of park and take your body for a spin!

Hey! There's a footprint in my breakfast!

Well, you ordered an omelette and told me to step on it!

I'm the dish everyone's talkin' about!

The Gift of Crab

Coconut crab cakes with mango-banana-curry sauce

You'll be *gabbing* about these coconut crab cakes to your friends! *Mango* crazy for them, and women do, too!

Sauce

1 cup diced fresh mango

½ cup diced banana

¼ cup each light coconut milk and plain, low-fat yogurt or light sour cream

2 tbsp hoisin sauce

1 tsp grated gingerroot

½ tsp curry powder

Crab Cakes

1 cup unseasoned dry bread crumbs, divided

1 lb fresh, frozen, or canned lump crabmeat (see tip below)

¼ cup flaked coconut

¼ cup light coconut milk

2 tbsp minced red bell pepper

2 tbsp minced fresh cilantro

2 tbsp minced green onions

1 tbsp hoisin sauce

1 tbsp grated gingerroot

1 egg

1 tsp minced garlic

½ tsp salt

¼ tsp freshly ground black pepper

2 tsp each olive oil and butter

Makes 12 crab cakes and 1¼ cups sauce

- To prepare sauce, whirl together all sauce ingredients in a food processor or blender until smooth. Refrigerate until ready to use. Sauce may be served cold or warm. To warm, heat over medium heat in a small saucepan, stirring constantly.

- For crab cakes, spread ½ cup bread crumbs on a small plate. Place remaining ½ cup bread crumbs in a large bowl and add remaining ingredients, except olive oil and butter. Mix well using your hands. To form crab cakes, fill a ¼-cup measuring cup with crab mixture and pack it down firmly. Flip the measuring cup over and shake it so the crab cake lands in your hand, then shape it a little so it's nice and round and about ½-inch thick. Handling crab cake very gently, dip each side in bread crumbs, then place crab cake on a plate until all of them are formed. (At this point, many recipes suggest refrigerating the crab cakes for 1 hour to help them hold together. However, as long as you're gentle with them, they shouldn't fall apart.)

- Heat olive oil and butter in a large, non-stick skillet over medium-high heat. Carefully place crab cakes in skillet. Cook for about 3 to 4 minutes per side, until crab cakes are golden and completely heated through. Serve hot with cool or warm sauce.

PER CRAB CAKE

calories	total fat	saturated fat	protein	carbohydrate	fiber	cholesterol	sodium
95	3.4 g	1.4 g	8 g	9 g	0.4 g	46 mg	301 mg

PER 2 TBSP SAUCE

calories	total fat	saturated fat	protein	carbohydrate	fiber	cholesterol	sodium
32	0.5 g	0.3 g	1 g	7 g	0.6 g	1 mg	56 mg

Cooking TIP

When cooking with crabmeat, whether fresh lump crabmeat, frozen, or canned, pick over the pieces to remove any bits of shell or cartilage. The tastiest crab cakes are always made with fresh crabmeat, but it's very expensive. Canned lump crabmeat is a good alternative. The way we see it, crab cakes made with canned crabmeat are better than no crab cakes at all! If you choose to use canned crabmeat, drain it well, soak it in ice water for 10 minutes, then drain it again and pat dry. This will help the crabmeat taste fresher. Imitation crabmeat (flavored pollock) is fine for crab salads and hot crab dips, but isn't recommended for crab cakes.

Dilly Whoppers

Pan-fried fresh salmon patties with dill and feta cheese

They're *dill*ightful! They're *dill*icious! They're *dill*ovely! And healthy, too? Yup, according to the Better Burger Bureau, these heart-smart salmon burgers with whopping good flavor won't make you a fatty Patty.

1 ½ lbs boneless, skinless
  salmon fillet,
  cut into chunks
1 cup fresh whole wheat bread
  crumbs (see tip in margin)
½ cup crumbled light feta
  cheese (2 oz)
¼ cup minced shallots
1 tbsp honey mustard
1 tbsp freshly squeezed
  lemon juice
1 egg
1 tbsp minced fresh dill
1 tsp grated lemon zest
¼ tsp each salt and freshly ground black pepper

- Place salmon chunks in a food processor. Pulse on and off until salmon is chopped into very small pieces. (If you don't have a food processor, use a very sharp knife and mince the salmon by hand.) Transfer salmon to a large bowl. Add remaining ingredients. Mix well using your hands.

- Form mixture into 6 patties, about ³⁄₄ inch thick. Place patties on a large plate, cover with plastic wrap, and refrigerate for 1 hour. (Chilling will help the patties hold their shape while cooking.)

- Spray a large, non-stick skillet with cooking spray and heat over medium-high heat. Add patties and cook for about 4 minutes per side, until salmon is cooked through. Be careful not to overcook the patties, and be gentle when flipping them so they don't fall apart. If you don't have a high-quality (unscratched!) non-stick pan, you might want to cook the patties in a tablespoon or two of olive oil.

- If desired, serve patties on small, whole wheat hamburger buns with sliced tomatoes, lettuce, and honey mustard, or top them with a spoon of low-fat tartar sauce (see recipe in margin) and serve with a salad.

Makes 6 servings

PER SERVING

calories	total fat	saturated fat	protein	carbohydrate	fiber	cholesterol	sodium
236	10.4 g	2.8 g	26 g	9 g	1.1 g	106 mg	333 mg

Cooking TIP

Fresh bread crumbs are simple to make: Just break up a slice of bread (preferably whole wheat) into several smaller pieces and place in a food processor or mini chopper. Pulse on and off a few times to create fluffy soft crumbs. An average slice of bread will make about ½ cup fresh bread crumbs. Dry, store-bought bread crumbs are more compact (and drier, of course!), so if a recipe calls for fresh crumbs and you'd rather use dry, cut the amount in half. To make low-fat tartar sauce for this and other yummy fish dishes, mix together ½ cup low-fat mayonnaise, 1 tbsp minced fresh dill, 1 tbsp sweet pickle relish, and 2 tsp each prepared horseradish and freshly squeezed lemon juice. Refrigerate until ready to use.

Fear Factor, Reality Check
. . . .

We're scared. We're really scared. We're afraid of pollution in our air, chemicals in our water, germs in our food, mysterious new viruses, and dangers that might be lurking in power lines and cell phones. Perhaps some of these fears are justified. But more often than not, our perceptions of risk don't always match reality. We worry ourselves sick over terrorism, yet smoke a pack a day. We scale back on fish because the morning paper talks of toxins in our waters—yet we scarf down two donuts and a large coffee while reading the headlines. The only time we break a sweat is when we swat frantically at mosquitoes. Honestly! What's more likely to kill us: West Nile Virus or being overweight and sedentary? Scientists are still trying to come to grips with the risks presented by the trappings of modern life, but this much is already known: Smoking can truly kill you. Eating too much and exercising too little is a lethal combination. The bottom line is this: Yes, wash your hands often, swat those mosquitoes, and don't talk on your cell phone while lying in a tanning bed, but keep your perspective. Focus on lowering the truly big health risks, put your butts out, and get your butt moving!

The shape of your figure can shape your future.

Fat or Fiction?

An apple a day keeps the doctor away, but if you've got an apple-shaped core, you might want a doctor on standby. Tons of studies show that abdominal fat isn't just a cosmetic issue—it's far more dangerous than lower-body fat, putting you at risk for heart disease and other health complications. In fact, a groundbreaking 12-year study (Iowa Women's Study) found that women with the thickest waist circumferences were more likely to die early. And a study at Harvard showed that allowing your belt size to increase by just five inches during adulthood can double your risk for diabetes. Yikes! How 'bout them apples! Though researchers aren't exactly sure why belly fat raises the risk of premature death, they point out that this type of fat sits close to critical organs like the heart and liver, and that abdominal fat may also be metabolized differently than other types of fat, contributing to higher cholesterol, blood fats, and blood pressure. Those symptoms, in combination with an apple shape, are often a sign of insulin resistance, a precursor to diabetes also referred to as Syndrome X or Metabolic Syndrome. Basically, insulin resistance means your pancreas is fed up with your reckless eating. To figure out if your figure is putting your health in jeopardy, get out a tape measure (and don't suck in your gut!). A waist size of more than 35 inches for women or 40 inches for men is a signal to tighten your belt by shaping up and slimming down. Given all the health risks surrounding belly fat, don't diddle when trimming your middle!

Star-Kissed Tuna Melts

Seasoned tuna on toasted multigrain bread with melted cheddar

Sorry, Charlie. Only our tuna melts have star quality. Get ready to roll out the *bread* carpet!

2 cans (6 oz each) water-packed tuna, drained
1 cup broccoli slaw mix (see tip below)
¼ cup light ranch or light creamy cucumber and dill salad dressing
¼ cup minced red onions
2 tbsp light mayonnaise
1 tbsp freshly squeezed lemon juice
½ tsp granulated sugar
¼ tsp each salt and freshly ground black pepper
4 slices multigrain bread with flaxseed, toasted
1 large tomato, thinly sliced
4 slices light cheddar cheese (¾ oz each—see tip below)

- Preheat broiler. In a medium bowl, combine tuna, broccoli slaw mix, dressing, onions, mayonnaise, lemon juice, sugar, salt, and pepper. Mix well.

- Place toasted bread on a baking sheet. Distribute tuna mixture evenly over bread. Top with tomato slices. Place under broiler, about 6 inches from heat source, for 2 minutes, or until tuna is warmed. Remove from oven and top each open-faced sandwich with cheese slice. Return to oven and broil for 1 minute, until cheese is completely melted. Serve hot.

Tip: Look for broccoli slaw mix where you find regular coleslaw mix in the produce aisle of your grocery store. It usually contains grated carrots and red cabbage as well as shredded broccoli, which makes this sandwich colorful. You can use any type of cheese you like to top this melt. Light Swiss and provolone cheeses are good substitutes for the cheddar.

Makes 4 servings

PER SERVING

calories	total fat	saturated fat	protein	carbohydrate	fiber	cholesterol	sodium
275	8.7 g	3.4 g	26 g	24 g	3.7 g	25 mg	628 mg

Awe, Shucks!

Seared sea scallops with Alfredo sauce and bacon

In our humble opinion, these succulent scallops are totally awesome. *Seariously*, you'll be awestruck after just one taste. *Sea* for yourself!

20 large, plump sea scallops
   (about 1 lb—see tip below)
Salt and freshly ground black pepper
3 slices bacon
½ cup dry white wine
⅓ cup minced shallots or red onions
1 tsp minced garlic
½ cup light Alfredo sauce
Grated zest of 1 lemon
1 tbsp chopped fresh parsley

- Rinse scallops under cold water and pat dry thoroughly with paper towels. Sprinkle lightly with salt and pepper and set aside.

- Heat a 10-inch, non-stick skillet over medium-high heat. Add bacon and cook until crisp (but not burnt!). Drain bacon on paper towels, reserving drippings in skillet. Crumble bacon and set aside.

- Drain off all but 1 tbsp bacon drippings in skillet. Add scallops and cook (sear) over medium-high heat for about 2 minutes per side, until lightly browned. Remove from skillet and keep warm.

- Add wine, shallots, and garlic to same skillet. Reduce heat to medium. Cook and stir for 2 minutes, until shallots are tender and wine has evaporated a bit. Stir in Alfredo sauce and lemon zest. Mix well. Return scallops to skillet and gently stir so that they're coated with sauce. Cook 1 more minute. Remove skillet from heat. Sprinkle crumbled bacon and parsley over scallops and add a bit more freshly ground black pepper. Serve immediately.

Tip: What's the difference between sea and bay scallops? Sea scallops are the big ones and bay scallops are the weensy ones. You want the big sea scallops for this recipe.

Makes 4 servings

	PER SERVING						
calories	total fat	saturated fat	protein	carbohydrate	fiber	cholesterol	sodium
231	9.3 g	3.9 g	22 g	8 g	0.2 g	57 mg	418 mg

"SAY IT AIN'T SO!"

Tall. Grande. Venti. Frappuccino. Cappuccino. Mochaccino. Sure is a whole *latte* lingo goin' down at the gourmet coffee shop—and a whole *latte* calories! In fact, with the help of an interpreter and some nutritional detective work, you'll soon discover your Mocha-coca-java can hava-lotta-fattuccino, too! Depending on the size of your drink, the type of milk and syrup you choose, and whether you said "yes" to whipped cream, you can transform an innocent beverage into an insulin-spiking, belt-busting milk shake. Here's proof: a Starbucks Strawberries & Crème Frappuccino has an unthinkable, drinkable 600 calories, 17 grams of fat (10 of them saturated), and 87 grams of sugar—that's almost 22 teaspoons! If that kind of coffee's your daily grind, you're in big, fat trouble, Joe! Choose tall (small), skinny (nonfat milk), and skip the whip. And remember that beverage calories do count—venti (large)!

Heavy Metal Banned

No need to scale back on fish just because you've heard reports that it contains the toxic metal, mercury. Just don't swim with the sharks. Fish with higher levels of mercury include shark, swordfish, king mackerel, and tilefish. These fish are at the top of the food chain, they're large, and live a long time, so they accumulate more mercury. They're the fish that government health regulators suggest limiting to one meal per month for women of childbearing age and young children. The following species are low enough in toxic metal levels that even pregnant women can enjoy them a couple times per week: sardines, trout, haddock, shrimp, catfish, summer flounder, and wild Pacific salmon. Hooked on tuna sandwiches? The fish used in canned tuna are small, so they don't accumulate as much mercury. But don't overdo it. Once or twice per week is fine. And keep in mind that the fatty acids, vitamin E, and selenium contained in fish itself provide protection from mercury. Still smells fishy to you? Then remove the skin and fat, where toxins are likely to lurk, and avoid frying, which can seal in chemical pollutants. Grilling and broiling helps drain them away. We'd write more, but we've got bigger fish to fry!

During Captain James Cook's great voyage to explore the Pacific in 1772, he ordered thousands of pounds of _____ to help prevent scurvy among his crew members:

a) Flintstone vitamins
b) navel oranges
c) water chestnuts
d) sauerkraut

Answer: (d) Made from fermented cabbage, sauerkraut is high in vitamin C.

My idea of exercise is a good brisk sit.
Phyllis Diller

Tinbucktuna
Mild and creamy tuna and rotini stovetop casserole

You don't have to travel halfway across the planet looking for obscure, exotic, highly unusual ingredients when you're just tryin' to put a tasty, healthy meal on your family's dinner table. There's no weird stuff (just good stuff!) in our delicious tuna and rotini casserole. Plus, it's cheap and easy (like Janet!).

8 oz uncooked rotini pasta (about 3 cups—see tip below)
2 cups frozen mixed vegetables (see tip below)
1 tbsp butter
1 cup diced onions
1 tsp minced garlic
1 can (10.75 oz) condensed, reduced-fat cream of broccoli soup, undiluted
¾ cup packed shredded light old (sharp) cheddar cheese (3 oz)
¼ cup light sour cream
¼ cup grated Parmesan cheese
1 tbsp minced fresh dill or fresh basil leaves, or 1 tsp dried
½ tsp dry mustard powder
¼ tsp freshly ground black pepper
2 cans (6 oz each) chunk light tuna in water, drained, or boneless, skinless salmon, drained

- Cook pasta according to package directions, adding frozen vegetables to the boiling water for the last 5 minutes of cooking time. Drain pasta and vegetables.

- Meanwhile, prepare sauce. In a large, non-stick pot, melt butter over medium heat. Add onions and garlic. Cook and stir until onions are tender, about 5 minutes. Add soup, shredded cheese, sour cream, Parmesan cheese, dill, mustard powder, and black pepper. Mix well and cook until sauce is bubbly and cheese has melted. Remove from heat. Stir in pasta, vegetables, and tuna. Serve hot.

Tip: Try using whole wheat rotini to make this meal even healthier. For the vegetables, use a frozen mixture of carrots, beans, and green peas, or a broccoli, cauliflower, and carrots combo (sometimes referred to as California Blend).

Makes 6 servings

PER SERVING

calories	total fat	saturated fat	protein	carbohydrate	fiber	cholesterol	sodium
349	8.7 g	4.8 g	24 g	14 g	2.6 g	35 mg	690 mg

A Chorus Loin

Broad ways with beef and pork

More than one... singular sensation

Roasted beef tenderloin with herbs • Lemon-rosemary barbecue pork chops • Beef stew with rosemary dumplings • Pork tenderloin with apple-Dijon sauce • Marinated flank steak • Apricot-mustard skillet pork chops • Asian-glazed pork tenderloin • Beef and vegetable kebobs • Slow cooker pot roast • Asian beef stir-fry • Grilled pork tenderloin with mango • Company pork loin roast • Pork tenderloin chop suey • Maple-mustard glazed ham

Ponderoasta

Mouthwatering, slow-cooked pot roast in a sweet and spicy barbecue sauce

It's a flavor *Bonanza*! A totally *Hoss*ome pot roast with a finger-lickin', lip-smackin' sauce that'll drive you wild! (Can you stand our *Little Jo*ekes?) Ring the cowbell and get ready for a stampede to the dinner table.

¾ cup root beer (not diet root beer)
⅓ cup hickory-flavored barbecue sauce
2 tbsp tomato paste
1 tbsp freshly squeezed lemon juice
1 tbsp grated gingerroot
2 tsp Worcestershire sauce
1 tsp minced garlic
½ tsp each ground cumin and chili powder
1 sirloin tip roast (3 to 3½ lbs)
Salt and freshly ground black pepper
2 tsp olive oil or vegetable oil
1 medium onion, cut into wedges
2 tbsp cornstarch

• To make sauce, combine root beer, barbecue sauce, tomato paste, lemon juice, gingerroot, Worcestershire sauce, garlic, cumin, and chili powder in a small saucepan. Bring to a boil over medium-high heat. Reduce heat to medium and let sauce boil gently for 2 minutes. Remove from heat. (The sauce is very strong and concentrated at this point—don't panic, it will "mellow" once it's cooked in the beef juices!)

• Pat roast dry with paper towels. Sprinkle lightly with salt and pepper. Heat oil in a large skillet or Dutch oven over medium-high heat. Add roast and brown it on all sides.

• Place browned roast in a slow cooker. Arrange onion wedges around roast. Pour sauce over roast. Cover with lid and cook on low heat setting for 8 hours. Note: It's tempting to lift the lid and peek inside, but each time you do this, you have to add about 15 minutes to the cooking time!

• Remove roast and onions from slow cooker (use a slotted spoon to scoop up onions). Pour sauce from slow cooker into a medium saucepan. Skim off as much fat as possible. In a small bowl or cup, mix cornstarch with an equal amount of water and stir until smooth. Add to sauce and bring to a boil over high heat, whisking constantly, until sauce has thickened slightly.

• To serve, slice roast thinly (it may be so tender that it falls apart!) and spoon hot sauce over top.

Tip: If you love mashed potatoes, they're a great accompaniment to this roast.

Makes 8 servings

PER SERVING

calories	total fat	saturated fat	protein	carbohydrate	fiber	cholesterol	sodium
230	8.7 g	2.8 g	28 g	8 g	0.5 g	85 mg	251 mg

Tomatoes and oregano make it Italian; wine and tarragon make it French.
Sour cream makes it Russian; lemon and cinnamon make it Greek.
Soy sauce makes it Chinese; garlic makes it good.

Alice May Brock

If you're working on changing your body shape, don't model it after supermodels or celebrities. It's tough to measure up (or more likely, down!) to the figures of Hollywood stars who have 24-hour private chefs, personal trainers, yoga gurus, tai chi instructors, and massage therapists (not to mention plastic surgeons to fix whatever problems are left). Then there's the airbrushing, good lighting, and other photographic wizardry. Let's face it, Hollywood isn't reality—it's a very small and distorted part of the world. If you're trying to whip your body into shape, be realistic to avoid disappointment, and do it for the right reasons: to develop a sense of well-being, improve self-esteem, and boost energy so you can enjoy life fully. Anyone, of any body type, of any age, can become fit through regular exercise and a healthy diet. It's smarter to make fitness—not thinness—your number-one priority. Besides, who wants to deal with all those paparazzi anyway?

Funky Factoid

Blondes have more f...ollicles! Natural blondes have more hair on their heads than redheads or brunettes. A blonde has about 120,000 strands of hair, while a redhead has about 20% fewer. Brunettes are somewhere in between the two. Four out of five hairstylists agree: Blondes have more *bun*!

Those steaks are charred!

Well, my doctor told me to burn more calories!

Wok This Way

Asian beef stir-fry with basil and red bell pepper

Ever dream of becoming a *wok* star? Well, now's your chance for fame and fortune cookies! This flavorful beef stir-fry with fresh basil, red bell pepper, and onions will get you *wokin'* and rollin'!

1 lb sirloin steak, trimmed of fat, thinly sliced
3 tbsp Asian fish sauce (see tip below)
2 tbsp reduced-sodium soy sauce
1 tbsp brown sugar
1 tbsp grated gingerroot
1 tsp minced garlic
½ tsp crushed red pepper flakes
1 tbsp peanut oil or canola oil
1 large red bell pepper, seeded and cut into strips
1 medium red onion, sliced
Lots of fresh basil leaves (at least 20)

- Place steak slices in a shallow bowl or casserole dish. In a small bowl, whisk together fish sauce, soy sauce, brown sugar, gingerroot, garlic, and crushed red pepper flakes. Pour over steak. Marinate steak at room temperature for 30 minutes.

- Heat oil in a large, non-stick wok over medium-high heat. Remove steak from marinade and shake off excess. Reserve marinade. Cook steak in hot oil just until cooked through, stirring constantly. Remove steak from wok and set aside. Add red pepper and onion to wok. Cook and stir for about 5 minutes, until vegetables are tender. Return beef to wok and add basil and reserved marinade. Cook 1 more minute, until basil leaves are wilted and beef is hot.

Tip: Asian fish sauce is an essential ingredient for authentic Thai flavor. Most grocery stores stock it near the soy sauce. For more information, see tip on page 179.

Makes 4 servings

PER SERVING

calories	total fat	saturated fat	protein	carbohydrate	fiber	cholesterol	sodium
258	9.5 g	3 g	26 g	17 g	2.8 g	68 mg	732 mg

A CHORUS LOIN

115

The Grill of My Dreams

Marinated, grilled pork tenderloin with mango and peppers

This one's not like all the other *grills*! Make our one-of-a-kind pork tenderloin masterpiece in the summertime when peppers are fresh and you can't stand the heat in the kitchen.

Marinade
3 tbsp reduced-sodium soy sauce
3 tbsp balsamic vinegar
2 tbsp toasted sesame oil
2 tbsp minced fresh basil leaves
1 tbsp liquid honey
1 tbsp grated gingerroot
2 tsp grated orange zest
1 tsp minced garlic
¼ tsp each salt and freshly ground black pepper

1 lb pork tenderloin
1 medium zucchini
3 large bell peppers (red, yellow, orange)
1 medium mango, peeled and sliced into wedges
Baby spinach leaves (optional)

- Whisk together all marinade ingredients in a small bowl. Reserve ⅓ cup marinade for basting and as a dressing. Place pork in a large, heavy-duty, resealable plastic bag. Add marinade and seal bag. Turn bag several times to coat pork with marinade. Marinate in refrigerator for at least 4 hours.

- Preheat grill to medium-high setting. Slice unpeeled zucchini lengthwise into four long strips. Seed peppers and cut each one in half. Place pork on a grill rack that has been coated with cooking spray or lightly brushed with oil. Grill meat until it's nicely browned on the outside and just slightly pink in the center, about 16 minutes. Be careful not to overcook pork. Add peppers and zucchini for the last 8 minutes of cooking time. Turn vegetables once to grill both sides, and baste with some of the reserved marinade.

- Remove pork and vegetables from grill and let pork rest for 5 minutes before slicing. Meanwhile, slice peppers into thick strips and cut zucchini strips in half crosswise. Place vegetables in a large bowl and add mango, thinly sliced pork, and a bit of reserved marinade. Toss well. Serve on a bed of baby spinach leaves, if desired. Top with freshly ground black pepper.

Tip: If you like onions, slice a medium red onion into thick rings and grill alongside pork.

Makes 4 servings

PER SERVING

calories	total fat	saturated fat	protein	carbohydrate	fiber	cholesterol	sodium
275	9 g	2.1 g	27 g	23 g	4.1 g	74 mg	449 mg

I'm on a high-protein diet. Can I eat red meat 'til the cows come home?

Ask Janet

Only if you want to *mooove* a kidney stone and have *udderly* bad breath! Convinced that the road to Slimville is paved with bunless burgers and all-you-can-eat prime-rib buffets, people are going mad over cow products, and that can spell disaster for their overall health. While animal protein is fine in moderation, science has proven that excess saturated fat is a staggering burden for your heart to handle. Beef it up morning, noon, and night, and there's not much room left for fiber and nutrient-packed plant foods. That paves the way for chronic constipation, headaches, bad breath, and hair loss, some of the common side effects experienced by high-protein dieters. Even worse, eating too much meat can make your body very acidic. That can lead to fatigue, bone loss, kidney and liver damage, and it's also the environment that disease—especially cancer—thrives in. Let's not lose sight of these effects just because our sights are set on losing weight. We run into trouble when we take things too far. Sure, including protein with each meal is a good idea, but that doesn't mean you should pile your plate sky-high with slabs of ribs and mountains of chicken wings and then go back for seconds. To trim the saturated fat from your healthy-carb lifestyle, choose protein sources like skinless chicken or turkey breast, fish, and lean cuts of pork or beef. Opt for low-fat dairy products and experiment with meatless sources of protein like beans, lentils, and nuts every once in a while. Most importantly, think smaller portions. Don't have a *whole* cow, man!

Sign on church bulletin:
Have trouble sleeping?
Try counting your blessings.

"SAY IT AIN'T SO!"

You can bring home the bacon and fry it up in the pan—just don't pig out on the stuff. Sodium nitrate, a common preservative used in bacon, packaged meats, cold cuts, hot dogs, and sausages, changes into something evil called "nitrosamines" when it mixes in the stomach with other compounds found in protein-containing foods. Trouble is, even small amounts of nitrosamines have been shown to cause cancer in animals. Good nitrate! Fortunately, there are more and more butchers who make their own preservative-free meats and sausages. Otherwise, look for nitrates (a.k.a. nitrites) on ingredients lists, and just don't overdo it. Most of us enjoy eating bacon every now and then, but you really shouldn't go hog wild. Plus, if you slice up plenty of veggies, legumes, and maybe some fruit on the side, their potent, cancer-fighting phytonutrients can help counteract the negative effects of nitrates.

Funky Factoid

The world's rarest coffee comes from Indonesia. At approximately $300 US per pound, kopi luwak is the end product (we really mean *end* product!) of a catlike marsupial, called the Paradoxurus, that loves eating coffee beans. The enzymes in the animal's stomach add a unique flavor, and the beans are collected only after they are excreted. Oh, come on! Don't pooh-pooh it until you try it!

The Loin King

Delicious marinated pork loin roast for company or Sunday dinner

It's the tastiest pork roast this side of the jungle... and we aren't *lion*, either!

Marinade
¼ cup each brown sugar and ketchup
3 tbsp balsamic vinegar
2 tbsp olive oil
1 tbsp reduced-sodium soy sauce
2 tsp minced garlic
1 tsp each curry powder, ground coriander, and ground ginger
½ tsp each salt and freshly ground black pepper

1 boneless pork loin roast (about 4 lbs)

- Whisk together all marinade ingredients in a medium bowl. Place pork in a large, heavy-duty, resealable plastic bag. Add marinade and seal bag. Turn bag several times to coat roast with marinade. Marinate overnight in refrigerator.

- Preheat oven to 325°F. Remove pork from bag and place on a rack set in a shallow roasting pan. Reserve marinade. Roast pork, uncovered, for about 1 hour and 45 minutes to 2 hours. A meat thermometer inserted in center of roast should read 155°F.

- While roast is cooking, pour reserved marinade into a small saucepan. Bring to a boil, then reduce heat to low and simmer for 1 minute. Brush roast generously with marinade during the last 20 minutes of cooking time.

- Remove roast from oven. Cover loosely with foil and let rest for 10 minutes before slicing. Slice thinly and serve with cranberry-onion relish on page 146, if desired.

Makes 10 servings

PER SERVING (WITHOUT RELISH)

calories	total fat	saturated fat	protein	carbohydrate	fiber	cholesterol	sodium
254	9.9 g	3.2 g	34 g	5 g	0.2 g	88 mg	220 mg

If a pig loses his voice, is he disgruntled?

Chop Soooo-ey!

Chop suey with marinated pork tenderloin and crunchy vegetables

Call your family to the dinner table for our much-tastier-than-takeout chop suey and they're bound to go hog wild! Squeals of approval guaranteed. Don't be disgruntled over the long ingredients list—it's actually soooo easy to make.

Ah, so good!

Marinade

1 tbsp reduced-sodium soy sauce
1 tbsp oyster sauce (see tip in margin)
2 tsp grated gingerroot
1 tsp each minced garlic, granulated sugar, and cornstarch

1 lb pork tenderloin, cut into strips

Sauce

½ cup beef broth
1 tbsp reduced-sodium soy sauce
1 tbsp oyster sauce
2 tsp cornstarch
1 tsp toasted sesame oil
¼ tsp crushed red pepper flakes

1 tbsp peanut oil or vegetable oil
2 cups sliced mushrooms
1 cup sliced celery (cut on the diagonal)
1 handful snow peas
2 cups bean sprouts
1 can (8 oz) sliced water chestnuts, drained
1 cup sliced green onions

- Combine all marinade ingredients in a medium bowl. Add pork and toss to coat with marinade. Let pork marinate for 15 minutes while you prepare remaining ingredients.

- To make sauce, whisk together broth, soy sauce, oyster sauce, cornstarch, sesame oil, and red pepper flakes in a small bowl and set aside.

- Heat peanut oil in a large, non-stick wok over medium-high heat. Add pork and any extra marinade. Cook and stir until pork is lightly browned on the outside, about 3 minutes. Add mushrooms, celery, and snow peas. Cook and stir for 3 to 4 more minutes, until mushrooms are tender. Add bean sprouts, water chestnuts, green onions, and reserved sauce. Cook and stir for 3 more minutes, until vegetables are tender-crisp and sauce is bubbly and has thickened. Serve immediately.

Makes 4 servings

PER SERVING

calories	total fat	saturated fat	protein	carbohydrate	fiber	cholesterol	sodium
271	9.1 g	2.1 g	29 g	20 g	5.7 g	74 mg	471 mg

Bone Appétit

Did you know that North Americans consume more dairy products than anyone else in the world? Sadly, North Americans also have the highest rate of osteoporosis on the planet, no bones about it. What gives? Isn't the calcium from dairy products supposed to prevent the thinning of our bones? Though we're milking dairy products for all they're worth, North Americans also consume more "calcium robbers" than anyone on earth, and it's definitely our loss. Some of the things that leach calcium from our bones are the same things most common to North American living: caffeine, sugar, soft drinks, alcohol, excessive protein, smoking, stress, and inactivity. Amazingly, poor dietary and lifestyle choices have more to do with calcium deficiency and bone loss than not taking in enough calcium. Before boning up on calcium supplements or eating more yogurt, start by repairing the calcium leaks. Beware the calcium bandits, get some exercise, and choose nutrient-filled foods more often.

Sir, can you fix my torn shoe?

What? And add insole to injury?

Fat or Fiction?

You are what you eat: Garbage in, garbage out.

Within a year, virtually every cell in your body will be replaced with a new cell. Out with the old, in with the new. Your skin, muscles, bones, even your organs, are constantly degenerating and regenerating. As sure as you're reading the words on this page, your body is in a constant cycle of renewal. Guess what the body uses to re-create itself? Food! That means *you* are the construction foreman who's responsible for choosing the raw materials to build your foundation. Knowing that, would you order fries to build your eyes? Choose Twinkies to become your pinkies? Pick chips to form your lips? Beer to shape your ear? When Elvis sang, "You ain't nothin' but a *hot* dog," was he referring to you? Most people don't have a clue what they're doing to their bodies as a result of poor eating habits. Nor are they aware how much better they could look and feel if they stopped eating mindlessly and started rebuilding themselves intentionally. If you constantly eat junk, you create an inferior, weaker version of what you're capable of being. Eat fresh, natural, nutrient-filled foods more often, and watch how you'll rejuvenate, replenish, and renew. What kind of structure are *you* building?

In the Middle Ages, it was customary for peasants to toss their daily food scraps and leftovers into iron pots simmering over open fires. They often had no idea what was actually cooking, so when an unexpected visitor was asked "to take pot luck," he was invited to dine on whatever was available in the pot. It was a matter of luck—what meal was actually in the pot and whether there would be enough of it to go around. Today, the expression refers to a gathering of people for a meal where each of the guests brings food to be shared by all.

The Blah-Shank Redemption

Baked bone-in ham with a maple-mustard glaze

We've turned a plain ol' boring ham into something sensational! Why *confine* yourself to the same mundane recipe every Easter dinner? *Break out* of the rut and *escape* the ordinary with our delectable, yet simple, maple-mustard glazed ham. We've kept the recipe under lock and key until now.

1 fully-cooked, smoked, bone-in ham (about 8 lbs)
Whole cloves
¼ cup pure maple syrup
3 tbsp grainy Dijon mustard
1 tbsp cider vinegar
1 tsp ground ginger
Pineapple chutney (optional; see recipe, page 158)

- Preheat oven to 325°F. Move oven rack to bottom third of oven.

- Using a sharp knife, score surface of ham crosswise and lengthwise, forming a crosshatch pattern about ¼ inch deep and 2 inches apart. Push a clove into the center of each square.

- Place ham on a rack in a shallow roasting pan. Cover loosely with foil. Roast for 1 hour and 40 minutes.

- While ham is cooking, prepare glaze. Combine maple syrup, mustard, vinegar, and ginger in a small bowl.

- Remove ham from oven and brush with glaze. Use all of it and cover every square inch of ham. Return to oven and roast, uncovered, for 20 to 30 more minutes, until a meat thermometer inserted in deepest part of ham registers 140°F.

- Let ham rest for about 10 minutes before slicing. Slice thinly and serve hot with pineapple chutney, if desired.

Makes 16-20 servings

PER SERVING (BASED ON 20 SERVINGS)

calories	total fat	saturated fat	protein	carbohydrate	fiber	cholesterol	sodium
169	5.6 g	1.8 g	25 g	3 g	0 g	55 mg	1329 mg

Cottage cheese diet: Eating your curds and weigh.

The Great Pretenderloin

Roasted whole beef tenderloin with rosemary and thyme

Actually, there's no use pretending—this is truly the most succulent, mouth-watering beef you'll ever taste. A real showstopper! You might want to save it for special occasions or holidays, though. It costs a lotta *moo*-la, but it's worth every penny.

Only you... can make this roast just right

Seasoning Rub
- **1 tbsp softened butter or olive oil**
- **1 tbsp Dijon mustard**
- **1 tbsp brown sugar**
- **1 tbsp steak sauce (such as A1)**
- **1 tbsp minced fresh rosemary**
- **1 tbsp minced fresh thyme**
- **2 tsp minced garlic**
- **1½ tsp salt**
  (we like sea salt)
- **1 tsp freshly ground**
  black pepper
- **1 tsp grated lemon zest**

1 whole beef tenderloin (about 3 lbs), trimmed of visible fat

- Preheat oven to 450°F. Move oven rack to bottom third of oven.

- Mix together rub ingredients in a small bowl. Rub all over beef. Let stand at room temperature for 30 minutes. Place beef on a rack in a shallow roasting pan. Place pan in oven and reduce temperature to 400°F.

- Roast meat, uncovered, for 45 to 55 minutes, or until meat thermometer inserted in the center registers 140°F for medium-rare. Remove roast from oven and let stand, uncovered, for 10 minutes before slicing. (Note: Exact cooking time will depend on thickness of roast. Temperature will continue to rise as meat rests.)

Makes 8 servings

PER SERVING							
calories	total fat	saturated fat	protein	carbohydrate	fiber	cholesterol	sodium
225	11.3 g	4.6 g	26 g	3 g	0.2 g	82 mg	533 mg

There has always been a food processor in the kitchen. But once upon a time she was usually called "Mom."

Sue Berkman

THE E FILES

Having a bad *air* day? If you're a shallow breather, you may not be getting enough oxygen to your body's cells, and that can leave you feeling foggy, fatigued, and a little stressed. What's more, lack of oxygen could be contributing to your growing gut! Say what? Well, you need oxygen to burn fat, which is why aerobic exercise (the intense kind that boosts your heart rate and gets you breathing heavily) is necessary if you want to unveil those six-pack abs. But exercise aside, you can avoid bad air days by learning deep-breathing techniques. Deep breathing not only helps detoxify your body, but also kicks up the level of oxygen in your cells, boosting your metabolism. Plus, it helps tone your midsection by putting the brakes on cortisol. (Cortisol is the nasty stress hormone that promotes weight gain around our middles, giving them the dreaded Pillsbury Doughboy look.) Deep breathing also triggers an automatic relaxation response in your body, which lowers blood pressure and heart rate, reduces tension, and sharpens thinking. Phew! A little breathing sure goes a long way! Whether you buy a book on deep-breathing techniques or sign up for a class, you'll be accumulating valuable air miles.

The ancient Egyptians recommended a concoction of half an onion mixed with beer foam as a method of...

a) warding off death
b) repelling insects
c) neutralizing bad breath
d) preventing a mummy's hair from turning gray

Answer: (a) Apparently, its effectiveness wasn't very impressive, as research indicates that all ancient Egyptians are, in fact, dead.

Lick Your Chops

Juicy pork loin chops in a zesty lemon-rosemary barbecue sauce

The lemon and molasses give 'em zest and zing. It's a "lick your lips, lick your fork, lick your plate" kinda thing. You'll make them lickety-split, too!

Sauce

½ cup ketchup

2 tbsp freshly squeezed lemon juice

2 tbsp molasses

2 tbsp minced shallots or onions

1 ¼ tsp chili powder

1 tsp minced garlic

1 tsp grated lemon zest

½ tsp dried rosemary

¼ tsp freshly ground black pepper

4 boneless pork loin chops (about 5 oz each)

- To make sauce, combine all sauce ingredients in a small saucepan. Bring to a boil over medium-high heat. Reduce heat to low and simmer for 2 minutes, stirring occasionally.

- Preheat grill to medium-high setting. Place pork chops on a grill rack that has been coated with cooking spray or lightly brushed with oil. Grill pork chops for about 6 minutes per side, depending on thickness of chops. Pork should be just slightly pink in the center. Be careful not to overcook them or they will be dry. Brush pork generously with sauce during last 5 minutes of cooking time.

- Brush any remaining sauce on pork chops just before serving.

Note: If you have the time, you can marinate the pork chops in the sauce overnight. You don't have to cook the sauce first. Then, just throw the chops on the grill and wait for the standing ovation you're sure to receive!

Makes 4 servings

PER SERVING

calories	total fat	saturated fat	protein	carbohydrate	fiber	cholesterol	sodium
282	9 g	3.1 g	36 g	13 g	0.6 g	91 mg	403 mg

RETURN TO SLENDER

Though we aren't crazy about diets in general, we actually love them when we make them up ourselves. Just kidding! Actually, the following week-long "Janet and Greta Mini Diets" truly are beneficial because they can help improve your overall eating habits. At week's end, take stock of which foods you missed and which you could live without. (1) *The Think Outside the Box Diet*: No packaged or processed foods. Eating out of packages, boxes, and bags can boost your intake of calories, sodium, trans fats, and saturated fat. Instead, prepare simple meals using fresh foods; (2) *The Meatless in Seattle Diet*: By-pass the meat market and get your protein by eating beans, fish, nuts, whey protein shakes, yogurt, and other low-fat dairy products; (3) *The BYOF (Bring Your Own Food) Diet*: That means no meals of fast food, take-out, or convenience food. Instead of waiting for someone at work to show up with a box of Krispy Kremes, eat breakfast at home. When you brown-bag it for lunch and snacks, you can pack some balanced blends of protein, fat, and fiber, a combination that'll keep you full until dinner time. Incidentally, a man from Port Huron, Michigan, combined all three diets and lost over 100% of his body weight in seven days. (Just making sure you're still reading!)

A ham walked out of the hospital and said, "I'm cured!"

Putting the C.A.R.T.S. Before the Hearse

If you want to add years to your life and life to your years, then beware the five deadly dietary sins: **C**affeine, **A**lcohol, **R**efined foods, **T**rans fats, and **S**ugar. Known as "anti-nutrients," these nutritional fiends don't contribute to your health, but take away from it, draining precious vitamins, minerals, and antioxidants from your body. They also make your liver work double overtime to mop up their toxic mess. Abuse them day in and day out, and there's a good chance you'll experience the worm-ridden fruits of their labor: heart disease, stroke, cancer, obesity, and diabetes. Even if they don't cut your life short, they can slowly make it miserable by contributing to nasty, nagging conditions like arthritis, allergies, osteoporosis, depression, chronic fatigue, poor sleep, and even premature aging. The bottom line is this: It's about self-control! We're not suggesting you give up your favorite food vices (Greta loves her Quarter Pounders!), but you should limit them. Occasionally savoring special treats is okay. Habitually pigging out on them is not. The good news is there's a whole lotta great-tasting food that's also very healthy (see pages 20 to 190 for details!).

If you regularly hire the television as your babysitter, you may be paying an awfully dear price. The latest statistics show that the average North American watches 28 hours of television per week. That means that by the end of high school, the average child has wasted three years of his life in a sedentary TV trance. Better turn off the tube, or your kids may end up looking like *Telechubbies.*

A nickel will get you on the subway, but garlic will get you a seat.

Old New York Proverb

Just Stew It!

Slow-simmered beef stew with rosemary dumplings

This meal is *stew*pendous! Now, don't be scared off by a lot of ingredients— it's simple to make. Honest! You can do it! Just put your mind to it. C'mon, just stew it!

2 lbs stewing beef, cut into 1½-inch cubes
2 tbsp all-purpose flour
2 tsp olive oil, divided
1½ cups chopped onions
1 cup chopped celery
2 tsp minced garlic
2 tsp Herbs de Provence (see tip, page 84)
2 cups beef broth
2 tbsp balsamic vinegar
2 tbsp tomato paste
2 tsp granulated sugar
½ tsp each salt and freshly ground black pepper
2 cups chopped carrots
½ cup light sour cream
2 tbsp each cornstarch and chopped fresh parsley
½ cup frozen green peas
1½ cups Bisquick baking mix
⅓ cup 1% milk
½ tsp dried rosemary, or 1 tbsp chopped fresh parsley

- Trim beef of fat and sprinkle with flour. Heat 1 tsp olive oil in a large, non-stick pot over medium-high heat. Add half the beef cubes and cook until lightly browned. Remove from pot and set aside. Repeat process with remaining 1 tsp olive oil and beef cubes.

- Return all beef cubes to pot. Add onions, celery, and garlic. Cook and stir until onions begin to soften, about 5 minutes. Stir in herbs. Cook 1 more minute. Add broth, vinegar, tomato paste, sugar, salt, and pepper. Bring to a boil. Reduce heat to low, cover, and simmer for 1 hour. Add carrots and simmer 20 more minutes.

- Combine sour cream, cornstarch, and parsley in a small bowl. Add to stew along with green peas. Mix well. To make dumplings, combine baking mix with milk and rosemary in a medium bowl. Stir with a fork until smooth. Drop dough by teaspoonfuls over hot stew. Cover with a tight-fitting lid. Simmer 20 minutes without lifting lid. Dumplings should be puffed up and dry to touch. Serve hot.

Makes 6 servings

PER SERVING

calories	total fat	saturated fat	protein	carbohydrate	fiber	cholesterol	sodium
362	11.7 g	3.5 g	24 g	41 g	4.1 g	53 mg	744 mg

Jellystone Pork

Grilled pork tenderloin with a tangy apple jelly and Dijon mustard sauce

When you *bearly* have the energy to prepare dinner, and you can't see the forest for the trees, try this scrumptious pork tenderloin recipe with an amazing (and simple!) apple-mustard sauce. It's approved for all taste buds by both the *Pork* Ranger and the *Loin* Ranger!

Sauce
1 tbsp butter
⅓ cup finely minced shallots
2 tbsp grated gingerroot
1 tsp minced garlic
⅓ cup apple jelly (see tip below)
3 tbsp Dijon mustard
2 tbsp cider vinegar
**¼ tsp salt and freshly
   ground black pepper**
¼ cup light sour cream

2 pork tenderloins (12 oz each)
Salt and freshly ground black pepper

- Before grilling pork, get all of the sauce ingredients ready so you can whip up the sauce while the cooked pork is resting.

- Preheat grill to medium-high heat. Sprinkle pork with salt and pepper. Place pork on a grill rack that has been coated with cooking spray or lightly brushed with oil. Grill pork for about 16 minutes, turning occasionally. The outside should be nicely browned and the center should have just a trace of pink. Transfer pork to a plate, cover with foil, and let rest while you make the sauce. (You could also roast pork in the oven: Brush pork lightly with olive oil, then sprinkle with salt and pepper. Roast at 350°F for about 40 minutes.)

- To make sauce, melt butter in a small, non-stick skillet over medium heat. Add shallots, gingerroot, and garlic. Cook and stir until shallots begin to soften, about 2 minutes. Be careful not to burn them.

- Add apple jelly, Dijon mustard, vinegar, salt, and pepper. Mix well. Cook and stir for 3 minutes, until jelly completely melts and sauce begins to thicken. Reduce heat to low if it's bubbling too much. Remove from heat and stir in sour cream.

- To serve pork, slice it thinly and arrange on a small platter. Drizzle sauce over pork.

Tip: Look for apple jelly near other jams and spreads at your grocery store.

Makes 4-6 servings

PER SERVING (BASED ON 6 SERVINGS)

calories	total fat	saturated fat	protein	carbohydrate	fiber	cholesterol	sodium
226	6.5 g	2.6 g	25 g	16 g	0.2 g	80 mg	241 mg

Cooking TIP

With juicy, delicious pork tenderloin on th menu, dinnertime doesn't have to be *boaring*! Next to chicken and turkey breasts, pork tenderloin is about the leanest cu of meat around. A three-ounce serving contains just 140 calories and four grams of fat! Use it in stir-fries, pan-fried as medallion roasted or grilled whole, and even stuffed. When roasting or grilling pork, try not to overcook it, since it can end up dry as a bo A meat thermometer is a good investment (w like the digital kind) and when inserted in the center of the tenderloin, it should read 155° for medium doneness. The pork should still have a hint of pink in the middle. Let the pork rest for minutes or so before you slice it. This'll give the juices time to wor their flavor magic.

The Nail Files

Did you know that your fingernails grow faste on the hand you favor? If you're right-handed your right fingernails will grow faster, and vic versa. And just to keep your manicurist on he toes, the middle fingernail grows faster than any other nail. Also, nails can be a telltale sign of nutrient deficiencies. White spots mig indicate a zinc deficiency. Longitudinal striations on your fingernails may mean you'r not properly absorbing minerals, such as calcium and magnesium. Concave, spoon-shaped nails are commonly associated with c iron deficiency. And no, biting nails is not a good source of iron!

A burger without a bun is a "light" choice.

Buns away! We're not exactly fans of processed, white-flour bread. If you banish the bun, you'll save about 150 calories and prevent a little spike in blood sugar. But don't fool yourself into thinking you've magically converted your ground beef patty topped with processed cheese and fat-soaked bacon into a "diet" food. Somehow, volumes of scientific data on how too much saturated fat clogs your arteries and stifles your heart have been thrown out the drive-thru window along with the bun. Remember, Wimpy wasn't exactly fit! Let's be frank about burgers. We all love them! But there's a way to enjoy burgers—great taste and all—without becoming fatty like the patty. Try making your own so you can use extra-lean ground beef and avoid the evil trans fats lurking in some fried fast-food burgers. Pile on lots of healthy vegetable fixin's. Skip the fatty mayo, special sauces, bacon, and fat-filled cheeses when ordering from a fast-food menu. And yes, Annie, get your bun. Just choose the whole-grain variety instead of the plain, gluey, white kind (many restaurants now offer whole wheat buns). Not only do they taste better, but they're also a good source of fiber (your weight-loss ally), and you'll get more magnesium, zinc, and B vitamins than if you choose the lowly, nutrient-poor, albino kind. Follow these suggestions, choose the better bun, and you won't set off a burger alarm!

During which of the following world-famous events did the pizza industry report the highest number of pizza deliveries?

a) the final episode of Survivor I
b) Superbowl XXXXVII
c) the O.J. Simpson Bronco chase
d) the opening night of the first Gulf War

Answer: (c) Be honest! There's no way you got this one right! Interestingly, O.J. later claimed that he, himself, was out delivering pizzas that night. When it was pointed out that there were no pizzas in his Bronco, he accused the police of eating them.

Flank 'n' Stein

Beer and spice marinated, grilled flank steak

If you're *Igor* to tame a monstrous appetite, here's a little *tipsy*: Beer will cure what *ales* ya—plus it adds a bit of zing to this juicy, grilled steak! It tastes delicious with grilled or roasted vegetables or in fajitas. And let's be *flank*, the *lager* you marinate it, the better!

Marinade
½ cup light beer
⅓ cup hickory-flavored barbecue sauce
1 tbsp freshly squeezed lemon juice
2 tsp Montreal steak spice
1 tsp grated lemon zest
1 tsp balsamic vinegar
¼ tsp dried rosemary, crushed

1½ lbs flank steak, trimmed of fat

Hicc!

- Whisk together all marinade ingredients in a medium bowl. Place flank steak in a large, heavy-duty, resealable plastic bag. Add marinade and seal bag. Turn bag several times to coat steak with marinade. Marinate in refrigerator for at least 2 hours or as long as 24 hours.

- Preheat grill to high setting. Remove steak from bag and transfer marinade to a small saucepan. Bring sauce to a boil and continue to boil for 1 minute. Remove from heat.

- Place flank steak on a grill rack that has been coated with cooking spray or lightly brushed with oil. Grill for about 6 minutes per side, or to desired degree of doneness. Baste often with reserved marinade during last few minutes of cooking time (you will use about half the marinade).

- Let steak rest for 5 minutes before slicing. To serve, slice steak thinly across the grain using a very sharp knife.

Makes 4 servings

| | PER SERVING | | | | | | | |
calories	total fat	saturated fat	protein	carbohydrate	fiber	cholesterol	sodium
279	12.2 g	5.2 g	33 g	6 g	0.1 g	80 mg	493 mg

Never eat raw meat unless it's a rare occasion.

Life in the Fast Loin

Skillet pork loin chops drizzled with apricot-mustard sauce

Suppertime rush hour got you frazzled? Here's the ticket:
A speedy and simple stovetop pork chop recipe that'll shift your family's appetite into high gear.

Sauce
²/₃ cup water
½ cup no-sugar-added apricot preserves
2 tbsp each balsamic vinegar and Dijon mustard
¾ tsp ground ginger
¼ tsp each salt and freshly ground black pepper

4 boneless pork loin chops (about 5 oz each)
Salt and freshly ground black pepper
1 tbsp olive oil

- Whisk together all sauce ingredients in a medium bowl and set aside.

- Sprinkle both sides of pork chops with salt and pepper and let stand for a few minutes. Heat olive oil in a 10-inch, non-stick skillet over medium heat. Add pork chops and cook for about 6 minutes per side, until nicely browned on the outside and just slightly pink in the center. Cover skillet with lid if they're splattering.

- Remove pork chops from skillet, cover with foil, and keep warm. Pour sauce into same skillet. Using a whisk, cook and stir sauce for about 5 minutes, or until it thickens. Make sure you scrape up any brown bits on the bottom of the skillet for added flavor. Serve pork chops drizzled with hot apricot-mustard sauce.

Makes 4 servings

PER SERVING

calories	total fat	saturated fat	protein	carbohydrate	fiber	cholesterol	sodium
267	9.9 g	2.7 g	30 g	13 g	0.3 g	89 mg	260 mg

Funky Factoid

Oh, what a tangled, psychedelic web we weave! NASA scientists tested the effects of certain human drugs on a spider's ability to spin webs. A spider on marijuana tried to make a web, but gave up when it was only half done. Spiders on Benzedrine (speed) spun webs quickly, but left huge holes in them, making very odd patterns. Spiders on caffeine spun only some random threads, while those on sleeping pills never even bothered to start a web, apparently preferring to catch a few zzz's over a few flies. The moral of the story? Stay clean and keep your spider senses tingling!

"SAY IT AIN'T SO!"

S.O.S.! S.O.S.! Save Our Smoothies...from wreaking havoc on our waistlines! Think you're doing your body a favor by chugging a frothy, fruit-filled concoction every day? With flavored syrups as their main cargo, some smoothies rock the boat with more than 500 calories and enough sugar to jolt your pancreas into abandoning ship. At the smoothie stand, avoid the *hipwreck* and ensure *smoothie* sailing by choosing blends made with fresh, whole fruits (berries are best!) instead of fruit juices, and low-fat or nonfat dairy products. Be on the lookout for the words chocolate, heavy syrup, fructose, fruit nectar, ice cream, cream, or whole milk—ingredients that are destined to cruise straight to your waistline! Even better, make your own smoothies so you can focus on fruit and whey protein powder, while bailing out on the extra sugar and empty calories.

My father was a dentist and my mother was a manicurist. No wonder they fought tooth and nail!

Chew the Right Thing

Did you know that it takes 50 hours for a snake to digest one frog? If you did, you have way too much time on your hands! Actually, the snake is not alone in battling digestion problems. Today, millions of folks are suffering from digestive difficulties, largely due to our "standard" diet of processed, refined junk foods. Unfortunately, foul play in the gut is often a major contributor to serious, chronic illness. Here's a simple tip to get your body on the right digestive track: Chew your food! You've probably heard that it takes about 20 minutes for the brain to compute what's going on in the stomach and register the feeling of satiety (fullness). So chewing slowly might mean you'll eat less. But thoroughly chewing each bite is also important because the process of digestion actually begins in the mouth. There's an enzyme in saliva that starts breaking down starches as you chew. When you scarf down an order of fries like Janet on a box of Turtles, your stomach's left to deal with your mouth's hasty, incomplete work. That would be fine if we had an extra set of teeth in our stomach, but since we don't, your stomach can't do its job properly. That puts a huge burden on your pancreas, which is responsible for supplying the remaining digestive enzymes. After years of dealing with poor chewing and poor *chewsing*, your pancreas can become exhausted and wave the white flag. A whole chain reaction occurs right through your digestive tract, with organs straining and suffering from overexertion. By the time those fries end up in your large intestine, they're an incompletely digested mass of spuds just sitting there and fermenting—perfect feed for the disease-causing bacterial critters that live in that organ. Gross! If you want to get on the right health track, then train yourself to chew. Chew, chew, train!

Beijing Beauty

Asian-glazed, grilled pork tenderloin

This sensational, grilled pork tenderloin is a beauty and a feast, not difficult in the least. Just baste and repeat 'til it's ready to eat!

Glaze

¼ cup hoisin sauce
2 tbsp freshly squeezed lemon juice
1 tbsp each Dijon mustard and liquid honey
1 tbsp each toasted sesame oil and reduced-sodium soy sauce
1 tbsp grated gingerroot
2 tsp minced garlic
2 tsp grated lemon zest

3 pork tenderloins (12 oz each)

- To make glaze, combine all glaze ingredients in a small bowl and mix well. Set aside.

- Preheat grill to medium-high setting. Spray grill rack with cooking spray or brush lightly with oil. Grill pork for about 16 minutes, turning occasionally. Pork should be just slightly pink in the center. Do not overcook pork or it will be dry.

- Brush pork generously with glaze during last 5 minutes of cooking time. Baste, baste, baste! The more you baste, the better the taste!

- Place pork on a cutting board, cover loosely with foil, and let rest for 5 minutes. Cut pork into thin slices and serve.

Makes 6 servings

PER SERVING

calories	total fat	saturated fat	protein	carbohydrate	fiber	cholesterol	sodium
267	8.7 g	2.4 g	37 g	9 g	0.5 g	111 mg	362 mg

Did you hear about the farmer who planted bulbs in his garden so it would get more light?

Kebob's Your Uncle

Marinated, grilled beef kebobs with pineapple and vegetables

And ke*barb*'s your aunt! Don't be surprised if all of your long-lost relatives show up at the door when you throw these juicy beef kebobs on the grill. As long as you're not a monkey's uncle, who cares? You *kin* make enough for the whole clan.

Marinade
- **½ cup unsweetened pineapple juice**
- **¼ cup barbecue sauce**
- **¼ cup chopped fresh basil leaves**
- **¼ cup chopped green onions**
- **2 tbsp reduced-sodium soy sauce**
- **2 tbsp balsamic vinegar**
- **1 tbsp grated gingerroot**
- **2 tsp minced garlic**
- **½ tsp freshly ground black pepper**
- **¼ tsp salt**

- **1¾ lbs sirloin steak or beef tenderloin steak, cut into 1½-inch cubes (aim for 24 pieces)**
- **16 chunks fresh pineapple**
- **16 chunks red or green bell pepper (or a combination of both)**
- **16 whole, medium-sized mushrooms**
- **8 12-inch metal skewers**

- Whisk together all marinade ingredients in a small bowl. Place steak cubes in a large, heavy-duty, resealable plastic bag. Add marinade and seal bag. Turn bag several times to coat steak with marinade. Marinate in refrigerator for at least 1 hour (longer if possible).

- Preheat grill to high setting. Alternately thread marinated beef cubes, pineapple, bell peppers, and mushrooms onto skewers. Place kebobs on a grill rack that has been coated with cooking spray or lightly brushed with oil. Grill for 8 to 10 minutes, turning occasionally, until meat is cooked to desired degree of doneness. If you want to baste kebobs with the leftover marinade, boil it first to kill any bacteria.

Makes 8 kebobs

PER KEBOB

calories	total fat	saturated fat	protein	carbohydrate	fiber	cholesterol	sodium
166	5.3 g	2 g	21 g	8 g	1.2 g	59 mg	204 mg

THE E FILES

Afraid of becoming a hulky, bulky she-man if you start lifting weights? Relax, gals! First of all, if you're over age 35, you've been losing muscle for years now, so in most cases, you're just replacing what was there in your younger, slimmer days. Secondly, your hormones won't allow you to become The Incredible Hulk. Women don't produce as much of the growth-enhancing hormone testosterone as men do—some men produce up to 30 times more. Female bodybuilders get their muscle magazine look only with Olympian-like training programs and possible steroid use. Mere mortal women who lift weights will lose fat, tone their muscles, and still look feminine in a dress! Remember, muscle is more compact than fat, so even if the scale registers weight gain, those extra pounds will appear smaller, shapelier, and sexier—not bulkier. You'll look great in your clothes and you might even need to shop for new ones. (Yee-ha! A reason to shop! Not that we need one.) Sleek, compact muscle will act like a girdle to shrink and define your waist, thighs, arms, and butt. Imagine! No more saddlebags! No more love handles! Adios adipose! Goodbye jiggly thighs! Farewell to jello arms!

Pop Quizine

Why would anyone prefer an apple with a worm in it to one without?

a) you'll only find a worm in an apple that's fully ripened

b) worms are an excellent source of fiber and protein

c) the presence of a worm indicates the absence of pesticides

d) it must be a very tasty apple if a worm likes it

Answer: (c) A medium apple, with or without a worm, contains about 5 grams of dietary fiber.

A Beautiful Grind

Brilliant uses for ground meat

Wowie Maui Meatballs

Grilled meatball and pineapple kebobs with sesame-ginger barbecue sauce

Zowie! When you taste these meatballs, you'll scream "Wowie!" If you liked our Wowie Maui Chicken recipe in *Looneyspoons*, you'll love the similar flavor of these grilled meatball and pineapple kebobs.

Sauce

⅓ cup your favorite barbecue sauce

5 tsp reduced-sodium soy sauce

1 tbsp grated gingerroot

2 tsp liquid honey

1 tsp toasted sesame oil

32 precooked lean meatballs (see tip in margin)

32 1-inch chunks fresh pineapple

16 1-inch chunks red bell pepper

16 1-inch chunks green bell pepper

8 12-inch metal skewers

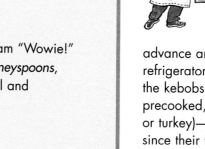

- To make sauce, whisk together barbecue sauce, soy sauce, gingerroot, honey, and sesame oil in a small bowl. Set aside.

- Preheat grill to high setting. For each skewer, thread meatballs, pineapple, red pepper, and green pepper in this order: 1 meatball, 1 piece pineapple, 1 piece red pepper, 1 meatball, 1 piece pineapple, 1 piece green pepper, then repeat, so that each skewer contains 4 meatballs, 4 pieces pineapple, 2 pieces red pepper, and 2 pieces green pepper.

- Spray grill rack with cooking spray or brush lightly with oil. Grill skewers for 12 to 15 minutes, turning and basting generously with sauce every 2 minutes.

Tip: If you're not a fan of bell peppers, just omit them. Increase the number of meatballs and pineapple chunks to 40 each, so you'll be threading 5 meatballs and 5 pieces pineapple on each skewer.

If you have the time, prepare the meatballs on page 139 up to step three. Let them cool before using them in this recipe. Or, make them a day in advance and keep them covered in the refrigerator until you're ready to assemble the kebobs. Alternatively, buy frozen, precooked, lean meatballs (beef, chicken, or turkey)—preferably *not* Italian meatballs, since their flavor would be an odd match for our yummy soy-ginger sauce. Make sure you thaw the frozen meatballs before threading them onto the skewers. Finally, buy some metal skewers (they're cheap!) so that you'll always have them on hand for making shish kebobs. Metal skewers don't burn like wooden skewers, don't need to be presoaked in water, and help heat the food from the inside, since metal conducts heat. Plus, they double as knitting needles, you can use them to pin up your hair in a groovy hairstyle, and the kids can use the round end to blow bubbles (just kidding!).

Everyone is familiar with the famous pink luncheon meat in a can, but do you know what the name SPAM stands for?

a) Salty Pork Army Meal
b) it's an abbreviation of "spiced ham"
c) Savory Processed Artificial Meat
d) Slimy Pink Awful Meatloaf

Answer: (b) While attending a New Year's Eve party thrown by Jay Hormel in 1936, Kenneth Daigneau won $100 for suggesting the now-famous name.

We have just received news that Betty Crocker has passed away. Funeral services are being held tomorrow at 3:50 for 25 to 30 minutes.

Makes 8 skewers

PER SKEWER

calories	total fat	saturated fat	protein	carbohydrate	fiber	cholesterol	sodium
178	6.3 g	3.1 g	11 g	20 g	2.6 g	27 mg	556 mg

The Farm Pharm

Good ol' Hippocrates sure knew what he was talking about when he said, "Let food be your medicine and medicine be your food!" There are nutrients in certain foods that, when consumed regularly and in proper amounts, allow the body to be its own best pharmacy—to protect and heal itself. In fact, virtually all foods have "drug-like" effects. (Just think about the high you get from eating a big slab of chocolate cake!) Some foods help improve your health while others destroy it. For instance, when you eat bad fats from a greasy burger and fries, many of your body's cells will falter for hours. Eat too much sugar and you throw your hormones out of whack and dull your immune system. We can either overdose on the wrong kinds of food like these, or we can buy into a healthy prescription of foods that contain the nutrients our bodies need to flourish. The healthiest products on the market are those packaged and delivered by the world's premier food manufacturer— Mother Nature! Her ideal prescription includes fresh, natural, whole foods—some cooked, some raw, seasonal and local, and organic if possible. Follow Ma's lead and you'll find the formula for vibrant health at the farm, not the pharmacy.

Funky Factoid

The terms "big cheese" and "big wheel" originated in medieval times out of envious respect for those who had money to buy whole wheels of cheese at a time—an expense few could afford. Both terms are often used sarcastically today to describe an important, influential person.

More Than Meatza Pie

Bacon-double-cheeseburger
meat loaf pizza

What'sa matta you? You kids-a no like-a you cookin'? Well, dey gonna eatza every last bite-a dis pizza. Dats a fact!

- 1¼ lbs extra-lean ground beef
- 8 oz light mild Italian sausage, casing removed (see tip below)
- ⅓ cup Italian-seasoned bread crumbs
- ⅓ cup minced onions
- ⅓ cup + ½ cup pizza sauce
- ¼ cup grated Parmesan cheese
- 1 egg
- 2 tsp minced garlic
- ¼ tsp each salt and freshly ground black pepper
- 1 cup packed shredded light old (sharp) cheddar cheese (4 oz)
- ½ cup diced tomatoes
- 4 slices bacon, cooked and crumbled
- 2 tbsp chopped green onions

- Preheat oven to 375°F. Spray two 8-inch round cake pans with cooking spray and set aside.

- Combine ground beef, sausage, bread crumbs, onions, ⅓ cup pizza sauce, Parmesan cheese, egg, garlic, salt, and pepper in a large bowl. Mix ingredients together using your hands. Divide mixture in half. Press divided mixture evenly over bottom of cake pans, spreading to edges. Bake for 25 minutes, until meat is no longer pink.

- Remove pans from oven and drain off any liquid. Carefully transfer "crusts" to a cookie sheet. Blot tops dry with paper towels. Spread ¼ cup pizza sauce over each "crust." Top with cheese, followed by tomatoes, crumbled bacon, and green onions.

- Bake for 10 more minutes, until cheese is completely melted. Serve hot.

Tip: If you'd rather omit the Italian sausage, increase the ground beef to 1¾ lbs and add ½ tsp crushed dried fennel seeds to the raw meat mixture.

Makes 8 servings

PER SERVING

calories	total fat	saturated fat	protein	carbohydrate	fiber	cholesterol	sodium
239	12.8 g	6.6 g	24 g	8 g	0.9 g	88 mg	672 mg

No Weigh, José! Mexican Lasagna

Layered Mexican casserole with chicken, beans, tortillas, and cheese

José, can you see...that your meal's really light? It's hard to believe that a scrumptious Mexican lasagna like this one won't produce a paunch under your poncho, but with tons of veggies, beans, and other lean good stuff, there's no *weigh*!

Eats unbelievable!

1½ lbs extra-lean ground chicken
1 cup each diced red onions and diced green bell pepper
2 tsp minced garlic
1 cup canned black beans, drained and rinsed
1 cup diced tomatoes
½ cup frozen or canned corn
1½ tsp chili powder
1 tsp ground cumin
2 cups your favorite tomato pasta sauce
1 cup medium salsa
¼ tsp freshly ground black pepper
2 tbsp minced fresh cilantro
4 large or 8 small whole wheat flour tortillas
1½ cups packed shredded light old (sharp) cheddar cheese (6 oz)
¼ cup chopped green onions
1 cup light sour cream

- Preheat oven to 375°F. Spray a 9 x 13-inch casserole dish with cooking spray and set aside.

- In a large, non-stick pot or skillet, cook ground chicken, onions, green pepper, and garlic over medium-high heat until meat is no longer pink. Break up any large pieces of chicken as it's cooking.

- Add black beans, tomatoes, corn, chili powder, and cumin. Cook and stir for 2 more minutes. Add pasta sauce, salsa, and black pepper. Bring to a boil. Reduce heat to low. Cover and simmer for 5 minutes, stirring occasionally. Stir in cilantro and remove from heat.

- To assemble lasagna, spread ⅓ sauce mixture over bottom of casserole dish. Top with ½ the tortillas, overlapping and cutting them as necessary to fit. Top with ⅓ sauce mixture, followed by ½ the cheese. Cover cheese with remaining tortillas, followed by remaining sauce. Sprinkle remaining cheese over sauce and top with green onions.

- Cover with foil and bake for 35 minutes. Uncover and bake 10 more minutes. Let lasagna stand for at least 10 minutes before slicing for easier serving. Top each piece with a dollop of sour cream.

Hint: If you prefer, you can substitute extra-lean ground beef for ground chicken and Monterey Jack cheese for cheddar cheese.

Makes 8 servings

PER SERVING

calories	total fat	saturated fat	protein	carbohydrate	fiber	cholesterol	sodium
319	7.9 g	3.7 g	31 g	30 g	5.5 g	73 mg	749 mg

Part of the secret of success in life is to eat what you like and let the food fight it out inside.

Mark Twain

RETURN TO SLENDER

If you want to shed pounds, don't fall victim to the "last supper" syndrome. You know...tomorrow you're "officially" starting that trendy, new diet that's all the rage in Beverly Hills. So today, your final day of food freedom, you devise your own eating strategy—the Beverly Fillbelly Diet—recklessly hoovering down everything you can get your hands on and then some. "Cut me some slack! For the next month, all the foods I love will be off limits!" And that's precisely why you're doomed. For lots of folks, just the anticipation of going on a diet can trigger drastic overeating, sending them into the vicious, unhealthy cycle of bingeing and crash dieting. Let's face it: Diets stink! They're unrealistic, ineffective, and temporary. Depriving yourself of occasional indulges in the foods you love is *not* the way to lose pounds and keep them off forever. In restrictive diets, so many tasty foods are taboo, it's only natural that these will become the foods you desperately crave. We're only human, right? We've said it before and we'll say it again: Dieting is only wishful shrinking! So, forget about dieting and try the balanced approach instead: Choose a variety of natural, satisfying, nutrient-rich foods most of the time, but slip in the occasional treat so you won't feel deprived. And don't forget that healthy foods can also be great-tasting and satisfying. (You're holding the proof!)

The Ladle in Red

Everyone's favorite classic beef chili.
A staple recipe!

Never seen you cookin' so healthy
as you did tonight.
Never seen you dine so right.
You were amazing.
I hardly know...
this chili by my side.
Never forget...
the way you cooked, tonight.

1 ½ lbs extra-lean
    ground beef
2 tsp minced garlic
1 cup each diced celery,
    diced green bell pepper,
    and diced red onions
1 ½ tbsp chili powder
1 ½ tsp each ground cumin
    and dried oregano
1 tsp ground coriander
¼ tsp ground black pepper
1 can (14.5 oz) diced
    tomatoes, undrained

2 cups tomato sauce
1 ¼ cups beef broth
¼ cup chopped celery leaves
1 tbsp hickory-flavored
    barbecue sauce
1 can (15.5 oz) red kidney
    beans, drained and rinsed
1 can (16 oz) beans in
    tomato sauce (see tip below)
3 tbsp chopped fresh cilantro
1 tbsp freshly squeezed
    lime juice
2 tsp liquid honey

- Cook beef and garlic in a large, deep, non-stick skillet or pot over medium-high heat until beef is no longer pink. Stir in celery, green pepper, and red onions. Cook and stir for 3 minutes, or until vegetables begin to soften.

- Stir in chili powder, cumin, oregano, coriander, and black pepper. Cook for 1 more minute. Add undrained tomatoes, tomato sauce, beef broth, celery leaves, and barbecue sauce. Bring mixture to a boil. Reduce heat to low. Cover and simmer for 20 minutes, stirring occasionally.

- Add beans and simmer, covered, for 10 more minutes. Remove from heat. Stir in cilantro, lime juice, and honey. Serve hot.

Tip: If you can, make this chili one day before you want to serve it. It thickens as it sits overnight and tastes even better the next day! Heinz Vegetarian Beans in Tomato Sauce are a good choice for this recipe and are usually available in every grocery store.

Makes 8 servings

PER SERVING

calories	total fat	saturated fat	protein	carbohydrate	fiber	cholesterol	sodium
270	7.8 g	3.9 g	24 g	28 g	10 g	53 mg	680 mg

Turk du Soleil

Flavorful Thai-inspired turkey burgers with zesty peanut sauce

In a daring feat of culinary acrobatics, we've teamed extra-lean ground turkey with a *Thai*rific circus of bold flavors to create a showstopping burger that'll make everyone flip!

⅓ cup bottled light peanut sauce
1 tsp toasted sesame oil
1 tsp reduced-sodium soy sauce
1 tsp grated lemon zest
1 tsp grated gingerroot
1½ lbs extra-lean ground turkey
   or chicken
1 cup fresh whole wheat bread crumbs, or
   ½ cup dry unseasoned bread crumbs
¼ cup finely minced green onions
2 tbsp minced fresh cilantro
1 egg
½ tsp salt
¼ tsp freshly ground black pepper
6 multigrain or sesame-seed burger buns
Lettuce and sliced tomatoes

- To make sauce, combine peanut sauce, sesame oil, soy sauce, lemon zest, and gingerroot in a small bowl. Mix well and set aside.

- In a large bowl, combine ground turkey, bread crumbs, green onions, cilantro, egg, salt, pepper, and 3 tbsp of the sauce (you will use the rest of the sauce to baste the burgers). Mix gently using your hands. Form mixture into 6 patties, about ½ inch thick. Cover and refrigerate until ready to grill.

- Preheat grill to high setting. Spray grill rack with cooking spray or brush lightly with oil. Grill burgers for about 5 minutes per side, or until cooked through and no longer pink in the center. Brush burgers with reserved sauce during last 2 minutes of cooking time.

- Serve burgers on lightly toasted buns with lettuce and sliced tomatoes, or any of your favorite burger toppings.

Note: The label on the package of hamburger buns will give you the nutritional information per roll. Just add these numbers to our analysis below to get the most accurate nutritional count.

Funky Factoid

Let's talk turkey! When you quit an unhealthy, addictive behavior abruptly—like smoking, drinking, or watching reality TV—it's said that you quit "cold turkey." That expression actually originates from the goose bumps and chalky complexion that accompany withdrawal from narcotics like heroin. When an addict stops using drugs, blood is directed toward the internal organs and away from the skin, which then resembles that of a plucked, cold turkey. How *fowl*!

THE E FILES

Boing! Boing! Boing! NASA has long recognized the enormous benefits of bouncing, or rebounding, beginning with its own use of mini trampolines years ago to help astronauts recover from prolonged periods of weightlessness. Get bouncing on a mini trampoline and you might experience *weigh-less-ness*, too. Making like a kangaroo for as little as 10 minutes per day can help you shed pounds, tone muscle, and conquer cellulite. It also helps protect against cancer, heart disease, and many degenerative conditions. That's because with each up and down movement, sixty trillion body cells are pitted against the earth's gravitational force (G-force), and the demand on your body's cells to adjust makes them grow stronger. Plus, when cells get squished from all that bouncing, that stimulates your lymphatic system (your internal vacuum cleaner) to force waste products out and bring nutrients in. Talk about *spring* cleaning! The result is a stronger immune system, renewed bone mass, and improved overall health. With a spongy landing surface, rebounding is easy on the joints, and you can do it just about anywhere or anytime: in your office, backyard, bedroom, or while watching TV, talking on the phone, or listening to music. Heck! Maybe you should let your kids bounce on their beds after all!

He always ate his burgers plain and gave his condiments to the chef.

Makes 6 burgers

PER BURGER (PATTY ONLY)

calories	total fat	saturated fat	protein	carbohydrate	fiber	cholesterol	sodium
229	11.2 g	2.6 g	26 g	8 g	1.2 g	105 mg	485 mg

All You Need is Loaf

Easy weekday meat loaf with barbecue sauce

Loaf, loaf, loaf. Tired of the same ol' song and dance for dinner *Eight Days a Week*? Don't worry, *We Can Work it Out*. Here's some *Help!*: A recipe you just can't *Beatle*—especially after *A Hard Day's Night*. Sure to *Please Please* everyone.

1½ lbs extra-lean ground beef
    or ground sirloin
½ cup dry unseasoned
    bread crumbs
½ cup your favorite barbecue
    sauce, divided
¼ cup chopped fresh parsley
⅓ cup minced onions
2 tbsp grated Parmesan cheese
1 egg
1 tsp minced garlic
½ tsp dried basil, thyme,
    or oregano
½ tsp each salt and freshly
    ground black pepper

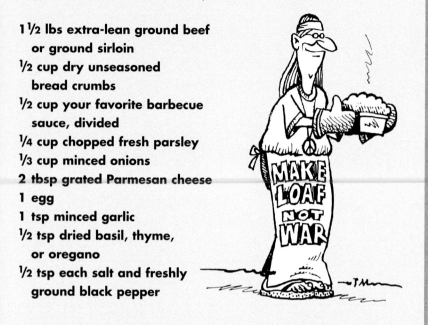

- Preheat oven to 350°F. Spray a broiler pan with cooking spray and set aside.

- Combine beef, bread crumbs, ¼ cup barbecue sauce, parsley, onions, Parmesan cheese, egg, garlic, basil, salt, and pepper in a large bowl. Mix well using your hands. Shape mixture into an oblong loaf, about 8 x 5-inches in size, and place directly on rack of broiler pan. Spread remaining barbecue sauce all over meat loaf.

- Bake for 50 minutes to 1 hour, or until meat loaf is nicely browned and meat is cooked through. Let stand 5 minutes before slicing.

Makes 1 loaf, 8 slices

PER SLICE

calories	total fat	saturated fat	protein	carbohydrate	fiber	cholesterol	sodium
187	8.3 g	4.3 g	18 g	10 g	0.6 g	80 mg	503 mg

Fat or Fiction?

Cutting fruit from my diet is a smart way to lose weight.

If you're cutting out fruit while following a low-carb diet, you've gone bananas! Yes, fruit contains simple sugars. But thanks to Mother Nature, that sugar comes strategically wrapped in high-fiber packaging, and fiber lessens the dreaded blood-sugar peaks, hormonal havoc, and weight gain that low-carb dieters fear. In fact, fruit's a fantastic fat fighter. Get two or three servings of fruit under your belt each day and there's less room for fattening junk food. Got a raging sweet tooth? Try some scrumptious raspberries, frozen bananas, or plump grapes to satisfy your cravings. Most fruits are high in fiber, low in calories, high in water content, great tasting, and convenient—what more could you ask for? How about a ton of disease-fighting antioxidants? Or hundreds of beneficial plant chemicals that scientists have recently discovered? In the same way these phytochemicals protect plants from the sun's damaging rays or from disease, they also protect us. They're a key to losing weight, feeling great, and ensuring good health. So, if you want to live to a ripe old age, don't cut out fruit—cut it up!

"SAY IT AIN'T SO!"

Shake your bon bon! Shake your groove thing! Shake your booty! Just don't shake your...shake! A large milk shake from a popular fast-food joint will shake you up with its seam-splitting 1,030 calories and 29 grams of fat. And to think that's just an "add-on" to your order of a burger and fries. It won't be a happy meal when you realize you'll need hours on the treadmill to shake it off.

People who eat candy with both hands are ambi-dextrose.

I'm cheesy, and so is this lasagna!

Ooh-la-la-sagna!

Italian sausage and beef lasagna with whole wheat noodles

Va-va-voom! This mighty meaty lasagna's got attitude, without a whole lotta *fattitude*! It's all dressed up but won't make you grow.

Sauce

8 oz light mild Italian sausage
8 oz extra-lean ground beef
1 cup chopped onions
2 tsp minced garlic
1 tsp dried oregano
¼ tsp crushed red pepper flakes
1 jar (26 oz) your favorite tomato pasta sauce
1 can (14.5 oz) tomatoes with Italian herbs, undrained, cut up
⅓ cup chopped fresh basil leaves
1 tbsp balsamic vinegar
½ tsp freshly ground black pepper

12 uncooked whole wheat lasagna noodles
2 cups light ricotta cheese (1 lb)
1 pkg (10 oz) frozen spinach, thawed, squeezed dry, and chopped
⅓ cup grated Parmesan, Romano, or Asiago cheese
1 egg
1½ cups packed shredded light mozzarella cheese (6 oz)

Makes 10 servings

- Spray a 9 x 13-inch baking dish with cooking spray and set aside.

- To make sauce, spray a large, non-stick pot or deep, non-stick skillet with cooking spray. Remove casing from sausage and break into small pieces in skillet. Add ground beef, onions, and garlic. Cook and stir over medium-high heat until meat is no longer pink. Stir in oregano and crushed red pepper flakes. Cook 1 more minute. Add pasta sauce, tomatoes, basil, vinegar, and pepper. Bring mixture to a boil. Reduce heat to low. Cover and simmer for 20 minutes.

- While sauce is simmering, cook lasagna noodles according to package directions. Drain. Rinse with cold water and drain again.

- In a medium bowl, mix together ricotta, spinach, Parmesan cheese, and egg. Refrigerate until ready to use.

- To assemble lasagna, spread 1 cup meat sauce over bottom of baking dish. Top with 4 lasagna noodles, cutting pieces to fit if necessary. Spread ⅓ remaining sauce over noodles, followed by ⅓ mozzarella. Top with 4 more noodles, ⅓ sauce, all of the ricotta mixture, and ⅓ mozzarella. For top layer: 4 noodles, ⅓ sauce, ⅓ mozzarella.

- Cover lasagna with foil and bake at 375°F for 35 minutes. Uncover and bake for an additional 15 minutes. Let lasagna stand, uncovered, for 15 minutes before serving.

PER SERVING

calories	total fat	saturated fat	protein	carbohydrate	fiber	cholesterol	sodium
311	10.5 g	5.7 g	25 g	29 g	4.2 g	68 mg	721 mg

*I feel about airplanes the way I feel about diets.
It seems to me that they are wonderful things
for other people to go on.*

Jean Kerr, The Snake Has All the Lines

Pie Caramba!

Mexican pizza with seasoned ground beef, black beans, tomatoes, and corn

Ai, ai, ai! It's a zesty pizza pie! If you want to experience the joy of Mex, say "sí" to this uniquely topped pizza that's bursting with fabulous southwestern flavor. It's hot, hot, hot!

8 oz extra-lean ground beef
⅓ cup minced onions
1 tsp minced garlic
½ cup diced grape tomatoes
¼ cup each grated carrots
   and diced green bell pepper
¼ cup frozen or canned corn
¼ cup canned black beans, drained and rinsed
1 tbsp minced fresh cilantro
1 tsp chili powder
½ tsp ground cumin
¼ tsp each salt and freshly ground black pepper
½ cup pizza sauce
1 12-inch, prebaked, thin-crust pizza shell
1 cup packed shredded light old (sharp) cheddar cheese (4 oz)
2 tbsp minced green onions
Light sour cream, salsa, and guacamole (optional)

- Preheat oven to 425°F.

- Spray a large, non-stick skillet with cooking spray. Add beef, onions, and garlic. Cook and stir over medium-high heat until beef is no longer pink. Add tomatoes, carrots, green pepper, corn, and beans. Cook and stir for 2 more minutes. Add cilantro, chili powder, cumin, salt, and pepper. Cook 1 more minute. Remove from heat.

- Spread pizza sauce evenly over crust. Top with half the cheese. Spoon beef mixture evenly over pizza. Top with remaining cheese, followed by green onions.

- Place pizza directly on middle oven rack and bake for 10 to 12 minutes, or until cheese is completely melted and crust is lightly browned.

- Tastes great with fajita-like accompaniments, such as sour cream, salsa, and guacamole.

Makes 1 pizza, 8 slices

PER SLICE

calories	total fat	saturated fat	protein	carbohydrate	fiber	cholesterol	sodium
186	6.8 g	3.4 g	12 g	18 g	1.9 g	28 mg	455 mg

The Steaks are High (in Fat!)

Hankering for a slab of beef? Even if you've sworn allegiance to the high protein way of life, realize that too much saturated fat is still, undoubtedly and proven by science, a staggering burden for your heart and the scale. So don't mosey into a steakhouse or a meat market until you know which cuts are the leanest.

Luckily, the most popular ones, top sirloin and filet mignon, are also the lowest in saturated fat (only round steak has less saturated fat). In fact, those cuts are A1 choices! It starts to go downhill from there, though. Choose a New York strip, rib eye, or T-bone, for instance, and you'll use up about a day's worth of saturated fat (20 grams). Porterhouse and prime rib are the worst bandits, rustling up almost two days' worth! *Steer* clear! Need another reason to trim all visible fat, choose the leanest cuts, and avoid excessive steak pig-outs? Environmental toxins, pesticides, and antibiotics taken in by the animal accumulate in the fat. *Lard* have mercy!

> Taco 'bout delicious!

They say that a relaxed, tranquil environment helps cows produce more milk, so some dairy farmers have employed the following strategy to increase their milk yields:

a) massaging the cows' udders with lavender-scented oil

b) burning incense in the barn

c) encouraging the cows to participate in weekly yoga sessions

d) playing light country tunes or classical music in the barn

Answer: (d) Their favorite composer? Moozart. Their least-favorite song? "Mammas Don't Let Your Babies Grow Up to be Cows."

"SAY IT AIN'T SO!"

It's *nacho* healthiest appetizer at the Mexican joint and it just may leave a huge paunch under your poncho! Top a mountain of fried tortilla chips with a third of a pound of melted cheese and a quarter pound of ground beef. Add high-fat sour cream and guacamole. Whaddya get? A fiesta for cardiologists and muchos pesos for folks in the weight-loss industry! A typical order of beef and cheese nachos will turn you into a piñata with approximately 1,300 calories and 80 grams of fat! Ai caramba! Share with a few amigos, or you can say adios to your waistline.

We must! We must! We must decrease our crust! Just because you're watching your weight doesn't mean you can't have a *pizza* the action. To lessen the blow from the dough, ask for whole wheat, thin-crust pizza instead of the regular kind that's fluffed up with white flour. You'll add fiber and subtract calories, so your pizza slices won't multiply all over your thighs. What about deep dish? Picture deep cellulite dimples. Stuffed crust? Only if you want stuffed fat cells. Choose thin to stay thin. Then pile your pizza with veggies, top it with lean protein, such as chicken or Canadian bacon, and ask for reduced-fat cheeses. And here's a simple trick to cut more grease: When your pizza arrives, blot it lightly with a paper towel (half a Bounty will do!) to soak up about a tablespoon (120 calories worth) of saturated fat. See! Healthy eating is a *pizza* cake!

Glad Thai Dings

Asian meatballs in a zesty, Thai-inspired sauce

Rejoice! Whether you serve these succulent meatballs with stir-fried vegetables, rice noodles, or alone as an appetizer, they're sure to bring your taste buds great comfort and joy.

Meatballs
- 1½ lbs extra-lean ground beef
- ¼ cup hoisin sauce
- ¼ cup dry unseasoned bread crumbs
- 3 tbsp finely minced green onions
- 1 tbsp minced fresh cilantro
- 1 egg
- 2 tsp minced garlic
- 1 tsp grated gingerroot
- 1 tsp toasted sesame oil
- ¼ tsp each salt and freshly ground black pepper

Sauce
- 1 cup light coconut milk
- ⅓ cup hoisin sauce
- 2 tbsp reduced-sodium soy sauce
- 2 tbsp light peanut butter
- 2 tbsp minced fresh basil leaves or fresh cilantro
- 1 tbsp grated gingerroot
- 1 tsp grated lemon zest
- ⅛ tsp crushed red pepper flakes

- Preheat oven to 400°F. Spray a rimmed cookie sheet or large baking pan with cooking spray and set aside.

- To make meatballs, combine all meatball ingredients in a large bowl (using your hands works best). Form meat mixture into 40 1- to 1½-inch meatballs. Place on prepared pan.

- Bake for 18 to 20 minutes, until meatballs are cooked through and nicely browned on the outside.

- While meatballs are cooking, prepare sauce. In a deep, non-stick skillet, whisk together all sauce ingredients. Heat over medium-high heat, stirring constantly, until sauce boils. Reduce heat to medium and cook, uncovered, for 3 minutes, stirring often. Sauce will thicken a bit.

- Add cooked meatballs to sauce and mix well. Serve hot.

Makes 40 meatballs

PER MEATBALL

calories	total fat	saturated fat	protein	carbohydrate	fiber	cholesterol	sodium
46	2.4 g	1.2 g	4 g	3 g	0.2 g	16 mg	125 mg

One Loaf to Love

Zesty vegetable-and-cheese-stuffed meat loaf

Our sensational stuffed meat loaf is nothin' like the old rubbery meat loaf they serve down at the *General Hospital*. We've dramatically improved this popular comfort food so it's not only *Bold*, it's *Beautiful*. *All My Children* (and yours) will adore it!

1 cup finely diced mushrooms
½ cup each finely diced red bell pepper,
 zucchini, and onions
1 tsp minced garlic
¼ tsp dried basil
1½ lbs extra-lean ground beef
1 cup fresh whole wheat bread crumbs, or
 ½ cup dry unseasoned bread crumbs
¼ cup + 2 tbsp barbecue sauce or ketchup
1 pkg (1.3 oz) hamburger seasoning mix
 (see tip below)
1 egg
¼ cup chopped fresh parsley
¼ tsp freshly ground black pepper
½ cup packed shredded light Monterey Jack,
 provolone, or mozzarella cheese (2 oz)

- Preheat oven to 375°F. Spray a medium, non-stick skillet with cooking spray. Add mushrooms, red pepper, zucchini, onions, and garlic. Cook and stir over medium heat until vegetables are tender, about 5 minutes. Add basil and cook 1 more minute. Remove from heat and set aside.

- In a large bowl, combine ground beef, bread crumbs, ¼ cup barbecue sauce, hamburger seasoning mix, egg, parsley, and pepper. Mix well using your hands.

- On a large sheet of waxed paper, form meat mixture into a 10 x 12-inch rectangle. Make sure edges are nice and straight, not jagged. Spread reserved vegetable filling over meat, leaving a ½-inch border. Sprinkle with cheese. Roll up meat loaf from the shorter (10-inch) end, lifting the waxed paper to help get it started. Roll it as tightly as possible. Pinch seam closed.

- Transfer meat loaf to a broiler pan that has been sprayed with cooking spray. Bake for 40 minutes. Remove from oven and spread remaining 2 tbsp barbecue sauce over meat loaf. Return to oven and bake for 10 more minutes, or until meat is cooked through and a meat thermometer inserted in the center registers 160°F.

- Let meat loaf stand for 5 minutes before slicing.

Tip: There are several varieties of dry hamburger seasoning mixes on the market, but we like Club House Superburger the best. It comes in a small envelope and you can usually find it in the aisle where gravy mixes are sold. You may also use Sloppy Joe or meatloaf seasoning.

Makes 1 loaf, 8 slices

PER SLICE

calories	total fat	saturated fat	protein	carbohydrate	fiber	cholesterol	sodium
204	9.3 g	5 g	20 g	12 g	1.6 g	84 mg	572 mg

It took scientists until 1970 to figure out what has been folk knowledge for centuries—that cucumbers really *are* cool. In fact, on a warm day, the inside of a field cucumber registers about 20°F lower than the air around it. How cool is that?

THE E FILES

Pop a pill or walk a hill? It's your choice. But a growing number of studies are showing that exercise has impressive mood-boosting effects and may even help fight clinical depression. A Duke University study asked people with major depression to exercise moderately for 45 minutes, three times per week, while others simply took their antidepressants. The result: Pills worked no better than push-ups and, in fact, exercise improved patients' symptoms faster than the antidepressants—and with pleasant instead of nasty side effects. Now, we're not suggesting you ditch the Prozac for a dose of Pro-activity, but it's encouraging to know that lifting weights can boost your spirits, and that regular exercise just might help you sweat the blues away!

For Christmas, my husband gave me a subscription to a science fiction magazine—Better Homes and Gardens!

Cowabunga Beef Burgers

Thick, juicy, smoky beef burgers with "kick"

Smokin'!

Hickory dickory, dude
Don't eat your burger nude
When the clock strikes one
Grab a whole-grain bun
Cowabunga!
That's kickin' food!

1 1/4 lbs extra-lean ground beef
3/4 cup fresh whole wheat bread crumbs, or
  1/3 cup dry unseasoned bread crumbs
3 tbsp hickory-flavored barbecue sauce
2 tbsp chopped fresh parsley
2 tsp prepared horseradish
1 egg
1 tsp minced garlic
1/2 tsp each salt and freshly ground black pepper
Extra barbecue sauce for basting burgers (optional)

- Combine all ingredients in a large bowl and mix gently using your hands. For juicier burgers, try to handle the meat as little as possible. Shape meat into 4 large patties, about 1 inch thick.

- Preheat grill to high setting. Spray grill rack with cooking spray or brush lightly with oil. Grill burgers for about 5 to 6 minutes per side, or to desired degree of doneness. Baste with extra barbecue sauce during last 2 minutes of cooking time, if desired. Resist the temptation to press down on burgers with a spatula. Every drop of juice and fat that you squeeze out makes the burgers that much drier.

- Serve burgers on whole-grain hamburger buns with your favorite burger toppings.

Makes 4 servings

PER SERVING (PATTY ONLY)

calories	total fat	saturated fat	protein	carbohydrate	fiber	cholesterol	sodium
271	12.9 g	6.6 g	29 g	12 g	1.4 g	141 mg	531 mg

Smackaroni and Cheese

Creamy stovetop macaroni and cheese with ground beef

Cheez! This sure is a *whiz* to make! And you won't believe your kids are gobbling up veggies and whole wheat macaroni, either. Totally *un*-gourmet and totally yummy!

1 can (12 oz) evaporated 2% milk
2 tbsp all-purpose flour
½ tsp dry mustard powder
1 cup light Cheez Whiz
¼ cup grated Parmesan cheese
¼ tsp freshly ground black pepper
1 lb extra-lean ground beef (see tip below)
1 cup diced onions
½ cup diced zucchini
1 to 2 tsp minced garlic
1 can (14.5 oz) tomatoes with Italian herbs, well drained
4 cups cooked whole wheat elbow macaroni (about 1½ cups dry)
½ cup packed shredded light old (sharp) cheddar cheese (2 oz)

- In a medium, non-stick pot, whisk together milk, flour, and mustard powder until smooth. Heat over medium-high heat, whisking constantly, until mixture bubbles and thickens. Reduce heat to low. Add Cheez Whiz, Parmesan cheese, and pepper. Stir until cheeses are melted. Remove from heat and set aside.

- In a deep, 10-inch, non-stick skillet, cook beef, onions, zucchini, and garlic over medium-high heat until meat is no longer pink. Break up any large pieces of beef while it's cooking. Drain off any liquid or fat in pan. Stir in tomatoes and cook 1 more minute.

- Add cooked pasta and reserved cheese sauce. Mix well and cook just until heated through. Remove skillet from heat. Sprinkle macaroni mixture with shredded cheddar. Cover and let stand 5 to 10 minutes before serving.

- Serve hot with a sprinkle of freshly ground black pepper and a salad on the side.

Tip: You can substitute ground chicken or turkey for ground beef if you prefer.

> Lip smacking good!

With all the recent fus over low-carb diets, is low-fat passé?

Ask Janet

Fat chance! For the sake o your hips, heart, and overall health, you still need to mind your fats. The problem is, when you single out one nutrient and try to eliminate it from your diet, it inevitably backfires. People took low-fat dieting too far, believing that all fats were unhealthy and taboo. Ditto for the low-carb craze: All carbs (even fruit!) were banned and blamed for bulging waistlines. Remember: Healthy eating isn't all or nothing; it's about balance. If you focus or good carbs and good fats most of the time, then healthy eating is a (small) piece of cake Like the researchers say, we should aim to ge no more than 30% of our daily calories from fat, and it's important to choose the good, health-promoting kind versus the bad, disease-causing variety. Here's the skinny on fat:

Sources of healthy fats
(eat regularly): Fish and fish oils, olive oil, flaxseed oil, avocados, raw nuts and seeds, nut butters, chickpeas, lentils, and tofu. (For good overall health, think omega-3's!)

Sources of okay fats
(eat moderately): Skinless poultry, lean, unprocessed meats (with fat trimmed), low-fat dairy products, omega-3 eggs, and butter. Look for expeller-pressed, unrefined versions of the following oils: canola, sesame, peanut, sunflower, and safflower.

Sources of unhealthy fats (limit):
Processed, packaged foods made with hydrogenated or partially hydrogenated vegetable oils (trans fats), such as some margarines, shortening, cookies, crackers, donuts, potato chips, french fries, snack foods, candies, and deep-fried foods. Read the labels! Some manufacturers have done a good job of removing trans fats from foods that formerly contained them. Also, limit saturated fat intake from fatty red meats and full-fat dairy products.

Makes 8 servings

PER SERVING

calories	total fat	saturated fat	protein	carbohydrate	fiber	cholesterol	sodium
319	9.5 g	5.2 g	25 g	35 g	3.4 g	58 mg	612 mg

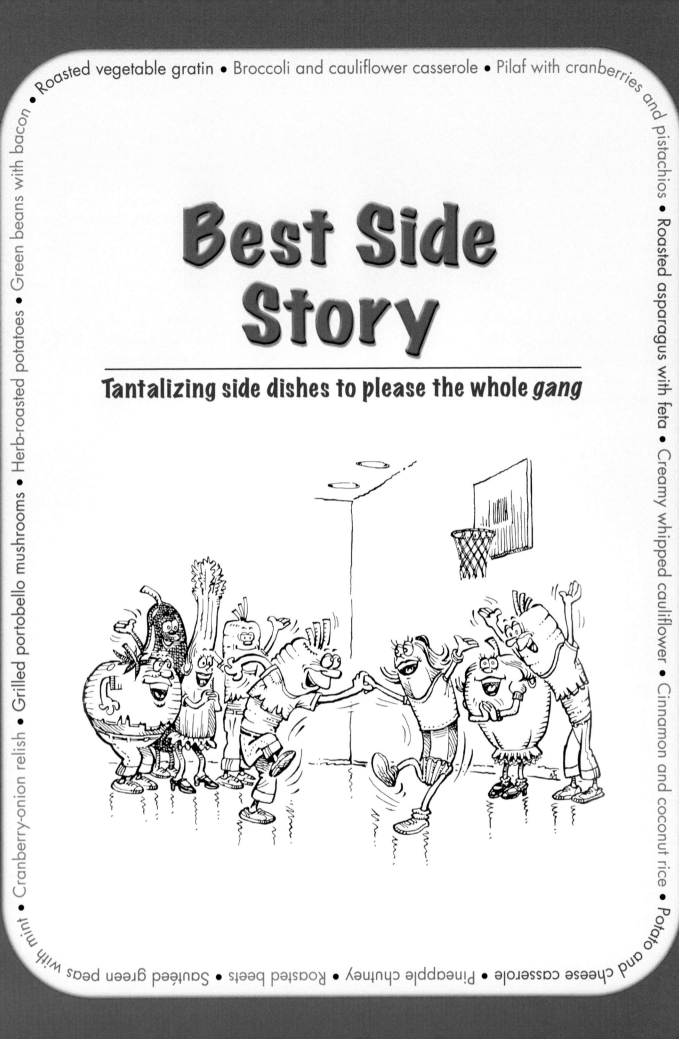

Best Side Story

Tantalizing side dishes to please the whole *gang*

Roasted vegetable gratin • Broccoli and cauliflower casserole • Pilaf with cranberries and pistachios • Roasted asparagus with feta • Creamy whipped cauliflower • Cinnamon and coconut rice • Potato and cheese casserole • Pineapple chutney • Roasted beets • Sautéed green peas with mint • Cranberry-onion relish • Grilled portobello mushrooms • Herb-roasted potatoes • Green beans with bacon

These Beets Were Made For Walkin'

Roasted beets and whole shallots with fresh thyme

There's no way these beets will get the boot! They're so darn tasty, they'll walk off the dinner table in no time.

6 medium-sized whole fresh beets (about 1 ½ lbs)
12 small to medium-sized shallots, peeled
1 tbsp olive oil
2 tsp minced fresh thyme
1 tsp balsamic vinegar
Salt and freshly ground black pepper to taste

- Preheat oven to 425°F. Wrap beets individually in foil. Place on middle oven rack and roast for about 1 hour, until beets are tender (you can pierce them with a fork), but not soft. Exact roasting time will depend on size of beets.

- While beets are roasting, prepare shallots. Place peeled shallots in an 8 x 8-inch baking pan. Add olive oil and thyme and toss to coat. Set aside.

- When beets are finished roasting, remove from oven and place pan of shallots in oven. Unwrap beets and let cool while shallots are roasting. Roast shallots for 15 minutes, stirring once, halfway through cooking time.

- When beets are cool enough to handle, peel them. If you cut off the stem end, the skin should come off very easily. Slice each beet into six wedges. Place in serving bowl. Add hot shallots and any olive oil and thyme you can scrape from the pan (using a rubber spatula helps). Sprinkle with balsamic vinegar, salt, and pepper and toss lightly. Serve hot.

Most people don't like beets because they've eaten them boiled, canned, or pickled. These beets are totally different—a million, trillion, bazillion times better! It's bit tedious to peel the shallots, but it's worth it. You could use small, quartered onions if you prefer, but we recommend the shallots fc added flavor and a prettier presentation.

Fat or Fiction?

All grains are bad carbs that make you fat.

Grain, grain, go away? Not if you want to lose weight, lower your cholesterol, keep your blood sugar on an even keel, stay regular, and prevent disease. Yes, there's a grain of truth to the claim that carbohydrates will make you fat. Today's grocery store shelves are filled with highly refined, overly processed, high-calorie products made from grains: crackers, cakes, cookies, white bread, pizza, bagels, nacho chips, sweetened cereals, and white rice, to name a few. These "bad" carbohydrates are the type we're overeating and the kind you can blame for your plus-sized pants. But here's the whole truth: Genuine whole grains—the kind that haven't been processed to death, stripped of fiber, and depleted of nutrients—are "good" carbs. They're allies, not enemies, in the battle of the bulge because they fill us up, curb our hunger, and provide us with a steady supply of energy. And they contain much more than just carbohydrates. Loaded with fiber, vitamins, minerals, and phytochemicals, they promote overall health and reduce our risk of developing serious disease. Whole grains include brown and wild rice, true multigrain bread (the dense, coarse, chewy kind with visible seeds), multigrain pasta, slow-cooked oatmeal, barley, rye, quinoa, and cereals made with whole wheat, millet, flax, or spelt. Never *spelt* "quinoa" in your life? Write it down on your shopping list and give it a try. For optimal health, don't go against the grain!

Makes 6 servings

PER SERVING

calories	total fat	saturated fat	protein	carbohydrate	fiber	cholesterol	sodium
87	2.5 g	0.3 g	2 g	15 g	3.2 g	0 mg	91 mg

Funky Factoid

In English pubs, ale is ordered by the pints and quarts. In Old England, when customers became unruly, the bartender would yell at them to mind their own "pints and quarts" and settle down. Legend has it that that's where we got the abbreviated phrase "mind your p's and q's."

RETURN TO SLENDER

Attention all parents! Refined, sugary cereals could be making your kids chunky—not to mention sabotaging their report cards! The typical commercial breakfast cereal is a starchy, high-glycemic meal that causes blood sugar to soar, then quickly crash. That can make little Suzie ravenous soon after, and fuel a cycle of overeating and weight gain. Frosted Twinkios cereal does *not* constitute the breakfast of chess champions, either. Sugar highs and lows can also affect brain functioning, causing mental fuzziness, fatigue, and impaired problem-solving abilities. To prevent weight gain and brain drain, a little parental guidance is suggested. Try replacing your kids' sugary cereal with a high-fiber one. Look for at least five grams of fiber per serving. Or, settle for a compromise: mix half of the sweet stuff with half of the high-fiber stuff. Some of the new, healthier offerings produced by cereal manufacturers should make your job easier. Think about varying what's served for breakfast, too. Whole-grain toast with nut butter, low-fat yogurt with fruit, poached eggs, or a whey-protein fruit smoothie are good fuel sources that'll keep blood-sugar levels balanced and brains sharp. Since breakfast variety is the spice of life, why not think outside the box?

Pea Diddy

Sautéed green peas with green onions and mint.

Why do peas get such a bad *rap?* Dress 'em up with some *bling* (a.k.a. green onions and mint), and they're the tastiest thing! *Hip hop* to it!

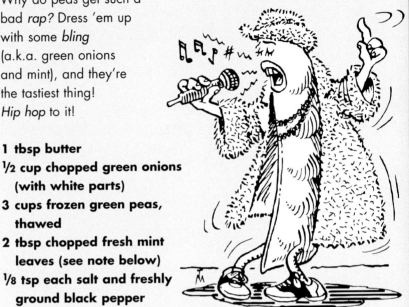

1 tbsp butter
1/2 cup chopped green onions (with white parts)
3 cups frozen green peas, thawed
2 tbsp chopped fresh mint leaves (see note below)
1/8 tsp each salt and freshly ground black pepper

- Melt butter in a medium, non-stick skillet over medium heat. Add onions. Cook and stir until onions are softened, about 3 minutes. Add peas. Cook and stir until peas are heated through, about 3 more minutes. Add mint, salt, and pepper. Mix well and remove from heat. Serve immediately.

Note: Please don't use dried mint for this recipe. It's just not the same as fresh mint and your peas won't be very tasty.

Makes 6 servings

			PER SERVING				
calories	total fat	saturated fat	protein	carbohydrate	fiber	cholesterol	sodium
72	2.3 g	1.2 g	4 g	10 g	3.3 g	5 mg	200 mg

Relish the Thought

Super-simple cranberry-onion relish

Think you need something to spruce up your Thanksgiving turkey? Thought so. Delight in the fact that this cranberry-onion relish is a snap to make and tastes wonderful when paired with roast turkey or pork.

1 tbsp butter
1 cup diced onions
1 tsp minced garlic
**⅓ cup packed
  brown sugar**
½ tsp ground ginger
**¼ tsp each ground
  cinnamon and nutmeg**
3½ cups frozen whole cranberries
½ cup orange juice
⅓ cup dried currants or raisins
2 tsp grated orange zest

- Melt butter in a 10-inch, non-stick skillet over medium heat. Add onions and garlic. Cook and stir until onions are tender, about 5 minutes. Add brown sugar, ginger, cinnamon, and nutmeg. Continue cooking and stirring until brown sugar is melted.

- Stir in cranberries, orange juice, currants, and orange zest. Bring mixture to a boil. Reduce heat to low and simmer, uncovered, for about 5 minutes, until cranberries begin to pop open. Remove from heat and cool completely. Cover and refrigerate before serving.

Makes 2½ cups

PER SERVING (2 TBSP)							
calories	total fat	saturated fat	protein	carbohydrate	fiber	cholesterol	sodium
40	0.6 g	0.4 g	0 g	9 g	1.1 g	2 mg	2 mg

*I see few die of hunger; of eating,
a hundred thousand.*

Benjamin Franklin

THE E FILES

Here's an important, yet little publicized reason to exercise: Your lymphatic system depends on it! "My nymphatic what?" That's *lymph* from the Latin word for "water goddess." If the liver is your body's filter, the lymphatic system is its drainage or sewer system. Through a complex series of teensy tubes running throughout your body, the lymph system continually drains excess fluid from cells and carries away waste materials and potentially harmful pollutants, making room for new blood with fresh nutrients. What happens when the sewer stops flowing? Nutrients from the food you eat don't get absorbed properly, your immune system gets bogged down with foreign invaders, and you get sick. And if your high-school reunion's approaching, take note: When your drainage pipes are backed up, your tissues can swell, adding 10 to 15 pounds to the scale! Here's where exercise comes into the picture: Unlike blood, which is pumped by the heart, lymphatic fluid (lymph) has no pump. Instead, what pumps the lymph through its many ducts and tunnels is good ol' movement. That's right—exercise is the liquid Drano that keeps our pipes clear! The fact our lymph system relies on voluntary movement is proof that Mother Nature intended us to be physically active creatures, constantly in motion, not sedentary couch potatoes or Internet junkies chained to our desks. Baby, we were born to run!

Pop Quizine

What determines whether an eggshell is white or brown?

a) the breed of hen
b) the time of year the eggs were laid
c) whether the chicken is male or female
d) the nationality of the chicken

Answer: (a) Despite what many people think, brown eggs are not nutritionally superior to white eggs.

Steeping Beauty

Looking for a way to burn fat, protect against cancer, and delay the aging process? Duh! Who isn't? Well, the answer may lie in the tea leaves. No need to visit your local clairvoyant, though. We're talking green tea here! Green tea's creating a big brew-ha-ha because it's thermogenic. That's a fancy shmancy way of saying that it boosts your metabolism, helping you to burn more calories. (And you thought "thermogenic" meant "looks good in a Thermos." Ha!) Plus, green tea contains polyphenols, natural compounds also found in red grapes, kidney beans, prunes, raisins, and red wine that have been shown to be anticancer, antibacterial, and antioxidant. Seems like an antidote to just about everything that could ail us. With green tea, good health is in the bag!

"SAY IT AIN'T SO!"

Feel like a good cry? Then mosey on over to any one of the popular steakhouse chains and order their most drooled-over appetizer: a colossal, deep-fried, batter-dipped onion. Cut open to look like a pretty flower and served with creamy dipping sauce, it may score points for presentation, but its nutritional profile will bring you to tears. Each onion has more than 2,000 calories and 150 grams of fat, for crying out loud! You'd be a *bloomin'* idiot to eat one all by your lonesome. Even if you share half with a friend, you've consumed the same amount of fat and calories found in two burgers! And to think it started out as an innocent vegetable. Oh, what a *frying* shame!

May I tell you about our corn on the cob special?

Yes, give me an earful.

Doctored Bello's

Grilled portobello mushrooms with basil and Parmesan cheese

I Dream of in-*Jeannie*-ous side dishes! If you do, too, these flavor-packed, grilled portobellos are just what the dinner doctor ordered!

Magically delicious mushrooms? It's sheer jeannie-us!

- **⅓ cup bottled low-fat Italian dressing**
- **1 tbsp minced fresh basil leaves**
- **2 tsp balsamic vinegar**
- **⅛ tsp freshly ground black pepper**
- **8 medium portobello mushrooms (about 4-inch diameter), stems removed**
- **¼ cup freshly grated Parmesan cheese or ¼ cup crumbled light feta cheese (1 oz)**

- Combine dressing, basil, vinegar, and pepper in a small bowl. Set aside.

- Wipe mushrooms clean. Using a pastry brush, generously brush both sides of mushrooms with prepared dressing. Let mushrooms stand at room temperature while you preheat the grill to high setting.

- Spray grill rack with cooking spray or brush lightly with oil. Grill mushrooms for 2 to 3 minutes per side, until tender with nice grill marks. Remove from heat. Slice mushrooms and place in a serving bowl. Sprinkle with Parmesan cheese. Serve immediately.

Tip: You can substitute your favorite low-fat balsamic vinaigrette dressing for the Italian dressing and balsamic vinegar. Make sure you still add the fresh basil, though. It gives the dressing a fresh note and makes the mushrooms taste even better.

Makes 4 servings

PER SERVING

calories	total fat	saturated fat	protein	carbohydrate	fiber	cholesterol	sodium
92	4.5 g	1.1 g	5 g	11 g	2.6 g	6 mg	396 mg

Spud **Light**

Very simple, very delicious roasted
mini red potatoes and onions

Even if you're watching your weight,
there's no need to be a tater hater.
As long as you keep your eye
on portion sizes, this spud's
for you!

**2 lbs mini red potatoes,
unpeeled**
**1 medium red onion,
cut into 8 wedges**
2 tbsp olive oil
**1 tbsp chopped fresh
rosemary or fresh thyme,
or a bit of both**
2 tsp balsamic vinegar
1 tsp minced garlic
Salt and freshly ground black pepper to taste

- Preheat oven to 425°F. Spray a 9 x 13-inch baking pan with
  cooking spray. Cut potatoes in half, or in quarters if they're
  larger, and place in baking pan. Add onion, olive oil, rosemary,
  vinegar, and garlic. Toss vegetables until well coated.

- Roast, uncovered, for about 30 minutes. Check for doneness of
  potatoes. Can you stick a fork in them? If not, stir the vegetables
  around a bit, return to oven and continue to roast until potatoes
  are tender. (It's a bit tricky to predict how long to cook the
  potatoes, since it depends entirely on their size.)

- Remove vegetables from oven and transfer to a serving dish.
  Sprinkle with salt and pepper and serve immediately.

Tip: You can substitute 8 large, peeled shallots for the red onion wedges.

Makes 8 servings

PER SERVING

calories	total fat	saturated fat	protein	carbohydrate	fiber	cholesterol	sodium
148	3.5 g	0.5 g	3 g	27 g	2.8 g	0 mg	81 mg

**When you apply for a job at Coca-Cola,
do they give you a pop quiz?**

**What's the scoop on th
Glycemic Index?
Should I care?**

Ask Greta

Here's the deal on the GI,
Joe: Initially designed to hel
diabetics maintain steady
blood-sugar levels, the
Glycemic Index was
developed by researchers at the University of
Toronto in 1981. Scientists came up with a
ranking of foods (on a scale of 0 to 100)
based on how quickly they raise your blood-
sugar levels. High-GI foods (above 70), such
as sweets and white bread, produce rapid
blood-sugar swings that are believed to cause
hunger, hormonal fluctuations, and weight
gain. Low-GI foods (less than 55), such as
most veggies, nuts, and whole grains, produc
a gradual rise in blood sugar that's
supposedly better for the body. But it's actuall
more complicated than that. The GI value of
food isn't definitive; it depends on how the
food is processed, stored, ripened, cut, and
cooked. Plus, the GI doesn't tell the whole
story. For example, white bread is assigned
almost the same value as whole wheat bread,
even though the latter has more nutrients and
fiber. Selecting foods strictly based on their G
value can lead to some bizarre choices—a
Snickers bar over carrots or potato chips over
cantaloupe. Is that cuckoo or what? Popular
diet books make it sound as if the GI is a
proven scientific theory but, in fact, it's one of
the most hotly debated topics in nutrition
research. Most obesity experts, including those
who believe in the Glycemic Index, agree tha
more long-term evidence using bigger trials is
needed, and that the GI is only one part of
the weight-loss and nutrition puzzle. Other
factors, including calories, saturated-fat
content, and general nutritional requirements,
are important considerations in choosing a
healthy diet. My advice? You probably don't
need a list of GI numbers to tell you what you
already instinctively know: In the name of
good health and svelte thighs, eat your fruits
and vegetables (carrots, corn, and potatoes
included) and don't become obsessed with
tedious bean-counting. Common sense is a
good guide. It doesn't take a degree in
nutrition to figure out that Frosted Choco Puffy
Stuff cereal is worse for you than slow-cooked
oatmeal. Generally, the more processed and
sugary a product is, the greater chance it's a
high-GI food. But if it's close to its natural
form—wrapped in fiber and filled with
nutrients—it's probably a food that'll do your
body good.

Tooth or Consequences

Your good ol' toothbrush may be one of the best tools for protecting your heart and your brain. Recent studies suggest that regularly flossing and brushing your teeth could cut your risk of stroke in half. In a 12-year study of 14,000 men, researchers found that those with the healthiest teeth and gums were also the least likely to have a stroke. That's because the bacteria that causes periodontal disease can sometimes sneak into the bloodstream, damaging blood vessels and increasing the risk of stroke. Our *flossify*? To maintain healthy arteries, avoid plaque like the plague.

"SAY IT AIN'T SO!"

This news just in: There are reports of a scandal cookin' down at the bakery! Looks like several members of the Baked Goods team have tested positive for steroids. That's right. Sweets on steroids! They're bigger than ever! Mammoth muffins, cuckoo-sized cookies, and donuts that could double as flotation devices have all been busted by the I.O.C. (International *O-Slim-Pick* Committee). That much sugar and white flour teamed up gives fat cells an unfair competitive advantage. And let's not overlook their high fat levels from all the butter, oil, chocolate, and cheese they're made with. Investigations are still underway but, in the meantime, the gold medal for "baked snack with the least impact on fat cells" goes to…biscotti! Yes, this slender, crunchy cookie is lower in sugar, calories, and fat than the others, and that's why it's sure to score a perfect 10.

Mr. Bean

Steamed green beans tossed with lemon, honey mustard, and bacon

We realize preparing dinner is no laughing matter, so we've concocted a tasty bean side dish that's *unspeakably* simple. It *mutters* not whether you can cook. You really can't *goof* up this one.

1 lb fresh green beans, trimmed
2 slices bacon, chopped
    into small pieces
½ cup minced red onions
    or shallots
1 tsp minced garlic
1 tbsp each honey mustard and
    freshly squeezed lemon juice
Salt and freshly ground
    black pepper to taste

- Place beans in steamer basket over boiling water. Steam for about 6 minutes, until beans are tender-crisp.

- While beans are steaming, cook bacon, onions, and garlic over medium heat in a 10-inch, non-stick skillet until bacon is crisp and onions are tender, about 5 minutes. Be careful not to burn them.

- Remove skillet from heat. Add honey mustard and lemon juice. Mix well. Add beans and stir to coat beans with onion-bacon mixture. Sprinkle with salt and pepper and serve immediately.

Tip: You can substitute frozen cut green beans for fresh beans if you prefer.

Makes 6 servings

PER SERVING

calories	total fat	saturated fat	protein	carbohydrate	fiber	cholesterol	sodium
62	2.4 g	1 g	2 g	8 g	1.9 g	3 mg	106 mg

Mine!

No, it's mine!

What do you call cheese that doesn't belong to you?
Nacho cheese!

Viva Las Veggies

Roasted vegetable gratin with tomatoes, zucchini, mushrooms, and onions

When the stakes are high and you feel like adding some glitz and glamour to ordinary veggies, bake this *sin*sational side dish and get your dinner party swingin'! It makes *slots*, so there's enough to feed everyone. Just remember: What happens in the kitchen, stays in the kitchen.

4 medium tomatoes, cut into chunks
2 medium zucchini, chopped
2 large portobello mushrooms, chopped (see tip in margin)
1 medium red onion, coarsely chopped
1 tsp minced garlic
1 tbsp each olive oil and balsamic vinegar
1 tbsp chopped fresh herbs, such as rosemary, basil, oregano, or thyme
¼ tsp each salt and freshly ground black pepper
1 cup fresh whole wheat bread crumbs (see tip in margin)
½ cup freshly grated Parmesan cheese (see tip in margin)
½ tsp dried thyme

- Spray a 9 x 13-inch baking dish with cooking spray. Add tomatoes, zucchini, mushrooms, onion, and garlic. Mix well (using your hands works best). Add olive oil, vinegar, herbs, salt, and pepper. Mix again to coat vegetables with dressing.

- Roast, uncovered, at 425°F for 25 minutes. While vegetables are roasting, prepare topping. Combine bread crumbs, Parmesan cheese, and thyme in a small bowl and mix well.

- Remove vegetables from oven. Sprinkle crumb mixture evenly over vegetables. Return to oven for 5 minutes, until cheese is melted and crumbs turn a light golden brown. Serve hot.

Makes 6 servings

		PER SERVING					
calories	total fat	saturated fat	protein	carbohydrate	fiber	cholesterol	sodium
139	5.7 g	2 g	8 g	18 g	4.1 g	7 mg	323 mg

150

Cooking TIP

Using a small spoon, scrape off (and discard) the gills from the underside of the portobello mushrooms before using them in this recipe. Making your own fresh bread crumbs is a snap, but you'll need a food processor or mini chopper. Tear a slice of multigrain or whole wheat bread into large pieces and place them in the food processor. Pulse on and off a few times and voilà! Homemade fresh bread crumbs. One slice of bread will yield about ½ cup of crumbs. The bread crumbs you buy at the grocery store are just a bit too dry for this type of recipe but, if that's all you have, you'll need to add 1 or 2 tbsp melted butter to the topping to help hold it together. Please buy fresh Parmesan cheese and grate it yourself. The cheap stuff you buy in the pasta aisle is fine on spaghetti, but it doesn't really melt, so you need to buy a small chunk of the good stuff to make this gratin.

Studies show that our taste buds change with age, including a declining sensitivity to bitterness. Fortunately, this makes many healthy foods more appealing to us as we get older. Eight in 10 older people reported a growing preference for green vegetables, whole-grain foods, and bitter fruits like grapefruits and lemons. And you thought Grandma's puckered face came from misplaced dentures!

An old wives' tale suggests putting _____ in your socks to keep your feet toasty warm during cold weather:

a) toaster crumbs
b) gunpowder
c) herbal tea leaves
d) cayenne pepper

Answer: (d) Likewise, walking barefoot on May 1st before sunrise was believed to combat sweating feet! The early morning grass would have a soapy effect and act as an astringent on the skin.

Florets Nightingale

Broccoli and cauliflower florets with
cheese sauce and a crumb topping

You can *nurse* a growling, grumbling tummy with this
nutritious, delicious broccoli and cauliflower
casserole. It's at the *head* of its class!

1 head broccoli
1 head cauliflower

Topping
½ cup fresh whole wheat bread crumbs
3 tbsp grated Parmesan cheese
1 tbsp chopped fresh parsley

Sauce
1 can (12 oz) evaporated 2% milk
⅔ cup 1% milk
3 tbsp all-purpose flour
1 tsp olive oil
¼ cup minced onions
1 tsp minced garlic
½ cup packed shredded light old (sharp)
  cheddar cheese (2 oz)
⅓ cup grated Parmesan cheese
1 tbsp Dijon mustard
¼ tsp each salt and freshly ground black pepper
Pinch ground nutmeg

- Chop broccoli and cauliflower into medium-sized
  florets, discarding tough stems. Place cauliflower in
  steamer basket over boiling water. Cover and steam
  for 3 minutes. Add broccoli florets and steam
  4 more minutes. Vegetables should seem just slightly
  undercooked.

- While florets are steaming, make topping and sauce.
  For topping, combine crumbs, Parmesan cheese, and
  parsley in a small bowl. Set aside.

- For sauce, whisk together evaporated milk, 1% milk,
  and flour in a medium bowl. Set aside. Heat olive oil
  in a medium, non-stick pot over medium heat. Add
  onions and garlic. Cook and stir until onions begin to
  soften, about 2 minutes. Add milk mixture. Cook and
  stir with a whisk until sauce bubbles and thickens.
  Remove from heat. Add both cheeses, mustard, salt,
  pepper, and nutmeg. Stir until cheese melts.

- Remove florets from steamer basket and place in a
  9 x 13-inch baking dish that has been sprayed with
  cooking spray.

- Pour sauce over florets in casserole dish. Top with
  reserved crumb mixture. Bake, uncovered, at 400°F
  for 20 minutes.

Makes 8 servings

	PER SERVING						
calories	total fat	saturated fat	protein	carbohydrate	fiber	cholesterol	sodium
175	5.8 g	2.6 g	13 g	20 g	5.5 g	18 mg	398 mg

*If we always break New Year's resolutions,
why don't we resolve to gain weight and
exercise less?*

Jim Mullen, Entertainment Weekly

THE E FILES

Here's proof that physical activity really can be addictive: A study in the journal *Behavioral Neuroscience* found that mice who were prevented from running for exercise experienced the same neurological response as if they were being denied a fix of cocaine, morphine, alcohol, or nicotine. Of mice and men, it looks like there really is such a thing as a *runner's high*.

Merry-Go-Brown

Brown-rice pilaf with cranberries and pistachios

Round and round it goes... your wooden spoon, that is, as you cook up a batch of this berry nutty, berry wholesome brown-rice pilaf. It's the fairest of the *fare*!

- **2 tsp olive oil or butter**
- **2 cups finely chopped mushrooms (see tip in margin)**
- **1 cup minced red onions**
- **1 tsp minced garlic**
- **1 cup whole-grain brown rice (see tip in margin)**
- **2 cups chicken or vegetable broth**
- **½ tsp salt**
- **¼ cup each chopped dried cranberries and chopped pistachios (see tip in margin)**
- **2 tbsp chopped fresh parsley**
- **2 tsp grated lemon zest**

- Heat olive oil in a medium, non-stick saucepan over medium-high heat. Add mushrooms, onions, and garlic. Cook and stir until vegetables begin to soften, about 3 minutes.

- Stir in rice. Cook 1 more minute. Add broth and salt. Bring to a boil. Reduce heat to low and simmer, covered, for about 45 minutes (check suggested cooking time on rice package).

- Remove from heat. Stir in cranberries, pistachios, parsley, and lemon zest. Let stand, covered, for 10 minutes before serving.

Makes 6 servings

PER SERVING

calories	total fat	saturated fat	protein	carbohydrate	fiber	cholesterol	sodium
202	5 g	0.7 g	6 g	34 g	3 g	2 mg	329 mg

The first person to mass-produce candies made a mint.

Britney's Spears

Roasted asparagus with balsamic vinegar and feta

Oops! We did it again! We've created a sensational side dish that'll have everyone in your family singing and dancing with delight.

1¼ to 1½ lbs asparagus spears
1 tbsp olive oil
1 tsp minced garlic
2 tsp balsamic vinegar
Salt and freshly ground black pepper to taste
¼ cup crumbled light feta cheese (1 oz) or ¼ cup freshly grated Parmesan cheese

- Preheat oven to 450°F. Trim tough ends off asparagus.

- Spray a small baking sheet with cooking spray. Arrange asparagus in a single layer. Drizzle with olive oil and sprinkle with garlic. Mix asparagus around a bit to make sure they're well coated with oil and garlic (use your hands for this…it's the easiest way).

- Roast for 12 to 15 minutes, depending on thickness of asparagus. Be careful not to overcook them. Soggy asparagus is no fun and no yum!

- Arrange cooked asparagus on a serving plate. Sprinkle with vinegar, salt, and pepper. Top with crumbled feta and serve immediately.

Tip: You can substitute fresh, whole green beans for the asparagus.

Makes 6 servings

PER SERVING							
calories	total fat	saturated fat	protein	carbohydrate	fiber	cholesterol	sodium
55	3.5 g	1.1 g	3 g	5 g	2 g	4 mg	152 mg

BEST SIDE STORY

I was going to marry a gardener, but he was too rough around the hedges.

Code 8! Code 8! We've got an emergency in the produce aisle! You probably noticed that most produce at the grocery store carries a four-digit price look-up code (PLU). The cashier isn't fondling your melons for nothin', you know! If the produce is organically grown, a "9" precedes that code. If the produce is genetically modified, it's identified with an "8" instead of a 9. (Psst: We wanted to make a joke about Bo Derek's melons being coded with a perfect 10, but decided it was inappropriate.)

In the healthy eating game, we all know that vegetables win the Most Valuable Player Award hands down, helping us to control weight and feel great. Low in calories, fat, and simple sugars, and high in fiber, nutrients, and cancer-fighting phytochemicals —no wonder health experts keep hounding us to eat five servings every day! But those aren't the only reasons why veggies are an indispensable tool in the weight watcher's arsenal. They have a very high water content, and that means they're also high in oxygen (hence the "O" in the H_2O formula, in case you spent chemistry class catching up on your zzz's). In order for your lean muscle tissue to burn fat, it needs oxygen to help convert that fat into energy. When you eat your greens (and yellows and reds and oranges), you flood your body with water, increasing oxygen levels, improving your metabolism, and helping you to burn fat. *Weigh* to go, veggies! Gimme five!

Cooking TIP

Using onion dip in this recipe is a great shortcut that saves both time and money! It takes the place of at least 4 or 5 different ingredients that you'd need to add to give the cauliflower such a delicious, creamy taste. Look for onion dip made with cream cheese, such as Philadelphia Dips. Ideally, the dip you choose should have no more than 3 grams of fat per 2 tablespoon serving.

You Go, 'Gurt!

Ever wonder why your doctor tells you to eat yogurt after you've been taking antibiotics? Well, when antibiotics go about gobbling up the "bad" bacteria that make you sick, they also kill off the "good," health-promoting bacteria that live in your intestines. Yes, you have friendly Bugs Buddies inside you! When the good are overtaken by the bad in your gut, it can turn ugly, and contribute to a variety of ailments from acne to allergies to arthritis. That's where yogurt enters the battle. It contains armies of gut-friendly bugs like acidophilus and bifidus, so by eating yogurt after a course of antibiotics, you're replenishing the troops, so to speak. Unfortunately, most commercial yogurts are overly pasteurized, and that kills off most of the good bacteria. Plus, the muck at the bottom of fruity yogurts is a sugar-laden buffet for the nasty critters. When possible, choose plain yogurt with live bacterial cultures and add your own chopped fruit or nuts. Organic yogurt is even better, since it's made from milk that's certified to be free of antibiotics or hormones. If you don't like yogurt, you can also buy good bacteria or "probiotics" in capsule form at a health-food store. By the way, antibiotics aren't the only things that help bad bacteria knock out the good. Poor diet (especially too much sugar, caffeine, refined foods, and alcohol) and even too much stress contribute to the enemy's cause.

The torch of love is lit in the kitchen.

French Proverb

Mashed Fauxtatoes

Creamy whipped cauliflower "potatoes"

It's a brilliant disguise! Whipped cauliflower does its best mashed potato impersonation in this creamy side dish that just might fool the staunchest starch connoisseur.

1 large head cauliflower (about 2½ to 3 lbs)
½ cup low-fat, cream-cheese-based onion dip (see tip in margin)
¼ tsp salt

- Place a steamer basket inside a large pot and add 1-inch water. Cut cauliflower into uniform-sized florets. Add cauliflower to pot. Cover and steam for about 15 to 20 minutes, or until cauliflower is very tender but not mushy (cooking time depends on size of florets).

- Transfer cauliflower to a blender. You will need to work in batches. Whirl cauliflower until smooth (no lumps!). This might take a bit of fiddling and poking at first, depending on the strength and size of your blender. Hang in there…it's worth it! Add onion dip and salt to the last batch. Transfer batches of whipped cauliflower to a serving bowl and mix well to distribute seasoning before serving. You may need to reheat it in the microwave if it has cooled.

Makes 8 servings

PER SERVING

calories	total fat	saturated fat	protein	carbohydrate	fiber	cholesterol	sodium
61	1.6 g	0.8 g	4 g	10 g	3.9 g	5 mg	322 mg

All That Jasmine

Sticky cinnamon-and-coconut-scented Thai jasmine rice

You can *jazz* up your dinner when you pair jasmine rice with fragrant spice. They make beautiful music together!

1 cup light coconut milk
1 cup chicken or vegetable broth
¼ tsp salt
1¼ cups uncooked
   jasmine rice,
   rinsed and drained
   (see tip in margin)
¼ cup dried currants
2 tsp olive oil
¾ cup diced onions
2 tsp grated gingerroot
¾ tsp ground cinnamon
¼ tsp each ground
   coriander and ground ginger
2 tbsp minced fresh cilantro

- Combine coconut milk, broth, and salt in a medium saucepan. Bring to a boil over high heat. Stir in rice. Reduce heat to low. Cover and simmer until liquid is absorbed and rice is tender, about 12 minutes. Remove from heat and stir in currants. Cover and let stand for 10 minutes.

- Heat olive oil in a large, non-stick skillet over medium heat. Add onions. Cook and stir until onions are tender, 3 to 4 minutes. Remove from heat. Add gingerroot, cinnamon, coriander, and ginger. Mix well. Return to heat. Add cooked rice. Cook and stir for 2 more minutes, until mixture is well blended and spices are evenly distributed. Stir in cilantro and serve hot.

Makes 6 servings

			PER SERVING				
calories	total fat	saturated fat	protein	carbohydrate	fiber	cholesterol	sodium
207	3.7 g	2.2 g	4 g	40 g	1.8 g	1 mg	174 mg

Cooking TIP

Similar to Indian basmati rice, jasmine rice is a fragrant rice from Thailand and it must be rinsed before cooking. Place the uncooked rice in a sieve and rinse under cold running water for a minute or so. Drain well. You can substitute basmati rice for the jasmine rice if you prefer.

THE E FILES

Excuses, excuses, excuses. Here's a popular one: "I'm too tired to exercise!" When you have the energy level of a slug, you're destined to end up flaked out on the couch with Dr. Philyerbelly. But it's a scientific fact that exercise actually *creates* energy. It's true. Give it a try! Tomorrow when you get home from work, bypass the sofa and keep on movin'. Go for a walk, cut the grass, play with your dog—as long as you're moving faster than a glacier, you'll get your heart pumping and oxygen flowing. Do it for at least 30 minutes, and we guarantee you'll feel more energetic than when you started. Now that you've been infused with energy, you'll be amazed at how much more you can accomplish during the evening. The more energy you have, the better you feel. The better you feel, the more you want to do. And after a few weeks, when your body becomes stronger and more efficient, you'll even get things done faster. Hey! Now you can't use that other well-worn excuse: "I can't find time to exercise." You've actually created *more* time by exercising!

What's the best nutritional supplement to take if you have straight hair? Curling iron.

Potatoes are evil.

Like bread and rice, people are shunning the potato based on its high score on the Glycemic Index. The theory is that potatoes send your blood-sugar levels skyrocketing, then plummeting, prompting hunger, overeating, and fat storage. That may be true in some instances, like when you eat a mountain of mashed potatoes and nothing else, but it's silly to think you can never play the *tuber* again without unleashing hormonal havoc, busting a seam, and sprouting a third eye. Remember, potatoes do contain valuable nutrients—people have been subsisting on them for generations, for gosh sakes! In fact, during the Klondike Gold Rush, potatoes were so valued for their vitamin-C content that miners traded them for gold. (They're also a good source of potassium and fiber when you leave their skins on.) If you dig potatoes, you simply need a strategy that allows you to eat them once in a while. First, keep your eyes on their size! Potatoes are a food we tend to overeat, and often in unhealthy forms: deep-fried, hash browned, or chipped 'n' dipped. Have a *small* portion (about half a cup) as an accompaniment to veggies and lean meat. Secondly, when you're hankerin' for a spud, make it a *spud light*. Choose new potatoes (a lower-glycemic option), and stick to healthier preparation methods such as baked, boiled, roasted, or mashed (without high-fat fixings). Finally, by pairing potatoes with protein, fiber, and fat, you'll transform the high-glycemic food into a moderate-glycemic meal. So, as long as you think portions, balance, and moderation, potatoes won't go to *waist*.

"SAY IT AIN'T SO!"

If you're craving an afternoon snack, don't let the office vending machine push your buttons. That's because nearly every processed snack food sold in vending machines contains partially hydrogenated vegetable oil and its wicked offspring, trans fats. Chocolate bars, licorice, chips, candy, and even a seemingly healthy snack like cheese popcorn can tip the trans-fat scale. A simple guideline: If the snack leaves your fingers feeling greasy, you can bet it'll leave your heart feeling queasy.

Darth Tater

Cheesy, gooey, roasted-potato casserole for a special occasion

If you think all potatoes are evil, think again! It's time to restore justice to the beloved spud with our lightened-up roasted-potato casserole. It's the best in the galaxy! A real life*saber* when you need a special side dish.

May the forks be with you!

2½ lbs unpeeled, thin-skinned potatoes (red or white)
1 cup chopped onions
1 tbsp olive oil
1 tsp minced garlic
½ tsp salt
¼ tsp each freshly ground black pepper, paprika, and dried thyme
1 can (10.75 oz) condensed cheddar cheese soup, undiluted
⅓ cup grated Parmesan cheese
2 tbsp chopped fresh dill or fresh parsley
½ cup packed shredded light old (sharp) cheddar cheese (2 oz)
1 green onion, chopped

- Preheat oven to 425°F. Cut potatoes into 1-inch chunks and place in a 9 x 13-inch casserole dish that has been sprayed with cooking spray. Add onions, olive oil, garlic, salt, pepper, paprika, and thyme and mix well. Roast potatoes for 30 minutes, stirring once, halfway through cooking time. Remove from oven and let cool slightly. Reduce oven temperature to 375°F.

- In a medium bowl, mix together soup, Parmesan cheese, and dill. Pour over potatoes. Mix well. Sprinkle grated cheddar on top, followed by green onion. Return potatoes to oven and bake, uncovered, for 25 minutes, until cheese is bubbly and potatoes are golden brown around edges. Let stand 5 minutes before serving.

Makes 10 servings

PER SERVING

calories	total fat	saturated fat	protein	carbohydrate	fiber	cholesterol	sodium
190	5.9 g	2.4 g	6 g	28 g	3.2 g	10 mg	454 mg

Chutney Houston

Sweet and spicy pineapple chutney

Our tangy pineapple chutney is an adult contemporary favorite that hits a high note where flavor's concerned. You may even need to hire a *bodyguard* to protect the leftovers! It's a *diva*vine topping for baked ham, pork chops, or pork tenderloin.

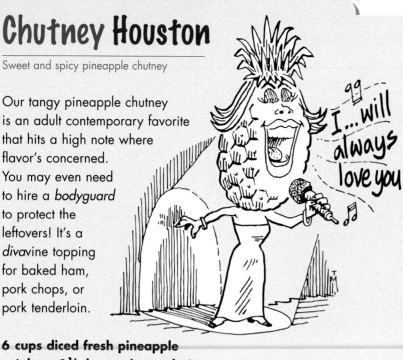

I...will always love you

6 cups diced fresh pineapple
   (about 1 1/2 large pineapples)
1/2 cup diced onions
1/2 cup dark brown sugar
1/3 cup cider vinegar
1/2 cup dried currants or raisins
1 tsp ground ginger
1 tsp minced garlic
1/2 tsp each salt and ground cinnamon
1/8 tsp cayenne pepper
1 tbsp cornstarch (optional)

- Combine all ingredients except cornstarch in a medium saucepan and bring to a boil over high heat. Reduce heat to low. Simmer, uncovered, for 20 minutes, stirring occasionally. If mixture is thin and you'd prefer it thicker, mix together 1 tbsp cornstarch and 1 tbsp water until smooth, add to chutney, and cook until thickened, about 1 minute.

- Let mixture cool slightly before serving. May also be served cold. To store, cover and refrigerate for up to 1 week.

Makes about 5 cups

			PER SERVING (3 TBSP)				
calories	total fat	saturated fat	protein	carbohydrate	fiber	cholesterol	sodium
43	0.2 g	0 g	0 g	11 g	0.6 g	0 mg	46 mg

I worked at a diet food company, but the chances for promotion were slim.

RETURN TO SLENDER

Are you in calorie denial? A handful of candy at the office. Forkfuls of your kid's leftovers. Food samples at the grocery store. Because these seemingly innocent nibbles aren't part of a planned meal, it's easy to convince yourself that they fall into a nutritional black hole, magically negating their calorie and fat counts. *You* can overlook the damage, but we have a *snacking* suspicion the scale won't! All those little bits and bites sure help explain why your knickers are *knot* fitting anymore. Consider the calories in these mindless mouthfuls (one measly tablespoon each): cake icing, 55 (still wanna lick the bowl?); cream cheese, 50; chocolate chip cookie dough, 70; jelly beans, 50; gravy, 40. Yikes! Eating in the No-Calorie Twilight Zone is scary stuff! To avoid surprises on the scale, plan your snacks ahead of time and choose well. That way you won't unconsciously nibble whatever's available. And keep a mental checklist of what you do eat. If you acknowledge the chocolate you had before lunch and admit to the pretzels you ate in the car, you're more likely to cut back on what you eat later on. Otherwise, *Snacks, Lies, and Videotape* could hit you with a shocking ending!

According to the National Safety Council, drinking coffee does not sober up a drunk person, and in many cases it may actually increase the adverse effects of alcohol. Coffee isn't the quicker-*perk*-me-upper that people think it is because the caffeine is just one more dose of toxic trouble for your liver. Your best bet to sober up? H_2O, on the rocks. So, when your friend offers you a cappuccino after a night of drinking vino, just say, *"Nay, Bob!"*

A Sweet Carb Named Desire

When you're craving dessert, these recipes take the cake

Sweet Home Alabanana

Banana bread with oat bran, pecans, and chocolate chips

Does your conscience bother you when all your banana *Skynyrds* are turnin' brown? Tell the truth! Here's a tasty solution: Whip up this guilt-free banana bread with crunchy pecans and mini chocolate chips—and make sure you save room for a *Second Helping*!

1¾ cups all-purpose flour
½ cup oat bran
2 tsp baking powder
1 tsp baking soda
1 tsp ground cinnamon
½ tsp salt
2 eggs
½ cup packed brown sugar
1½ cups mashed ripe bananas
    (about 4 medium or 3 large)
¾ cup buttermilk
2 tbsp vegetable oil
2 tsp vanilla
½ cup chopped pecans
⅓ cup mini chocolate chips

- Preheat oven to 350°F. Spray two 8 x 4-inch loaf pans with cooking spray and set aside.

- In a large bowl, combine flour, oat bran, baking powder, baking soda, cinnamon, and salt. Mix well and set aside.

- In a medium bowl, beat together eggs and brown sugar on medium speed of electric mixer for 2 minutes. Add bananas, buttermilk, oil, and vanilla. Beat again until well blended.

- Add wet ingredients to dry ingredients and mix just until dry ingredients are moistened. Do not use electric mixer for this step. Fold in nuts and chocolate chips. Do not over-mix batter.

- Divide batter evenly among loaf pans. Bake for 30 to 35 minutes, or until a toothpick inserted in center of loaves comes out clean. Cool loaves in pans on a wire rack for 10 minutes. Remove loaves from pans and (1) slice and eat warm, or (2) cool completely on rack, then store covered in plastic wrap (they won't last long!).

Note: You absolutely must use ripe bananas (with brown spots!) for this recipe. Most banana bread recipes use a lot more sugar than we use in ours, so the sweetness from the ripe bananas is really important.

Makes 2 small loaves, 8 slices each

PER SLICE

calories	total fat	saturated fat	protein	carbohydrate	fiber	cholesterol	sodium
173	6.4 g	1.3 g	4 g	28 g	1.9 g	27 mg	236 mg

What's the *Sweet'N Lowdown* on artificial sweeteners? Are they safe?

Ask Greta

Depends on who you ask! Artificial sweeteners have a long history of controversy. A quick search on the Internet for some "artificial intelligence" will reveal thousands of conflicting opinions about the safety of sugar substitutes. If aspartame *doesn't* cause migraines, reading about it sure will! It seem that Splenda (sucralose) is the only sweetene deemed splendid by just about everyone, but that could change over time. Personally, I try to limit the amount of aspartame, Splenda, saccharin, and other fake sugars I consume. I'd rather not be a human guinea pig while science figures out what's okay and what isn't. (That's why we decided not to use any artificial sweeteners in our dessert chapter.) Sure, I drink the occasional diet soda, and I'll even confess to sprinkling that little blue packet into my morning coffee. (Egads! Caffeine *and* chemicals!) But I don't overdo it, and neither should you. One problem with sugar substitutes is that they encourage people to make junky sweets and processed "diet" foods part of their everyday life. Daily dosages of sweet nothin's can add up and may leave a sour taste in your mouth. NutraSweet in your morning coffee, Splenda in your yogurt and orange juice, aspartame in your diet soft drink, xylitol in your energy bar, more aspartame in your chewing gum, plus sucralose in the ice cream you had for dessert. Eeek! That much fake is hard to take, especially for your tired, overworked liver! Also, just because those foods are sugar-free or low-calorie, doesn't mean they're healthy. Many of them are nutrient-free, too! More red flags: Recent studies show that artificial sweeteners can spur our appetites and boost insulin, the fat-storage hormone. And regular use of sugar substitutes can change your perception of what's sweet, making you crave more and more sugar in order to be satisfied. Some weight-loss aid, huh? Your best bet is to develop less of a taste for sweets in general, and view them as occasional, special treats. For people who need to lose weight, or for those who have to watch their blood-sugar levels because of diabetes, yes, too much sugar can be a problem. That's where moderate use of artificial sweeteners can come in handy. If you think moderation, you don't have to sweat the sweet stuff!

Fat or Fiction?

Skipping meals is the best way to save calories and lose weight quickly.

When you're trying to cut back on calories, it's tempting to speed up the weight-loss process by cutting out a meal entirely. Skipping breakfast or lunch seems like the most obvious tummy-trimming tactic in the world. Unfortunately, this strategy is a recipe for metabolic disaster! When you skip meals and become absolutely ravenous, not only do you experience unpleasant side-effects—dizziness, fatigue, irritability, and brain fog—but also your metabolism comes to a quick halt. Why? When you go half a day without food, your body thinks you're never eating again and shifts into survival mode. That means it'll hoard and ration the fuel you've already given it, with fat being the primary hostage since it lasts the longest in times of famine. Soon you can't process food as efficiently, and the calories you do eat are maximized. Say what? In simple terms, now you'll need to eat less just to *maintain* your weight. Plus, when you're starving, you're much more likely to overeat at your next meal, and with a system that's now ill-prepared to handle the extra calories, there's a good chance they'll end up strapped to your thighs. To avoid the metabolic meltdown, eat small meals throughout the day to keep your calorie-burning furnace stoked.

Goody Two Chews

Cranberry and peanut butter granola clusters

It actually takes more than two chews to get these tasty granola clusters down, but we just couldn't swallow the fact that our title didn't make sense, so we went with it anyway! A perfect treat for your perfect kids!

So good, you'll swear they're bad for you!

⅓ cup light peanut butter
⅓ cup pure maple syrup
2 egg whites
1 tsp pumpkin pie spice
2½ cups low-fat granola (see tip in margin)
¾ cup dried cranberries

- Preheat oven to 250°F. Spray a 12-cup muffin tin with cooking spray and set aside.

- In a medium bowl, beat together peanut butter and maple syrup on medium speed of electric mixer. Add egg whites and pumpkin pie spice and beat again until smooth.

- Stir in granola and cranberries. Divide mixture evenly among muffin cups. Bake on middle oven rack for 45 minutes. Remove from oven and cool completely on a wire rack before removing clusters from pan. Store in an airtight container.

Makes 12 clusters

PER CLUSTER

calories	total fat	saturated fat	protein	carbohydrate	fiber	cholesterol	sodium
124	3.2 g	0.5 g	4 g	22 g	1.2 g	0 mg	65 mg

Like I said before, you are what you eat.

Poppy Love

Light and lemony poppy seed bread

Once you've had a taste of our *pupular* lemon bread, you'll *dog-ear* this page for sure! It's a *doggone* simple recipe that everyone will fall in *loaf* with.

1 ¼ cups all-purpose flour
¾ cup granulated sugar
½ cup oat bran
1 tbsp poppy seeds
2 tsp baking powder
½ tsp salt
1 cup 2% milk
¼ cup melted butter
  or vegetable oil
1 egg
2 tbsp freshly squeezed lemon juice
2 tsp grated lemon zest

- Preheat oven to 350°F. Spray an 8 x 4-inch loaf pan with cooking spray and set aside.

- In a large bowl, mix together flour, sugar, oat bran, poppy seeds, baking powder, and salt.

- In a medium bowl, whisk together milk, butter, egg, lemon juice, and lemon zest. Add wet ingredients to dry ingredients and mix just until dry ingredients are moistened. Spread batter in prepared pan. Bake for 40 to 45 minutes, or until loaf is light golden brown and a toothpick inserted in center of loaf comes out clean.

- Cool loaf in pan on a wire rack for 10 minutes. Remove loaf from pan and cool completely on rack. Cover with plastic wrap and store at room temperature or in the refrigerator.

Makes 1 loaf, 12 slices

			PER SLICE				
calories	total fat	saturated fat	protein	carbohydrate	fiber	cholesterol	sodium
161	5.3 g	2.8 g	4 g	27 g	1.1 g	30 mg	197 mg

Anything that gets that hot without fire is from the devil.

Ellen DeGeneres,
speaking about microwave ovens

Lemons: The Quicker-Pucker-Upper

Cuts grease, dirt, and grime! Tackles tough stains! Eliminates soap scum! Tastes great in pie! Say what? The beloved lemon not only flavors the food we eat, but it's also used in household products because of its superior cleansing properties. It's not surprising then, that this unique citrus fruit is also prized for its *internal* cleansing abilities. Eating lemons helps cleanse the bloodstream and the liver. And your liver sure could use a good bath now and then! The liver is the body's waste filter, dealing with an onslaught of toxins such as caffeine, sugar, alcohol, trans fats, refined foods, artificial sweeteners, pesticides, preservatives, and pharmaceutical drugs. That's plenty of grease, dirt, and grime! But it's Mr. Lemon Clean to the rescue! Lemons also help balance the body's pH levels and promote healing. A gentle, effective way to keep your body clean 'n' pristine is to drink lemon water each morning. Simply squeeze the juice of half a lemon into a mug of warm, filtered water and drink. If you want a livelier liver, *pledge* to eat lemons more often!

Must…have…chocolate! If constant cravings are making you crazy, you can get rid of them in a pinch—quite literally. Try pinching your nostrils or earlobes for 10 seconds and the cravings should pass. Those spots are acupressure points, which means that how this method actually works is an ancient Chinese secret.

Lovin' My No-Oven Cheesecake

Light and velvety no-bake pumpkin cheesecake

Our famous no-bake pumpkin cheesecake is the perfect finish to Thanksgiving dinner. And you can make it no sweat, since you don't use an oven! Plus, we've *carved* out the heavy stuff and left in the light stuff, so even though you're feeling stuffed, you can still eat some sweet stuff.

Crust

1 ½ cups graham crumbs
2 tbsp brown sugar
½ tsp ground cinnamon
3 tbsp butter, melted

Filling

1 cup evaporated 2% milk
¼ cup frozen orange juice concentrate, thawed
2 envelopes (¼ oz each) Knox unflavored gelatine
1 ½ pkgs (8 oz each) light cream cheese, at room temperature
1 ¼ cups packed brown sugar
1 tbsp vanilla
2 cups light sour cream (not fat free)
2 cups canned pure pumpkin (not pumpkin pie filling)
2 tsp ground cinnamon
½ tsp each ground nutmeg, ground ginger, and ground allspice
Light whipped topping (optional)

Makes 12-16 servings

- To make crust, combine graham crumbs, brown sugar, and cinnamon in a medium bowl. Add melted butter and stir using a fork until crumbs are moistened. Spray a 9-inch springform pan with cooking spray. Press crumb mixture firmly and evenly over bottom of pan (not sides). Refrigerate for 1 hour.

- Meanwhile, to make filling, combine evaporated milk and orange juice concentrate in a small saucepan. Sprinkle gelatine over top and let stand for 5 minutes. Whisk gelatine into milk mixture and cook over medium-high heat, stirring constantly, until mixture just starts to boil. Remove from heat immediately and let cool while crust is setting.

- Beat together cream cheese, brown sugar, and vanilla on high speed of electric mixer until smooth. Add sour cream, pumpkin, and spices. Beat again on medium speed until well blended. Add milk mixture and beat again until well mixed.

- Pour batter over crust and smooth top. Cover with plastic wrap and refrigerate for at least 8 hours (overnight is best). To serve, run a sharp, thin knife around edge of pan to loosen cake. Remove sides of pan. Serve individual slices with light whipped topping, if desired.

PER SERVING (BASED ON 16 SERVINGS)

calories	total fat	saturated fat	protein	carbohydrate	fiber	cholesterol	sodium
227	7.8 g	4.6 g	6 g	33 g	1.5 g	24 mg	184 mg

I had a soft drink while catching up on the ironing. It was soda pressing.

Loaf Potion #9

Cranberry-orange loaf with zucchini, carrots, and walnuts

Meet the *loaf* of your life! A spellbinding combination of ingredients ensures love at first bite.

1 ½ cups all-purpose flour
⅔ cup oat bran
½ cup lightly packed brown sugar
1 tbsp baking powder
1 tsp baking soda
1 tsp ground cinnamon
½ tsp salt
⅔ cup chopped dried cranberries
⅓ cup chopped walnuts or chopped pecans
1 cup low-fat plain yogurt
3 tbsp vegetable oil
2 eggs
2 tbsp frozen orange juice concentrate, thawed
2 tsp grated orange zest
1 cup each grated carrots and grated, unpeeled zucchini

- Preheat oven to 350°F. Spray a 9 x 5-inch loaf pan with cooking spray and set aside.

- In a large bowl, combine flour, oat bran, brown sugar, baking powder, baking soda, cinnamon, and salt. Make sure you get all of the lumps out of the brown sugar. Stir in cranberries and nuts.

- In a medium bowl, whisk together yogurt, oil, eggs, orange juice concentrate, and orange zest. Stir in carrots and zucchini. Add wet ingredients to dry ingredients and mix just until dry ingredients are moistened.

- Spoon batter into prepared pan and smooth top. Bake on middle oven rack for 45 to 50 minutes, or until loaf is lightly browned and a toothpick inserted in center of loaf comes out clean.

- Cool loaf in pan on a wire rack for 10 minutes. Remove loaf from pan and cool completely on rack. Cover with plastic wrap and store at room temperature or in the refrigerator. To serve, cut loaf into 8 thick slices, then cut each slice in half. (This is easier than trying to cut 16 thin slices!)

Makes 1 large loaf, 16 slices

		PER SLICE					
calories	total fat	saturated fat	protein	carbohydrate	fiber	cholesterol	sodium
157	5.3 g	0.8 g	4 g	25 g	1.7 g	28 mg	268 mg

Pop Quizine

When is a nut not a nut? When it's a seed, like a cashew! The cashew "nut" is a member of...

a) the tuber family
b) the Nutella family
c) the poison ivy family
d) The Partridge Family

Answer: (c) The cashew used to be called the blister nut, named for the brown oil (actually a toxic fluid called cardol) between the inner and outer shell that blisters human skin. No reason to worry though—as consumers, we're never exposed to this oil.

Funky Factoid

Cranberries, hailed for their antibiotic effect in fighting urinary tract infections, are sometimes called bounce berries by growers in the Northeast. Though the origin of this term is lost to legend, here's the part of the story most agree upon: John Webb, a 19th-century New Jersey farmer who had lost one of his legs, was unable to lug all of his berries down from the hayloft where he stored them. Instead, he decided to pour them down the stairs, and discovered that the mushy, overripe berries would stick to the stairs, but the perfectly ripe, plump berries would bounce down to the floor below. To this day, leading cranberry producers like Ocean Spray separate their berries by bouncing them over a four-inch barrier.

Cooking TIP

The thick, creamy yogurt is the key to making this dessert taste rich and "non-diet-like." We recommend Dannon La Crème yogurt in plain strawberry and plain vanilla flavors. They're sold in small containers, so you'll have to buy a few of them. To lower the fat and carbohydrate count of this dessert, you can use low-fat, sugar-free yogurt instead, but try to find a brand that's really thick and creamy. If it's thin, the dessert won't hold its shape and it won't look nearly as pretty either!

THE E FILES

Step right up! Step right up to one of the most effortless exercise programs ever designed by man! Step right up…to 10,000 steps a day! A very popular and relatively painless first step to losing weight is by snapping on a nifty, inexpensive gadget called a pedometer to count the number of strides you take in a day. The secret power of the pedometer lies in its ability to motivate. When it's clipped to your waistband, you're reminded to get moving. Plus, it's satisfying to see the ticker ticking away. It's like getting a pat on the back—even if you're just walking down the hall to the restroom! Set your goal at a minimum of 10,000 steps—that's about five miles, which may sound like a lot, but it includes the steps you take during the regular course of a day as well as additional physical activity. The good news is, the more steps you take, the less you'll need to cut back at mealtime. However, if you try eating 75% of what you normally would in combination with stepping it up a notch, you're bound to lose weight at a safe rate of one to two pounds per week. What a cinch! Taking a step in the right direction is as easy as walking while talking on a cordless phone, strolling through the airport while waiting for a flight, or finding a lunch spot that's a 10-minute walk away. To accelerate your weight loss, step on it!

Strawberry Snortcakes

Mini strawberry shortcakes with creamy yogurt

You'll *oink* these down in no time! Here's the fastest, easiest, and yummiest way to make strawberry shortcakes. Choose this dessert when you want something that looks fancy and impressive, but that's really a cinch to make.

Oink! Oink! That looks berry delicious!

2½ cups sliced fresh strawberries
1 tbsp granulated sugar
6 prepared mini sponge cakes (0.8 oz each)
2 cups thick, creamy strawberry yogurt (see tip in margin)
½ cup thick, creamy vanilla yogurt (see tip in margin)
Mint leaves for garnish (optional)

- Combine strawberries and sugar and let stand at room temperature for 1 hour.

- To assemble dessert, place one sponge cake on each serving plate. Spoon a few sliced strawberries over cake. Top with ⅓ cup strawberry yogurt, followed by ⅓ cup sliced strawberries. Spoon vanilla yogurt on top of strawberries, like a dollop of whipped cream. Garnish with mint leaf, if desired. Serve immediately.

Tip: Assemble this dessert right before you serve it. Don't assemble it in advance, or it'll be soggy.

Makes 6 servings

PER SERVING

calories	total fat	saturated fat	protein	carbohydrate	fiber	cholesterol	sodium
226	6.2 g	2.9 g	6 g	39 g	1.6 g	32 mg	227 mg

Vegetables are a must on a diet.
I suggest carrot cake, zucchini bread,
and pumpkin pie.

Jim Davis, "Garfield"

Rhapsody in Blueberry

Blueberry crisp with oatmeal crumb topping

This *classical* dessert gets jazzed up with a symphony of flavors and textures that'll make your mouth water and your heart sing!

Filling
6 cups fresh blueberries
⅓ cup granulated sugar
2 tbsp cornstarch
2 tbsp freshly squeezed lemon juice
2 tsp grated lemon zest

Topping
1 cup quick-cooking rolled oats (not instant)
½ cup all-purpose flour
⅓ cup lightly packed brown sugar
½ tsp ground cinnamon
¼ cup butter, melted
2 tbsp apple juice or orange juice

1 cup low-fat vanilla yogurt or light whipped topping (optional)

- Preheat oven to 375°F. Spray a 9 x 13-inch baking dish with cooking spray. Add blueberries. Sprinkle blueberries with granulated sugar, cornstarch, lemon juice, and lemon zest. Mix well and set aside.

- To make topping, combine oats, flour, brown sugar, and cinnamon in a medium bowl. Add melted butter and juice. Using a fork, stir until mixture resembles coarse crumbs. Sprinkle crumb mixture evenly over coated blueberries.

- Bake for 30 minutes, until blueberries are bubbling around edge of pan and crumb topping is golden brown. Cool for 10 minutes before serving (it's hot!). Serve with a dollop of low-fat vanilla yogurt or light whipped topping, if desired. It's also tasty with a small scoop of vanilla frozen yogurt.

Tip: Make this recipe when fresh blueberries are in season. It just isn't the same when you make it with frozen blueberries.

Makes 8 servings

			PER SERVING				
calories	total fat	saturated fat	protein	carbohydrate	fiber	cholesterol	sodium
256	6.9 g	3.7 g	3 g	48 g	4.4 g	16 mg	12 mg

"SAY IT AIN'T SO!"

Talk about bad food combining! Don'tcha just love it when manufacturers mix together a few of our favorite food vices to launch what was already an indulgence into a whole new caloric stratosphere? As if your thighs really need a cheese-stuffed pizza crust. Or chocolate-chip cookie dough ice cream. Or gravy-covered, cheese-laden French fries. In most cases, the two-for-one whammy easily doubles your calories, bad fats, and pant size. They should really make it a *three-for-one* deal and include a prescription for cholesterol-lowering medication. Use common sense, practice moderation, and remember: Those who indulge, bulge!

Dig the Berried Treasure

Yo, ho, ho and a lot of yum! Berries not only satisfy our sugar cravings, but also are a treasure trove of amazing, health-promoting compounds. For instance, a cup of strawberries offers nearly double your daily vitamin C requirements and also contains a potent anticancer agent called ellagic acid. Both blueberries and cranberries help stave off urinary tract infections, and blueberries contain more antioxidants (compounds that ward off cancer, heart disease, and other age-related ills) than nearly any other fruit. In fact, feeding blueberry extracts to aging lab rats markedly improved their memory and balance. Imagine what blueberries could do for you? You'll remember where you left your keys, and you won't topple over trying to pick them up! All berries are nuggets of fiber, your best fat-loss buddy, and fresh berries contain live enzymes that improve digestion and act like spark plugs for your cells. Plus, they're low on the Glycemic Index, so they won't spike your blood sugar. You're making a big mistake if you cut *these* carbs out of your diet. They're as good as gold!

Drinking hard liquor is whiskey business.

Girl-Guy Cookies

A thin and chewy cross between a peanut butter cookie and a gingersnap

Dingdong! These peanut butter-gingersnap cookies are so scrumptious, you could easily make a fortune selling them door-to-door. Scouts honor!

¾ cup all-purpose flour
⅓ cup whole wheat flour
1 tsp baking soda
2 tsp ground cinnamon, divided
½ tsp ground ginger
¼ tsp each ground allspice and salt
2 tbsp granulated sugar
1 cup brown sugar
⅓ cup light peanut butter
3 tbsp butter, softened
2 tbsp molasses
1 egg
1 tsp vanilla

Guys love these!

Manly, yes. But I like them, too!

- Preheat oven to 350°F. (See tip in margin regarding oven temperature). Spray a large cookie sheet with cooking spray and set aside.

- In a medium bowl, stir together both flours, baking soda, 1 tsp cinnamon, ginger, allspice, and salt. Set aside. Combine granulated sugar and 1 tsp cinnamon in a small bowl. Set aside.

- In another medium bowl, beat together brown sugar, peanut butter, and butter on medium speed of electric mixer for about 1 minute. Add molasses, egg, and vanilla. Beat again until smooth.

- Using a wooden spoon, stir flour mixture into peanut butter mixture. You will be making a stiff dough. Using your hands, shape dough into 1½-inch balls. Roll balls in reserved cinnamon-sugar mixture. Place on cookie sheet at least 2 inches apart (they spread a lot while baking). Flatten cookies slightly using a fork.

- Bake cookies for 7 minutes. They may appear undercooked, but that's okay. Remove cookies from oven and immediately transfer from pan to a wire rack to cool.

Makes 20 cookies

PER COOKIE

calories	total fat	saturated fat	protein	carbohydrate	fiber	cholesterol	sodium
108	3.4 g	1.6 g	2 g	17 g	0.8 g	15 mg	100 mg

Cooking TIP

It's really important that your oven is properly preheated before you put the cookies in to bake. An oven thermometer is a good investment—ovens are notoriously inaccurate! Don't overbake the cookies or they'll be very dry. You want them chewy in the middle, not crispy. Seven minutes goes by very quickly, so don't start sorting socks or coloring your hair while the cookies are baking (promise?).

Barking Up the Right Tree

One of the oldest spices used by man, cinnamon is the inner bark of a tropical evergreen tree. After it's harvested, the bark curls as it dries, then it's cut into sticks or ground into powder.

Sprinkling cinnamon on your oatmeal or whole-grain toast may give you more than just a flavor boost: Research shows that cinnamon not only stimulates digestion, but it also stimulates the activity of insulin, helping the body process sugars much more efficiently. That's sweet news for diabetics and for those at risk for type 2 diabetes. By adding a half teaspoon to their daily diets, people with diabetes may help stave off complications related to impaired glucose metabolism, including fatigue, blurred vision, and increased risk of kidney failure. And if your taste buds crave adventure, consider the following little-known cinnamon factoid: In the fourth century AD, a Chinese Taoist alchemist wrote that if one ingested cinnamon along with toad brains for seven years, that person could walk on water and avoid aging, and even death! Interestingly, this hypothesis has not yet been tested by modern science. Wanna sign up for the clinical trials?

Sign at dairy farm:
You can whip our cream
but you can't beat our milk.

RETURN TO SLENDER

Patience is a virtue—especially when it comes to cooking heart-healthy oatmeal. The slower it cooks, the better it is for you. Instant, flavored oatmeal (the just-add-water variety) might be quick and easy, but you pay a price for that convenience. In order for your oatmeal to be ready in a flash, the oats are cut thinly and some of the good stuff (fiber and nutrients) is stripped out. Fortunately, you can beef up instant oatmeal's resume by adding your own sources of fiber. Fiber is like a sugar stopper, slowing its absorption into the bloodstream so you don't get the highs and lows that cause intense hunger and overeating later on. Some good "stir-ins" are berries, raisins, or chopped apples. Ground flaxseed and slivered nuts will add fiber, good fats, and flavor. If you have time, choose slow-cooking oats (ready in 15 minutes)—they haven't been processed to death. Even better is old-fashioned, steel-cut oatmeal (sometimes called Irish oatmeal). Nothing's been stripped from it—the nutrients and fiber are all intact. Stir in some plain yogurt for a creamier texture and a hit of calcium and protein. Now your oats are *oat*standing!

It was an emotional wedding. Even the cake was in tiers!

A Bundt in the Oven

Upside-down blueberry streusel coffee cake

Oh, baby! Whaaaaa smells so yummy? It's the tastiest treat from here to *maternity*—the mother of all coffee cakes! This easy-to-bake, scrumptious cake is guaranteed to *ward* off hunger and *pacify* a growing tummy.

Streusel Topping
¼ cup chopped pecans
3 tbsp all-purpose flour
2 tbsp brown sugar
1 tbsp butter, melted

Cake
2 cups Bisquick baking mix
1 cup all-purpose flour
1 cup granulated sugar
1 tsp ground cinnamon
¾ cup lemon yogurt (see tip below)
2 eggs
⅓ cup 1% milk
¼ cup vegetable oil
2 tsp grated lemon zest
1 tsp vanilla
2 cups fresh blueberries

This baby's ready to come out!

- Preheat oven to 350°F. Spray a bundt cake pan with cooking spray and dust lightly with flour. Set aside.

- To prepare streusel topping, combine all streusel ingredients in a small bowl and mix well using a fork. Set aside.

- Combine baking mix, flour, sugar, and cinnamon in a large bowl. In a medium bowl, whisk together yogurt, eggs, milk, oil, lemon zest, and vanilla. Add wet ingredients to dry ingredients and mix just until dry ingredients are moistened. Batter will be thick. Gently fold in blueberries.

- Spoon batter evenly into prepared cake pan. Sprinkle streusel topping evenly over batter. Bake for 40 to 45 minutes, or until a toothpick inserted in center of cake comes out clean. Cool cake in pan on a wire rack. Loosen edges using a knife or small spatula. Invert cake onto serving plate and then flip cake over, so the streusel is on top.

Tip: If you can't find lemon yogurt, use plain yogurt and add 2 tbsp freshly squeezed lemon juice plus 1 tbsp sugar to wet ingredients.

Makes 16 servings

			PER SERVING				
calories	total fat	saturated fat	protein	carbohydrate	fiber	cholesterol	sodium
228	8.5 g	1.8 g	4 g	36 g	1.5 g	29 mg	176 mg

Shocklate Cheesecake

Rich-tasting, double-chocolate cheesecake with a chocolate brownie crust

1 box (about 1 lb) low-fat brownie mix
   (such as Betty Crocker Fudge Brownies)
2 cups 1% cottage cheese
1 cup light sour cream (not fat free)
1 pkg (8 oz) light cream cheese,
   at room temperature
1 cup granulated sugar
1/3 cup unsweetened cocoa powder
1/4 cup all-purpose flour
6 oz semi-sweet (not unsweetened) chocolate squares,
   melted and cooled slightly (see tip below)
1 cup fat-free egg substitute or 4 whole eggs
1 tsp vanilla
Chocolate sauce for drizzling (optional)

Electrify your guests with this shockingly good cheesecake! It's chock-full of chocolate and its rich, decadent taste will send chills up your spine!

Only 9 grams of fat? Shocking!

- Spray a 10-inch springform pan with cooking spray. Prepare brownies according to package directions, baking in springform pan instead of regular cake pan. Brownies should bake in about 20 minutes. Remove pan from oven and reset temperature to 325°F. Set brownie crust aside to cool slightly while you prepare filling.

- To make filling, whirl cottage cheese, sour cream, and cream cheese in a blender until perfectly smooth. Scrape out mixture into a large mixing bowl. In a small bowl, sift together sugar, cocoa powder, and flour. Gradually add sugar mixture to cream-cheese mixture and beat on medium speed of electric mixer until well blended. Add melted chocolate and beat again, scraping down sides of bowl as necessary. Add egg substitute and vanilla. Beat just until eggs are incorporated into batter.

- Before pouring batter over crust, lightly grease sides of pan. This will help prevent cheesecake from cracking as it cools. Pour batter over brownie crust and smooth top. Place on middle oven rack and bake for 60 to 70 minutes. Cake will be puffed up and center will jiggle slightly when pan is shaken. Turn off oven, open oven door halfway, and leave cake in oven to cool for 1 hour. Remove from oven, run knife around edge of pan to loosen cake from sides, and cool completely. Cover with plastic wrap and refrigerate overnight.

- To serve, remove sides of pan, slice thinly (it's rich!), and drizzle chocolate sauce over individual pieces, if desired.

Makes 16 servings

PER SERVING

calories	total fat	saturated fat	protein	carbohydrate	fiber	cholesterol	sodium
291	9.3 g	4.6 g	10 g	44 g	1.3 g	13 mg	208 mg

Cooking TIP

To melt chocolate, place chocolate squares in a microwave-safe bowl and microwave on medium-low power until chocolate is melted. For 6 squares, it should take about 3 minutes, depending on the strength of your microwave. Be careful not to burn chocolate! Remove bowl from microwave and stir chocolate until smooth. Cool slightly before using in recipe. Is your cheesecake all that it's cracked up to be? More often than not, a baked cheesecake will crack when it's cooling. Talk about frustrating, especially when you follow instructions to the letter and still get cracks the size of the Grand Canyon! Don't panic if your cake does the splits after it's baked—it'll still taste terrific. Before serving, cover the cracks with sliced strawberries and a drizzle of chocolate syrup, and no one will know the difference.

Fat or Fiction?

If you're going for the gold, you want carbs in your corner. They supply the quick-burning fuel you need for energy, powering both your muscles and your brain. Cut them from your diet roster and you'll feel sluggish and unable to perform at your maximum intensity. What's more, without proper fuel from carbohydrates, your metabolism will take a nosedive. That's because your body has to turn to protein to create energy, diverting it from its primary job, which is to repair muscle and build other body tissues. So, you end up losing lean body mass, and that means you'll burn fewer calories at rest. Unfortunately, popular low-carb diets start you off at daily intakes as low as 20 grams of carbs—the equivalent of eating a weensy apple or a puny salad. That might prepare you for the Gerbil Olympics, but not for serious competition. You need at least 30 to 60 grams of carbs in just one post-game meal to replenish the glucose (fuel) you used up scoring the winning goal in overtime or lunging to return 120-m.p.h. tennis serves. But before you reach for that celebratory chocolate donut, realize that carbs that do a body proud aren't fries and white bread or cookies and pretzels. They're unrefined carbs like veggies, fruits, and whole grains. For your personal best, put *good* carbs to the test!

Little Miss Muffin Tops

Oatmeal, blueberry, and banana muffin tops

Elaine from *Seinfeld* made muffin tops famous. Your kids will love them! Look for muffin-top pans (sometimes called muffin-cap pans) in specialty bakeware stores. You may never make muffins in regular pans again!

You've never tried muffin like it!

- 1 cup quick-cooking rolled oats (not instant)
- 1 cup all-purpose flour
- ½ cup oat bran
- ½ cup granulated sugar
- ⅓ cup flaked coconut (optional)
- 1 tsp each baking powder and ground cinnamon
- ½ tsp each baking soda and salt
- 1 cup mashed ripe bananas
- ½ cup low-fat plain yogurt
- 3 tbsp butter, melted
- 1 egg
- 1 tsp vanilla
- 1 cup fresh blueberries

- Preheat oven to 375°F. Spray two 6-cup muffin-top pans with cooking spray and set aside.

- In a large bowl, combine oats, flour, oat bran, sugar, coconut (if using), baking powder, cinnamon, baking soda, and salt. Mix well.

- In a medium bowl, whisk together bananas, yogurt, butter, egg, and vanilla. Add wet ingredients to dry ingredients and mix just until dry ingredients are moistened. Batter will be thick. Gently fold in blueberries.

- Divide batter evenly among muffin-top cups. Bake for 12 to 14 minutes, or until muffin tops are puffed up and a toothpick inserted in center comes out clean. Remove muffin tops from pans and cool on a wire rack.

Makes 12 large muffin tops

PER MUFFIN TOP

calories	total fat	saturated fat	protein	carbohydrate	fiber	cholesterol	sodium
169	4.4 g	2.2 g	4 g	31 g	2.5 g	26 mg	108 mg

La Vida Mocha

Flourless chocolate cake with a hint of coffee flavor

½ cup evaporated 2% milk
¾ cup packed brown sugar
1 tbsp instant coffee granules
3 oz semi-sweet chocolate squares
2 tbsp butter
½ cup unsweetened cocoa powder
¼ cup light sour cream (not fat free)
2 egg yolks
1 tsp vanilla
5 egg whites
¼ tsp salt
Icing (confectioner's) sugar for
    dusting top of cake
3 cups sliced fresh strawberries
2 cups light whipped topping or
    low-fat vanilla frozen yogurt
Mint leaves for garnish (optional)

She bakes! She bakes! But there's no flour in her cake, her cake! Unlike traditional cakes made with flour, this cake is flat, very moist, and almost fudge-like. Your taste buds will go loca for the mocha!

- Preheat oven to 350°F. Spray a 9-inch springform pan with cooking spray. Cut a circle of wax paper or parchment paper to fit bottom of pan and place in pan. Spray paper with cooking spray. Set aside.

- In a small saucepan, whisk together evaporated milk, brown sugar, and coffee granules and cook over medium heat until mixture is almost boiling and sugar is completely dissolved. Remove from heat. Add chocolate squares and butter and stir until melted. Transfer chocolate mixture to a mixing bowl and let cool for 5 minutes. It will still be warm.

- Add cocoa powder, sour cream, egg yolks, and vanilla to chocolate mixture and beat on medium speed of electric mixer until smooth. Set aside.

- Thoroughly clean and dry the beaters. Place egg whites in a deep glass or metal mixing bowl and add salt. Beat on high speed until stiff peaks form. Fold egg whites into chocolate mixture in three additions until no white streaks remain. Do not use the mixer for this step! Pour mixture into prepared pan. Bake for 30 to 35 minutes, or until cake has risen and top feels dry to touch.

- Remove cake from oven and cool on a wire rack. It will fall dramatically as it cools, but that's what it's supposed to do, so don't worry! When cake is cool, run a thin, sharp knife around edge of pan and remove sides. Cover and refrigerate until cold, at least 3 hours. To serve, invert cake onto a large plate, remove wax paper, then invert it again onto a decorative serving plate. Dust with icing sugar and serve small slices of cake with fresh strawberries, whipped topping, and mint leaves, if desired.

Makes 12 servings

PER SERVING							
calories	total fat	saturated fat	protein	carbohydrate	fiber	cholesterol	sodium
187	7.2 g	4.5 g	4 g	27 g	2.5 g	43 mg	95 mg

Research tells us that fourteen out of every ten individuals like chocolate.

Sandra Boynton

Don't Be Afraid of the Dark

The proof is in the chocolate pudding! Not only is chocolate good for the soul, but scientists have confirmed that it's also good for the heart. Chocolate is rich in flavonoids, the natural antioxidants that are also credited with making red wine heart-healthy. Does that mean you should run to the supermarket and load your cart with Kit Kats and Milky Ways for "medicinal purposes"? *Whoa*, Henry! It's only the high-quality dark stuff that's good for you. In fact, the more cocoa in dark chocolate, the better for you. Sorry to burst your Aero bubble, but research published in *Nature* found that adding milk to chocolate seems to cancel out its antioxidant properties. Plus, the cheaper milk-chocolate bars usually contain partially hydrogenated oils (trans fats) and a lot more sugar than their darker cousins. According to researchers, one ounce per day is the heart-healthy target. Eaten slowly and mindfully, that should satisfy even the most serious chocolate cravings. Psst. One of the best-kept secrets on the market is the Dove Dark Chocolate bar. It's made with a specially processed cocoa and actually has four times the flavonoids of an apple. Could a Dove a day keep the doctor away?

Forget all those fitness fads. Walking is definitely the best exercise for you!

Bugsy's Fitness Emporium

A Bran New World

Scrumptious bran muffins with sweet potato and currants

Who says bran has to be bland? By keeping up with *currant* events, we've discovered a *bran* new way to load up on flavor and nutrition. *Muffin* compares!

1 cup cooked, mashed sweet potato (about 1 medium potato—see tip in margin)
1 cup buttermilk
1/2 cup packed brown sugar
3 tbsp vegetable oil
2 eggs
2 tsp grated orange zest
4 cups Bran Flakes cereal
1 1/4 cups all-purpose flour
1/2 cup dried currants
1/2 cup chopped pecans or chopped walnuts (optional—see tip in margin)
2 tsp baking powder
1 tsp baking soda
1 tsp ground cinnamon
1/2 tsp salt
1/4 tsp each ground nutmeg and ground allspice

At last! The discovery we've been waiting for!

Christopher Columbus

- Preheat oven to 375°F. Spray a 12-cup muffin tin with cooking spray and set aside.

- In a large bowl, whisk together sweet potato, buttermilk, brown sugar, vegetable oil, eggs, and orange zest. Add Bran Flakes and mix well.

- In another large bowl, combine flour, currants, nuts (if using), baking powder, baking soda, cinnamon, salt, nutmeg, and allspice. Add wet ingredients to dry ingredients and mix just until dry ingredients are moistened. Batter will be thick.

- Divide batter evenly among muffin cups. There's lots of batter, so fill the cups right up! Bake for 17 to 18 minutes, or until muffins are golden brown and a toothpick inserted in center of muffin comes out clean. Remove muffins from pan and cool slightly on a wire rack. Serve warm.

Makes 12 muffins

PER MUFFIN

calories	total fat	saturated fat	protein	carbohydrate	fiber	cholesterol	sodium
191	4.8 g	0.9 g	4 g	35 g	3.2 g	36 mg	363 mg

You're Pudding Me On

Warm banana bread pudding
with chocolate chips and pecans

It's foolproof!

You'll be a super *duper* when
you fool your friends with this
lightened-up banana bread pudding.
No one will believe it's lower in fat
and contains multigrain bread!
Better hide the recipe, *jest* in case!

**10 to 12 large slices multigrain
  bread (about 1 lb)**
2 cups 2% milk
2 cups mashed ripe bananas
1 cup low-fat vanilla yogurt
**1 cup fat-free egg substitute or
  4 whole eggs, lightly beaten**
3/4 cup packed brown sugar
1 tsp each vanilla and ground cinnamon
3/4 cup semi-sweet chocolate chips
2/3 cup chopped pecans

- Break bread into 1-inch pieces and place in a 9 x 13-inch glass
  baking dish that has been sprayed with cooking spray. Dish
  should be full.

- In a large bowl, whisk together milk, bananas, yogurt, egg
  substitute, brown sugar, vanilla, and cinnamon. Pour mixture over
  bread. Using your hands (yeah, it's a little messy), mix bread
  cubes with milk mixture so that all pieces are coated. Let stand
  for 15 minutes while you preheat the oven to 350°F.

- Just before popping dish into oven, mix in most of the chocolate
  chips and pecans, saving a little of each to sprinkle on top.
  Now, go ahead and sprinkle them on top!

- Bake for 50 to 55 minutes, until pudding is puffed up and
  golden brown and center is set. Remove from oven and let stand
  for 10 minutes before serving. You can cut the dessert into
  squares and serve it on a plate or spoon it into dessert bowls.
  If you feel like splurging, serve the sliced version with a small
  scoop of vanilla ice cream or frozen yogurt, and the spooned
  version with a drizzle of real whipping cream.

Time for the bar exam! Even though energy
bars might give off an aura of health, don't
go nuts eating them. Once in a while,
they're fine. But remember, in scientific
terms, "energy" means calories. And that's
exactly what you're getting—up to 350
calories, in some cases. Many energy bars
are really just glorified chocolate bars.
When you scour the fine print on the label,
you'll often uncover some not-so-good-for-you
ingredients near the top of the list, including
the usual suspects like glucose/fructose
(sugar!) and hydrogenated vegetable oil.
If a vitamin/mineral supplement is what
you're after, you don't need to pay top
dollar for it in the form of an energy bar.
The cheap, synthetic vitamins in some of
these bars might be more of a burden than a
blessing to your body if you go overboard.
When you need a snack and you're called
to the bar, look for those where natural,
high-fiber foods, such as oats, nuts, seeds,
and dried fruit are the main ingredients.
The final verdict: Eating an energy bar is
better than eating a bag of chips, but there's
a lot more nutrition packed in a handful of
almonds and an apple—bar none!

"SAY IT AIN'T SO!"

Bless me father, for I have *cin*namon buns!
Okay, okay. Just admit it. There you were,
just mindin' your own business at the mall
food court, nowhere near sniffing distance
(or so you thought), when all of a sudden
that devilishly irresistible aroma wafted over
and led you straight into temptation.
Oh well, it's just a little ol' harmless snack to
tide you over 'til dinner, right? The true
confession: This sinfully delicious pastry's
670 calories may stop you from fitting
between the Pearly Gates! Better split one
with a friend, and live by this
commandment: If you're praying for buns of
steel, don't covet buns of cinnamon!

Makes 12 servings

PER SERVING

calories	total fat	saturated fat	protein	carbohydrate	fiber	cholesterol	sodium
276	8.7 g	2.2 g	9 g	45 g	4 g	3 mg	221 mg

Naughty Biscotti

Lemon, cranberry, and pistachio biscotti

Let's go skinny dipping!

If you were to make a list of the tastiest low-calorie snacks ever, and you checked that list twice, you'd discover this biscotti's not naughty—it's nice! Nice to your waistline and nice to share with a good friend over a hot cup of tea.

- Preheat oven to 350°F. Spray a cookie sheet with cooking spray and set aside.

- Combine flour, baking powder, and salt in a medium bowl. Set aside.

- In a large bowl, beat together both sugars, eggs, egg white, butter, lemon zest, lemon juice, and vanilla on medium speed of electric mixer. Stir in flour mixture using wooden spoon, just until blended. Dough will be thick. Add cranberries and pistachios and mix well.

- Divide dough in half. On prepared cookie sheet, using lightly floured or greased hands, shape each half into an 8 x 3 x 3/4-inch loaf, placing loaves 3 inches apart.

- Bake on middle oven rack for 20 minutes. Remove loaves from cookie sheet and cool on a wire rack for 15 minutes. Reduce oven temperature to 275°F. Transfer loaves to a cutting board. Using a very sharp knife, cut each loaf crosswise on a diagonal into 9 slices. (You'll have some scraps from the end pieces, so go ahead and eat them. Everyone knows that scraps have zero calories.) Place slices, cut-side down, on same cookie sheet. Return to oven and bake for 8 minutes. Turn biscotti over and bake 8 more minutes. Cool completely on wire rack. Biscotti will harden as they cool.

2 cups all-purpose flour
1 1/2 tsp baking powder
1/4 tsp salt
1/3 cup granulated sugar
1/3 cup lightly packed brown sugar
2 eggs
1 egg white
2 tbsp butter, softened
1 1/2 tbsp grated lemon zest
1 tbsp freshly squeezed lemon juice
1 tsp vanilla
1/2 cup chopped dried cranberries
1/2 cup chopped pistachios

Tip: You can store these cookies for a month in the freezer in a resealable plastic bag.

Makes 18 biscotti

PER COOKIE							
calories	total fat	saturated fat	protein	carbohydrate	fiber	cholesterol	sodium
96	3.2 g	1.1 g	2 g	15 g	0.7 g	24 mg	77 mg

Biscotti, twice-baked Italian biscuits (cookies) served in hip coffeehouses, were part of Christopher Columbus's food supply on his long voyages because of their mold-resistant properties. In fact, biscotti have a shelf life of fourteen hundred and ninety-two years (give or take)!

J-Lo Pudding

Extra chocolaty, extra creamy,
old-fashioned chocolate pudding

Marc our words: If you've ever *Ben Afflected* by intense chocolate cravings, this rich chocolate pudding will leave you satisfied! It's the perfect marriage of dreamy and creamy—there's no *groom* for improvement!

½ cup packed brown sugar
⅓ cup unsweetened cocoa powder
3 tbsp cornstarch
1 can (12 oz) evaporated 2% milk
1¾ cups light (5%) cream
1 egg
1 tsp vanilla

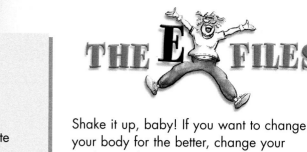

> I do, I do, I do, love this pudding!

- Combine brown sugar, cocoa powder, and cornstarch in a medium, non-stick saucepan. Whisk in milk and cream. Cook and continue whisking over medium heat until mixture is bubbly and has thickened. Don't rush it by cranking up the heat. You don't want the pudding to burn. Remove from heat but leave burner on. Reduce heat to low.

- In a medium bowl, beat egg using a fork. Add about 1 cup of the hot pudding mixture to the beaten egg and whisk quickly until well blended. Pour egg mixture into pot with remaining pudding and return to heat. Don't let it boil. Cook and stir for 1 more minute.

- Remove pudding from heat. Stir in vanilla. Spoon pudding into individual dessert dishes or a larger serving bowl. Press plastic wrap over surface of pudding to prevent skin from forming on top. Refrigerate until cold and set, at least 1½ hours for small bowls and 4 hours for larger bowl. Tastes great alone or with sliced bananas, strawberries, or raspberries. Best if eaten within 1 day.

Option: For a more "grown-up" taste, add 2 tbsp coffee-flavored liqueur, such as Kahlúa, when you add the vanilla.

Makes 6 servings

PER SERVING

calories	total fat	saturated fat	protein	carbohydrate	fiber	cholesterol	sodium
234	6.9 g	2.9 g	11 g	34 g	1.4 g	68 mg	156 mg

176

THE E FILES

Shake it up, baby! If you want to change your body for the better, change your workout. Often. Variety might be just what your body needs if you aren't seeing improvements in your fitness level. When you follow the same exercise routine over and over again, your body adapts, then gets bored, and pretty soon it's stuck in a rut. What's needed is a new challenge, a little stimulation, a few curves thrown your body's way. Try varying the exercises you do and the order in which you do them— even how often you exercise and how frequently you rest. Change up the weights you use and the number of repetitions. When you use your muscles and ligaments in a completely different way, they'll thank you with increased strength and better shape. Plus, you'll be amazed at how much you enjoy doing something new. If you've been sweatin' to the oldies for years, try kickboxing. If you've been faithful to yoga, try Pilates. If you always run on a treadmill, try running through your neighborhood. Or, be like Janet—she used to run off at the mouth, but now she jumps to conclusions!

Hershey's Kisses are appropriately named because...

a) the machine that makes them looks like it's kissing the conveyor belt
b) they're Gene Simmons's favorite candy
c) the foil they're wrapped in is puckered
d) they were introduced on Valentine's Day

Answer: (a) Milton Hershey began mass-producing his famous confection in 1907. Today, Hershey's makes more than 80 million Kisses daily at its chocolate factories.

Cashew: The sound a nut makes when it sneezes.

I'm Dreaming of a White Chili

Creamy and delicious tomatoless chicken chili

Unlike the ones you used to know, this dramatically different chili is an enticing blend of mostly white ingredients. Bing would sing of its zest and zing!

2 tsp olive oil
4 boneless, skinless chicken breasts (about 1½ lbs), cut into 1-inch cubes
1½ cups chopped onions
1 cup diced celery
2 tsp minced garlic
1 tbsp chili powder
2 tsp each ground cumin and dried oregano
½ tsp ground coriander
¼ cup all-purpose flour
3 cups chicken broth
1 can (12 oz) evaporated 2% milk
2 cans (15.5 oz each) navy beans, drained and rinsed
1 can (4.5 oz) chopped green chilies (look near taco kits)
½ tsp each salt and ground white or black pepper
¼ tsp cayenne pepper
1 cup light sour cream
2 tbsp minced fresh cilantro
Shredded light Monterey Jack cheese and chopped green onions for garnish (optional)

- Heat olive oil in a large, non-stick soup pot over medium-high heat. Add chicken and cook for 3 to 4 minutes, stirring constantly, until no longer pink. Add onions, celery, and garlic. Cook and stir for 4 to 5 more minutes, until vegetables begin to soften.

- Add chili powder, cumin, oregano, and coriander to chicken. Mix well and cook for 1 more minute. Add flour and stir until chicken is well coated. Stir in broth and evaporated milk. Bring mixture to a boil. Reduce heat to medium and simmer, uncovered, for 5 minutes.

- Add navy beans, green chilies, salt, pepper, and cayenne pepper to chicken mixture. Reduce heat to medium-low. Cover and simmer for 15 minutes, stirring occasionally.

- Remove chili from heat. Stir in sour cream and cilantro. Ladle chili into serving bowls and top with shredded cheese and a few chopped green onions, if desired.

Makes 6 to 8 servings

PER SERVING (BASED ON 8 SERVINGS)

calories	total fat	saturated fat	protein	carbohydrate	fiber	cholesterol	sodium
283	3.9 g	1.2 g	32 g	30 g	8.1 g	63 mg	770 mg

Eating eggs will make my cholesterol levels skyrocket.

Fat or Fiction?

Looks like the hype about eggs and cholesterol isn't all it's cracked up to be. Scientists are taking a closer look at eggs, and they're concluding that eggs can be an *okey-yolky* part of a healthy diet. According to the prestigious *New England Journal of Medicine*, in one study, a group of New Guinea natives (whose diets were extremely low in cholesterol), were fed eggs to measure their cholesterol-raising effect. Figuring that the subjects' blood-cholesterol levels would be blown off the charts, the scientists were surprised that egg consumption had no significant effect on blood cholesterol. Another study conducted by the American Cancer Society revealed that egg eaters actually had a lower death rate from heart attacks and strokes than non-egg eaters. (And this was a huge study involving more than 800,000 people!) Maybe that's because the cholesterol in eggs is balanced with lecithin, a substance that keeps cholesterol moving in the bloodstream, preventing it from depositing in the arteries—a great example of how Mother Nature creates balance and synergy in whole, natural foods. Unfortunately, when you scramble or fry eggs, the high heat causes structural changes (called oxidative damage) to the cholesterol in the yolk, and oxidized cholesterol can cause problems in our blood vessels. Poaching or boiling eggs is fine because these methods don't cause much damage. That's good news, because a boiled egg in the morning is *hard to beat*!

Did you split your pants again?

Yes, every time I bend over it's the seam old story.

Tongue Thai'd

Pad Thai: Stir-fried rice noodles
with shrimp and tofu

Cat got your tongue? Too bad. You won't be able to savor the flavor of this zesty, zingy Pad Thai recipe with shrimp and tofu. Never tried Thailand's most famous noodle dish? It's about *Thai*!

**3 tbsp each freshly squeezed lime juice and
    Asian fish sauce (see tip below)**
2 tbsp each ketchup and brown sugar
**1 tbsp each grated gingerroot and
    reduced-sodium soy sauce**
1 tsp toasted sesame oil
¼ tsp crushed red pepper flakes or hot pepper sauce
8 oz rice stick noodles, ideally ⅛ inch wide
2 tsp peanut or vegetable oil
½ cup very thinly sliced red onions or shallots
2 tsp minced garlic
1 medium red bell pepper, seeded and diced or thinly sliced
8 oz uncooked medium shrimp, peeled and deveined
1 cup diced extra-firm tofu (see tip below)
2 cups bean sprouts
½ cup chopped green onions
¼ cup chopped fresh cilantro
¼ cup chopped dry-roasted peanuts

I'm speechless!

23rd Annual Yummy Awards

- First, gather all the ingredients you'll need for this recipe and get them ready (i.e., chop the red pepper, peel the shrimp, etc.). Once you're ready to go, the meal comes together very quickly. You don't want to be hunting for the bean sprouts while the shrimp burns!

- To prepare sauce, whisk together lime juice, fish sauce, ketchup, brown sugar, gingerroot, soy sauce, sesame oil, and crushed red pepper flakes in a medium bowl. Set aside.

- Place rice noodles in a large bowl and pour boiling water over top. Let soak 7 minutes. Drain.

- While noodles are soaking, heat peanut oil in a large, non-stick wok. Add onions and garlic. Cook and stir over medium-high heat until onions are tender, about 2 minutes. Add red pepper and cook 2 more minutes, stirring often. Add shrimp and tofu. Cook and stir until shrimp turn pink, about 3 minutes. Add reserved sauce, noodles, bean sprouts, green onions, and cilantro. Toss and cook until mixture is hot, about 1 minute. Add peanuts and toss again. Serve immediately.

Makes 6 servings

PER SERVING

calories	total fat	saturated fat	protein	carbohydrate	fiber	cholesterol	sodium
308	7.3 g	1 g	15 g	47 g	2.8 g	57 mg	990 mg

Cooking TIP

This recipe might sound very exotic, but all of the ingredients can be found in well-stocked grocery stores. The fish sauce makes it authentic—please don't leave it out! Once you buy it, you can keep in forever (well, not forever, but for a long, long time). Look for it in the aisle where you find other Asian ingredients, like coconut milk, hoisin sauce, soy sauce, etc. You'll probably find the rice noodles there, too. The key is not to take a big whiff of the fish sauce. It smells awful, but tastes very good when mixed with other ingredients. You might want to hold your breath when adding it to the sauce (we're not joking!). Oh, and don't taste the raw sauce...you'll think we've "lost it" completely! Just trust us that the finished product will be wonderful. Try to stick with the recipe as printed, at least the first time you make it. Make sure you buy extra-firm tofu for this recipe or any stir-fry recipe that includes tofu. Soft or silken tofu will fall apart or turn to mush when you try to stir-fry it. For added flavor, look for Szechuan, teriyaki, or sesame-ginger tofu in the produce aisle of your grocery store.

A-lo-fat Hawaiian Pizza

Hawaiian pizza with Canadian bacon and fresh pineapple

Hawaii Five-Eh? There's a little bit of Canadian in our Hawaiian pizza. Fresh pineapple and Canadian bacon make it *pine* and dandy! A kid favorite.

**½ cup pizza sauce
(see recipe in margin)
1 12-inch, prebaked,
thin-crust pizza shell
2 tbsp grated Parmesan cheese
1 cup packed shredded light
mozzarella or Monterey Jack
cheese (4 oz), divided
6 slices Canadian bacon,
cut into quarters
½ cup diced fresh pineapple chunks
Chopped fresh parsley for garnish (optional)**

- Preheat oven to 425°F.

- Spread pizza sauce evenly over crust. Sprinkle Parmesan cheese over sauce, followed by half the shredded cheese. Top with bacon and pineapple. Sprinkle with remaining shredded cheese and a bit of chopped fresh parsley, if desired.

- Place pizza directly on middle oven rack and bake for 10 to 12 minutes, until cheese is completely melted and edges are lightly browned.

Makes 1 pizza, 8 slices

PER SLICE

calories	total fat	saturated fat	protein	carbohydrate	fiber	cholesterol	sodium
150	5 g	2.4 g	9 g	16 g	0.9 g	15 mg	480 mg

Cooking TIP

Make your own pizza sauce! It's easy and you can freeze it for months. Here's how: Heat 2 tsp olive oil in a medium, non-stick pot over medium heat. Add ½ cup minced red onions and 2 tsp minced garlic. Cook and stir until onions are softened, about 3 minutes. Stir in 2 cups tomato sauce, 1 can (5.5 oz/156 ml) tomato paste, 2 tsp dried oregano, 2 tsp balsamic vinegar, 2 tsp brown sugar, ½ tsp dried basil, ½ tsp dried rosemary, and ¼ tsp freshly ground black pepper. Bring to a boil. Reduce heat to low and simmer, covered, for 15 minutes. Cool before using. Makes about 2½ cups sauce.

THE E FILES

Flex your muscles on a regular basis, and you can forget about losing weight! Sound crazy? Actually, it's not. When you start building muscle, it's quite possible you'll get skinnier without losing any weight at all. That's because a pound of muscle takes up a lot less space than a pound of fat. So, every time you "trade" a pound of fat for a pound of muscle, you lose size without losing a lot of weight. To illustrate this point, let's compare a professional athlete, for example, a hockey player, to a couch potato who watches hockey on TV. Say each man is six feet tall and weighs 210 pounds. If weight really meant anything, they'd both wear the same size clothes and carry themselves the same way. But the pro athlete easily slips into size 32 slacks, while the couch potato stretches the seams of his size 38's. The athlete moves with the style, grace, and speed of a cougar while the couch potato clumsily trots along at a turtle's pace. Why the difference? The athlete's 210 pounds is mostly muscle while the couch potato's is mostly fat. So, the moral of the story is forget the scale and measure your progress in inches lost, not pounds.

The Flax of Life

With a list of health benefits as long as Michael Jordan's scoring records, it's no wonder scientists are going nuts over flaxseed! Without getting into too much nitty-gritty, scientific mumbo jumbo, here's why you need flaxseed in your diet: It's one of the richest sources of omega-3 fatty acids, a type of fat that your body can't manufacture. You can only get omega-3's from food, and sadly, due to our poor eating habits and (even poorer) food manufacturing processes, North Americans' diets are dreadfully deficient in them. But omega-3 fatty acids are vitally important to our health. In short, they keep our brains healthy (even easing depression), they fire up our immune systems to prevent illness, ease inflammation and arthritis, and help control diabetes. They're also heart-friendly and cholesterol-lowering, they protect against some cancers, make our skin glow, and relieve constipation. Heck, they even help us shed pounds. Imagine! A fat that helps fight fat! Seeding your body with omega-3's is a no-brainer—one of the smartest things you can do. Flaxseed oil is very sensitive to heat, air, and oxygen, so keep it refrigerated and don't ever cook with it (that makes the oil rancid). Make sure it's refrigerated when you buy it, too. Add a tablespoon of flaxseed oil to juice, smoothies, oatmeal, sauces, yogurt, or use it to make salad dressing. If you don't like the oil's taste, you can buy flaxseed oil capsules. Also, milled or ground flaxseed, full of cancer-fighting lignins and a great source of fiber, tastes great sprinkled on cereal, in smoothies, or used in baking. There you have it: The facts on flax!

The earliest known advocate of a high-fiber diet was Hippocrates. He urged his fellow countrymen to bake their bread with bran for its "salutary effect on the bowels." His being a big fan of bran surely has something to do with the Hippocratic *Oat*.

The Benefit of the Dough

Quick-rising, whole wheat and ground flax pizza dough

No doubt about this dough! It's the best-tasting healthy pizza crust you've ever tried. And it's a *pizza* cake to make—simple and quick enough for a weeknight supper.

1 cup all-purpose flour
1/2 cup whole wheat flour
2 tbsp flax meal or ground flaxseed
1 envelope (1/4 oz or 2 1/4 tsp) Fleischmann's quick-rising yeast
1/2 tsp salt
2/3 cup very warm water
2 tsp olive oil
2 tsp liquid honey
Olive oil cooking spray
1 tbsp cornmeal

- In a medium bowl, combine both flours, flax meal, yeast, and salt. Mix well.

- Measure warm water in measuring cup, then stir in olive oil and honey. Pour mixture over dry ingredients and mix using a wooden spoon to form a ball. Turn dough out onto a lightly floured surface. Knead for 2 minutes. Spray another medium bowl with olive oil spray and place dough inside. Cover with plastic wrap. Let rise in a warm place until double in size, about 20 minutes. Meanwhile, spray a 12-inch pizza pan with olive oil spray and dust with cornmeal.

- When dough has risen, turn out onto a lightly floured surface and, using a rolling pin, roll dough into a 12-inch circle. Transfer dough to prepared pizza pan. You can top it with your favorite toppings at this point and bake in a 425°F oven for about 15 minutes. Or, prick crust in several places with a fork and bake *untopped* for 6 minutes. Remove crust from oven, top with your favorite sauce and toppings, then slide pizza directly onto middle oven rack and bake for an additional 8 to 10 minutes.

Makes 1 12-inch pizza crust

PER SERVING (1/8 CRUST)

calories	total fat	saturated fat	protein	carbohydrate	fiber	cholesterol	sodium
122	2.8 g	0.3 g	4 g	21 g	2.6 g	0 mg	148 mg

Worth Every Penne

Whole wheat penne noodles with chicken, bacon, vegetables, and pesto sauce

To *coin* a phrase, "Pesto is the besto!" Okay, so it's a dumb phrase. We usually make perfect *cents*. Take this spectacular pasta recipe, for instance: It's *penne* wise, but not pound foolish, since we use high-fiber, whole wheat pasta and load up on the veggies and lean chicken. Worth the effort!

Sauce

2 tbsp basil pesto
2 tbsp balsamic vinegar
1 tbsp olive oil
1 tsp liquid honey
¼ tsp freshly ground black pepper

2 cups uncooked whole wheat penne noodles (about 8 oz)
4 slices reduced-sodium bacon, chopped
3 cups sliced mushrooms
1 cup chopped red onions
3 big handfuls baby spinach leaves
12 cherry or grape tomatoes, halved
3 cups chopped cooked chicken breast (see tip in margin)
¼ cup shaved Parmesan or Romano cheese, or ½ cup crumbled light feta cheese (2 oz)
Freshly ground black pepper to taste

- To prepare sauce, whisk together all sauce ingredients in a small bowl and set aside.

- Cook penne noodles according to package directions. Drain and keep warm.

- While pasta is boiling, cook bacon in a large, non-stick skillet or wok over medium-high heat for about 2 minutes. Remove and discard 1 tbsp bacon drippings from skillet. Add mushrooms and onions to skillet. Cook and stir until vegetables begin to soften, about 5 minutes. Add spinach leaves and tomatoes. Cook until spinach is wilted. Stir in chicken and cook just until chicken is heated through. Add cooked penne noodles and mix well. Add reserved sauce and mix again. Remove skillet from heat. Sprinkle pasta with Parmesan cheese and freshly ground black pepper. Serve immediately.

Makes 6 servings

PER SERVING

calories	total fat	saturated fat	protein	carbohydrate	fiber	cholesterol	sodium
331	10.6 g	2.9 g	27 g	31 g	5.7 g	50 mg	270 mg

To save work and time, buy a rotisserie chicken at your grocery store and chop up all of the breast meat for this meal. Save the dark meat for tomorrow's lunch. For a flavor variation, substitute the following super-simple sauce for the basil pesto sauce: Place ⅓ cup roasted tomato and oregano salad dressing (Kraft makes a tasty one!) and 6 large, fresh basil leaves in a small mini-chopper or food processor. Pulse on and off until mixture is smooth. Add to cooked penne mixture and mix well. Sprinkle with Parmesan cheese and freshly ground black pepper before serving.

"SAY IT AIN'T SO!"

When you lose weight on a very restrictive diet, at least one-quarter of that weight loss comes from water, muscle, and bone. Yes, bone! The faster you lose weight, the more bone you lose. And that's not just a bunch of *boney* baloney—it's true! In fact, doctors have found anorexic teens with bones as porous and brittle as women in their seventies and eighties—all a result of crash dieting. Maybe we should take a lesson from the French, who encourage eating with their famous expression, "*Bone* appétit!"

Pop Quizine

"Grunt" and "slump" are two words used to describe...

a) your husband
b) a cooking disappointment, such as a fallen soufflé
c) a fruit dessert with a biscuit topping
d) a pig with bad posture

Answer: (c) Similar to a cobbler, a "grunt," or "slump," is an old-fashioned New England dessert.

Thai Kwon Dough

Thai chicken pizza with zesty peanut sauce

Martial in the troops for this Thai-inspired work of *art*! It's a *kickin'* pizza topped with peanut sauce instead of tomato sauce, packing a real flavor *punch*!

Peanut Sauce

¼ cup light peanut butter
¼ cup hoisin sauce
1 tbsp freshly squeezed lemon juice
2 tsp toasted sesame oil
2 tsp grated gingerroot
1 tsp each liquid honey, reduced-sodium soy sauce, and red wine vinegar
1 tsp minced garlic
Pinch crushed red pepper flakes

1 cup chopped cooked chicken breast (see tip below)
1 12-inch, prebaked, thin-crust pizza shell
1 cup packed shredded light Monterey Jack cheese (4 oz), divided
⅓ cup bean sprouts
¼ cup each shredded carrots and chopped green onions
2 tbsp chopped roasted peanuts
1 tbsp minced fresh cilantro

- Preheat oven to 425°F.

- To make sauce, combine all sauce ingredients in a small saucepan and heat over medium-high heat until bubbly, stirring constantly. Remove from heat and let cool slightly.

- Mix 1 heaping tbsp of peanut sauce with chicken cubes and set aside. To assemble pizza, spread remaining peanut sauce evenly over crust. Top with half the shredded cheese. Distribute chicken cubes evenly over cheese. Top with bean sprouts (break them into smaller pieces if you prefer), carrots, green onions, and peanuts, in that order. Sprinkle remaining shredded cheese over toppings.

- Place pizza directly on middle oven rack and bake for 10 to 12 minutes, until cheese is completely melted and edges are lightly browned. Sprinkle with cilantro before serving.

Tip: We like using the breast meat from a rotisserie chicken because it's so moist. However, grilled chicken would work in this recipe, too, as long as it's not overcooked.

Slow down, you eat too fast…Gotta make the moment last… Just scarfin' pizza, gobblin' scones…Ate too much, *not* feelin' groovy! The purpose behind mindfully, slowly chewing your food is that it extends your eating time. And that's a good idea because there's a lag between when your belly begins to fill and when your brain notices it—about 20 minutes. Nowadays, when speed is valued in both the preparation of food (15 minutes or it's free!) and the consumption of food (wolfing down a burger in your car), our brains and bellies are barely on speaking terms. We eat so fast that we zoom right past the point of satiety and keep stuffing ourselves like Butterball turkeys. Besides chewing thoroughly, try starting your meal with a high-water-content food, such as soup or a small salad. That'll slow things down, begin the process of satisfying your hunger, and open up the lines of communication so your brain knows your belly's on the road to fullness. Ba, da, da, da, da, da, da…feelin' groovy!

*Bee*lieve it or not, honey is the only food that does not spoil. Honey found in the tombs of Egyptian pharaohs has been tasted by archeologists and found to be edible. Sweet!

Hi Honey! I'm home!

Makes 1 pizza, 8 slices

PER SLICE

calories	total fat	saturated fat	protein	carbohydrate	fiber	cholesterol	sodium
220	9.5 g	2.9 g	13 g	22 g	1.2 g	18 mg	442 mg

Lost in Trans-nation

For the sake of your family's health, you better tune in to trans fats—the evil, dietary bogeymen lurking below the surface of many popular foods. These man-made fats are created by bubbling hydrogen through vegetable oil. That gives packaged foods, such as potato chips, crackers, and cookies, the taste and texture we love, and embalms them so they can sit on store shelves forever. Trouble is, your body can't get rid of the stuff easily. How bad are they? Bad! Trans fats block our arteries, poison our hearts and our livers, interfere with our immune systems, inhibit fertility, and basically wreak hormonal havoc. Did we mention they make you fat? You've probably heard that trans fats are hiding in fried foods, donuts, some margarines, peanut butter, and shortening, but you might be shocked to find that these health corrupters have crept into some convenience foods that you've been feeding to your kids: pizza pockets and frozen pizzas, toaster waffles and pastries, microwave entrées, frozen fries, chicken nuggets, microwave popcorn, chocolate bars, nachos, candy, granola bars…even some breakfast cereals! Fruity O-no! Sound like your weekly shopping list? Don't panic. Manufacturers are being pressured to trash the trans and soon they'll have to spell it out for us on labels. In the meantime, become a grocery store detective and look for the words "hydrogenated vegetable oil" or "partially hydrogenated vegetable oil" on packages. The closer these words are to the top of the ingredients list, the more trans fats in the product and the more chance regular consumption will harm you. Our best advice? On your next shopping trip, make the transition to items that haven't made a pit stop at a factory en route from the farm.

*This is every cook's opinion—
no savory dish without an onion,
but lest your kissing should be spoiled
your onions must be fully boiled.*

Jonathan Swift

Silly Greek Chili

Zesty chicken chili with tomatoes, zucchini, chickpeas, and feta cheese

Greek chili? That's silly! Or so we thought, until we concocted this hearty, wholesome chicken chili that somehow got *mexed* up with Greek-style ingredients. It's food for the gods!

Honey, you're in a clash all by yourself

- **2 tsp olive oil**
- **3 boneless, skinless chicken breasts (about 1 lb), cut into 1-inch cubes**
- **1 cup chopped red onions**
- **1 cup diced zucchini**
- **½ cup chopped red bell pepper**
- **2 tsp minced garlic**
- **1 tbsp chili powder**
- **1 tsp each ground cumin and dried oregano**
- **1 can (14.5 oz) diced tomatoes with sun-dried tomato, undrained**
- **1½ cups your favorite tomato pasta sauce**
- **1 cup canned chickpeas, drained and rinsed**
- **1 tbsp brown sugar**
- **¼ tsp freshly ground black pepper**
- **2 tbsp minced fresh cilantro**
- **⅓ cup crumbled light feta cheese (1.5 oz)**

- Heat olive oil over medium-high heat in a large, non-stick pot. Add chicken. Cook and stir until chicken is lightly browned, but not cooked through, about 4 minutes. Add onions, zucchini, red pepper, and garlic. Cook and stir until vegetables begin to soften, about 3 minutes.

- Stir in chili powder, cumin, and oregano. Cook 1 more minute. Add tomatoes with their juice, pasta sauce, chickpeas, brown sugar, and pepper. Bring to a boil. Reduce heat to low. Cover and simmer for 15 minutes.

- Remove from heat. Stir in cilantro. Ladle chili into serving bowls and top with feta cheese.

Makes 5 servings

PER SERVING

calories	total fat	saturated fat	protein	carbohydrate	fiber	cholesterol	sodium
288	5.8 g	1.9 g	28 g	30 g	6.5 g	60 mg	698 mg

Phoney Pepperoni Pizzas

Turkey pepperoni, mushrooms, and green peppers on whole wheat pita crusts

We know what you're thinking: "Turkey on pizza? What a bunch of phoney baloney!" But here's the truth: Turkey pepperoni is an ideal kitchen counterfeit. After one slice you'll shout, *"Impostorble* taste!"

1 ½ cups thinly sliced mushrooms
½ cup thinly sliced turkey
   pepperoni or turkey
   pepperettes (see tip below)
½ cup diced green bell pepper
½ tsp dried oregano
1 cup pizza sauce
   (see recipe in margin, page 180)
4 7-inch whole wheat pitas
¼ cup grated Parmesan,
   Romano, or Asiago cheese
1 cup packed shredded light Monterey Jack
   or mozzarella cheese (4 oz)

I've got 'em all fooled!

- Preheat oven to 425°F.

- Spray a medium, non-stick skillet with cooking spray. Add mushrooms, pepperoni, and green pepper. Cook and stir over medium heat until mushrooms are tender. Stir in oregano and cook 30 more seconds. Remove from heat.

- For each pizza, spread about ¼ cup sauce over pita, leaving a ½-inch border. Sprinkle 1 tbsp Parmesan cheese over sauce. Top with ¼ pepperoni mixture, followed by ¼ shredded cheese.

- Place pizzas directly on middle oven rack and bake for 10 minutes, until cheese is completely melted and edges are beginning to brown. Transfer from oven to cutting board and let stand 1 minute before slicing.

Tip: Look for turkey pepperoni or turkey pepperettes where packaged cold cuts are sold at your grocery store.

Makes 4 servings

		PER SERVING					
calories	total fat	saturated fat	protein	carbohydrate	fiber	cholesterol	sodium
325	9.5 g	5.2 g	21 g	41 g	6 g	29 mg	827 mg

Life is too short to stuff a mushroom.

Shirley Conran

Ask Janet

Why is protein important for fat loss? How much should I eat each day?

Most of us have figured out that protein-rich foods are powerful appetite suppressants. They're filling, satisfying, and keep your blood sugar on an even keel so you won't crave junk food. But another interesting way that protein helps fight fat is through something called "the thermic effect of food." The actual process of digesting and absorbing the nutrients in a meal causes us to burn calories as heat. About 25% of protein calories are burned this way, 8 to 15% of carbohydrate calories, and less than 3% of fat calories. So, a high-protein meal generates more heat than a high-carb meal. Eat some chicken and get your calorie burner tickin'! Plus, you need muscle to burn fat, and adequate protein, along with exercise, prevents the loss of precious muscle. We know what you're thinking: "Cowabunga! Protein seems like a magic potion for weight loss!" Before you go hog wild, realize that eating too much protein can be detrimental to your health (see page 116 for details). If you'd rather look like Sharon Stone than Fred Flintstone, limit your stops at the Brontosaurus Burger Joint. Nutrition experts recommend getting between 20 and 30% of your daily calories from protein. A general guideline is to aim for small portions (10 to 25 grams) of lean protein with each meal. Some good choices: 3 oz chicken breast (21 g), a whey protein shake (25 g), ½ cup low-fat cottage cheese (15 g), 3 oz salmon (25 g), 1 cup chickpeas (12 g), 2 eggs (12 g), and ¾ cup yogurt (8 g).

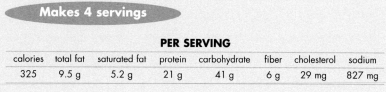

Pop Quizine

The word "burrito" is Spanish for...

a) little donkey
b) stuffed pancake
c) I'm hungry
d) heartburn

Answer: (a) And too many little donkeys can lead to one big ass.

Cooking TIP

We use low-fat, sun-dried tomato and basil croutons for this recipe. Look for bags of croutons in the produce aisle of your grocery store—you can usually find more interesting varieties there. Turkey kielbasa is a good substitute if you can't find light Italian sausage. It's already cooked, however, so just cut it up and heat it with the vegetables. The spiciness of the kielbasa will lend some flavor to the vegetables. If you prefer, you can replace the red bell pepper with ½ cup chopped roasted red peppers from a jar. You don't need to cook them with the other vegetables—just sprinkle them over the croutons with the sausage mixture.

Fat or Fiction?

Breakfast eaters are thinner, smarter, and nicer to be around.

Do you rise and shine, or just rise? Studies show that breakfast eaters not only have sunnier dispositions, but also fare better on memory and problem-solving tasks. When you skip breakfast, your blood-sugar levels take a nosedive, and that can make you a little weak in the bean—and irritable, too! Think that 10 a.m. coffee and Danish will perk you up? They'll only fuel the fire, sending your blood-sugar and energy levels soaring to the moon, only to violently crash down to earth a short while later. Your co-workers may not have thought it possible, but now you're even crankier! A hearty, healthy, high-fiber breakfast like oatmeal or whole-grain cereal with fruit does more than keep your brain cells, blood sugar, and relationships operating smoothly. It also jump-starts your metabolism, so you'll start burning fat and calories right out of the gate. Plus, eating breakfast prevents overeating at lunchtime, when you're sure to be famished if you've skipped your morning meal. No wonder experts say "breaking the fast" is crucial if you're serious about losing some weight. So, join the breakfast club and hang with the *thin* crowd!

Erik Eggstrata

Layered breakfast casserole with Italian sausage and vegetables

When the *CHiPs* are down, you can call on this satisfying breakfast strata to tame a hungry crowd. Colorful veggies and super-light ingredients mean you won't develop a *Ponch*.

3 cups low-fat, herb-seasoned croutons (see tip in margin)
8 oz light mild Italian sausage (see tip in margin)
1 cup diced zucchini
½ cup minced onions
½ cup diced red bell pepper (see tip in margin)
1 cup packed shredded light old (sharp) cheddar cheese (4 oz)
2 cups fat-free egg substitute or 8 whole eggs, beaten
1 cup evaporated 2% milk or light (5%) cream
¼ tsp each salt and freshly ground black pepper

- Spray an 11 x 7-inch casserole dish with cooking spray. Spread croutons evenly in bottom of dish. Set aside.

- Spray a medium, non-stick skillet with cooking spray. Remove and discard casing from sausage. Break or cut sausage into small pieces and add to skillet. Cook over medium-high heat until no longer pink, breaking up any large pieces. Add zucchini, onions, and red pepper. Reduce heat to medium. Cook and stir for about 3 more minutes, until vegetables begin to soften.

- To assemble strata, spoon sausage mixture evenly over croutons. Top with shredded cheese. Whisk together egg substitute, milk, salt, and pepper in a medium bowl. Pour egg mixture evenly over sausage and vegetables. Let strata stand for 10 to 15 minutes while you preheat oven to 350°F.

- Bake, uncovered, for 40 minutes, until eggs are completely set. Let stand 5 minutes before cutting.

Makes 8 servings

PER SERVING

calories	total fat	saturated fat	protein	carbohydrate	fiber	cholesterol	sodium
205	6.9 g	2.9 g	19 g	17 g	1.2 g	26 mg	657 mg

Wise Guy Pizza Pie

Italian sausage pizza with mushrooms and red onions

You wanna *pizza* me? Who can blame you! All da boys will wanna *pizza* the action, too. You'd be wise to double this recipe so you don't get mobbed when everyone wants more.

8 oz light mild Italian sausage
³⁄₄ cup thinly sliced red onions
2 cups thinly sliced mushrooms
1 tbsp minced fresh oregano or basil leaves, or 1 tsp dried
¹⁄₂ cup pizza sauce
1 12-inch, prebaked, thin-crust pizza shell
¹⁄₄ cup grated Parmesan or Romano cheese
1 cup packed shredded light provolone cheese (4 oz—see tip below)

It's really good, fellas.

• Preheat oven to 425°F.

• Spray a 10-inch, non-stick skillet with cooking spray. Remove and discard casing from sausage. Break or cut sausage into small pieces and add to skillet along with onions. Cook and stir over medium-high heat until sausage is cooked through and onions begin to soften, about 3 minutes. Break up any large pieces of sausage as it's cooking.

• Stir in mushrooms and cook until mushrooms are tender, about 5 more minutes. Add oregano, mix well, and remove from heat.

• Spread pizza sauce evenly over crust. Top with Parmesan cheese. Spoon sausage mixture evenly over cheese. Sprinkle shredded cheese evenly over sausage mixture.

• Place pizza directly on middle oven rack and bake for 10 to 12 minutes, until cheese is completely melted and edges are lightly browned.

Tip: If you can't find light provolone cheese, use light Monterey Jack instead.

Makes 1 pizza, 8 slices

PER SLICE

calories	total fat	saturated fat	protein	carbohydrate	fiber	cholesterol	sodium
184	7.4 g	3.5 g	13 g	17 g	1.3 g	24 mg	573 mg

Top o' the pizza to ya! According to purist Italian chefs, ingredients that should never appear on an authentic Italian pizza include bell peppers, pepperoni, and chicken. In Australia, the number-one topping for pizza is eggs. In Chile, the favorite topping is mussels or clams. In the United States, it's pepperoni. In Eastern Europe, ketchup is often used on pizza as a condiment. In Iceland, Domino's Pizza has Reindeer Sausage Pie on its menu—ho, ho, hold the antlers!

How Sweet it Isn't

Studies show that the sweeter your diet, the more nutrient deficient it is. Given that the average North American consumes about 150 pounds of sugar per year, no wonder chronic disease is on the rise. If you just can't yank your sweet tooth, at least choose "sweet somethin's" over "sweet nothin's." Cut back on refined sugar and artificial sweeteners that serve up nothing but empty calories. Instead, choose natural sweeteners that offer some beneficial, health-promoting properties. Honey, for instance, contains vitamins (the *Bee* vitamins?), minerals, and enzymes, plus antioxidants that protect against illness. And it won't jack up your blood sugar, either, because it has a moderate effect on insulin. Another good choice is organic molasses since it's grown in mineral-rich soil. It also contains the valuable B vitamins plus other important nutrients, like iron. For those who think a milk mustache is all the rage, a blackstrap molasses mustache may soon be a trend that really sticks—two tablespoons of the gooey stuff contains as much calcium as a glass of milk! Got molasses?

Waiter, this steak tastes like an asphalt shingle!

Sorry, sir. Meat prices have gone through the roof

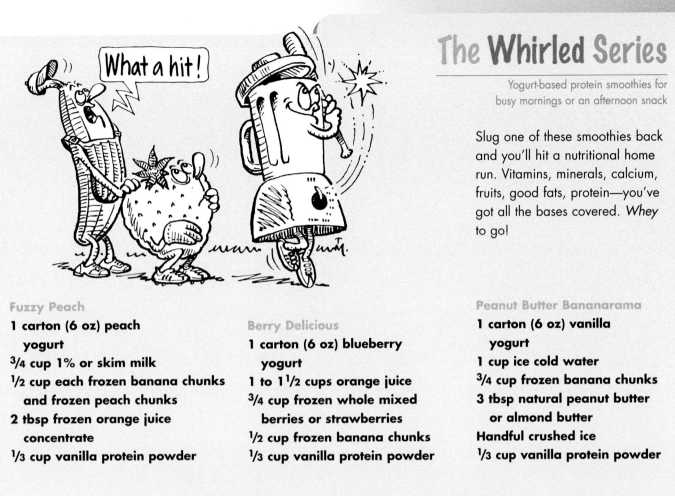

The Whirled Series

Yogurt-based protein smoothies for busy mornings or an afternoon snack

Slug one of these smoothies back and you'll hit a nutritional home run. Vitamins, minerals, calcium, fruits, good fats, protein—you've got all the bases covered. *Whey* to go!

Fuzzy Peach

1 carton (6 oz) peach yogurt
³/₄ cup 1% or skim milk
¹/₂ cup each frozen banana chunks and frozen peach chunks
2 tbsp frozen orange juice concentrate
¹/₃ cup vanilla protein powder

Berry Delicious

1 carton (6 oz) blueberry yogurt
1 to 1¹/₂ cups orange juice
³/₄ cup frozen whole mixed berries or strawberries
¹/₂ cup frozen banana chunks
¹/₃ cup vanilla protein powder

Peanut Butter Bananarama

1 carton (6 oz) vanilla yogurt
1 cup ice cold water
³/₄ cup frozen banana chunks
3 tbsp natural peanut butter or almond butter
Handful crushed ice
¹/₃ cup vanilla protein powder

- Please read note below for helpful smoothie-making tips!

- Directions for all smoothies: Place all ingredients except protein powder in blender. Whirl until smooth. Add protein powder and mix on low speed just until blended. Serve immediately.

Each recipe makes 2 servings

PER SERVING

calories	total fat	saturated fat	protein
219	1.3 g	0.7 g	19 g

carbohydrate	fiber	cholesterol	sodium
34 g	2.8 g	6 mg	106 mg

PER SERVING

calories	total fat	saturated fat	protein
234	1.4 g	0.6 g	16 g

carbohydrate	fiber	cholesterol	sodium
40 g	3.7 g	3 mg	55 mg

PER SERVING

calories	total fat	saturated fat	protein
302	12.4 g	2.4 g	22 g

carbohydrate	fiber	cholesterol	sodium
27 g	3.8 g	2 mg	67 mg

Cooking TIP

All fruit used in smoothies should first be frozen. The cold chunks of fruit act like ice cubes and make the smoothies nice 'n' cold. It is absolutely, positively essential that your bananas are frozen if you want a creamy texture. Peel bananas that are just starting to show brown spots and cut them into chunks. Put the chunks in a resealable plastic bag and pop it in the freezer. Seems like there's a gazillion types of protein powder on the market and each one has its own distinct taste and texture, so it's difficult to recommend a particular brand. Some powders make thin shakes and others make very thick shakes, so you'll need to adjust the amount of liquid in the recipes above to suit your brand of powder and your personal preference. To increase the fiber content of smoothies, try adding a tablespoon of ground flaxseed or chia seed, a "supergrain" that's not only very high in fiber, but also has more omega-3 fats (gram for gram) than salmon.

Spring Chickens

Warm chicken tortilla spring rolls with peanut sauce

Bounce for bounce, our nutritious, oven-baked chicken spring rolls with whole wheat tortillas are lower in fat and calories than traditional fried spring rolls. Your taste buds will flip when spring has sprung from the oven!

6 7-inch whole wheat flour tortillas (see tip in margin)
1 tbsp toasted sesame oil
3/4 cup packed shredded light Monterey Jack cheese (3 oz)
1 large cooked chicken breast, thinly sliced (see tip in margin)
2 tbsp chopped fresh cilantro
1/4 cup chopped green onions
6 thin strips red bell pepper
1/3 cup grated carrots
1/2 cup bean sprouts
3/4 cup bottled light peanut sauce for dunking (see tip in margin)

- Preheat oven to 450°F. Working one tortilla at a time, coat one side of tortilla with sesame oil using a pastry brush. Lay coated side down on your work surface. Evenly distribute about 1/6 of each ingredient (except peanut sauce) on lower half of uncoated side. Starting at edge closest to you, roll up tortilla into a tight cigar shape, tucking in sides as you roll, so filling is completely enclosed. Place tortilla seam-side down on a baking sheet. Repeat with remaining tortillas and filling. Make sure you space tortillas at least 1 inch apart on baking sheet.

- Bake tortillas on middle oven rack for about 8 minutes, until lightly browned and heated through. Slice warm tortillas in half (on an angle) and arrange them on a platter with a bowl of warmed peanut dipping sauce in the center.

Makes 6 servings

PER SERVING

calories	total fat	saturated fat	protein	carbohydrate	fiber	cholesterol	sodium
244	9.6 g	3.2 g	13 g	24 g	2.6 g	24 mg	503 mg

It is better to wear out than to rust out.

Frances E. Willard

When buying tortillas, make sure they're very soft and fresh. If they're a little old, they'll crack when you roll them (frustrating!). To revive slightly stale tortillas, just wrap them in a lightly dampened, clean tea towel and microwave them for 15 to 20 seconds (adjust time according to your microwave and the number of tortillas you're using). Don't buy the huge tortillas for this recipe—they're way too big. You want the smaller size. For the chicken, a roasted chicken breast tastes great in this recipe, as does grilled teriyaki chicken (see recipe, page 91). Nowadays, it's pretty easy to find a bottled peanut sauce that isn't loaded with fat. Look in the Asian food section at your grocery store or in the aisle where stir-fry sauces are sold.

THE E FILES

Muscle is a terrible thing to waste. But when you diet without exercising, that's exactly what you're doing. When you lose more than two pounds per week, typically half of the weight lost comes from muscle. That's bad news. Muscle is your calorie-burning, fat-incinerating furnace, using energy even when you're sleeping. Fat pretty much just sits there. Sure, if you starve yourself on a super-low-calorie diet, you'll lose weight. But it'll be an unfavorable type of weight loss. Though the scale says you're five pounds lighter, you've really just changed your body composition. You're simply a lighter fat person! That's not what you had in mind when you were subsisting on melba toast, was it? To make matters worse, when you go off the diet (and you will), you'll gain back the weight you lost and then some. By sacrificing muscle on the restrictive diet, you've turned your body into a less-efficient fat burner, so you'll gain weight even though you're eating less. What a great plan! To transform your body for the better, don't lose muscle—*use* muscle.

Died-and-Gone-to-Heaven Chocolate Layer Cake

Triple-decker, triple-decadent chocolate layer cake

If you've been a dietary saint all year, treat yourself to a little piece of heaven: A slice of divine chocolate cake that's packed with decadent, splurge-worthy ingredients. Go ahead! It's not like you're going to burn in hell or anything! Just make sure you burn off the calories later.

Cake

3 cups granulated sugar
2½ cups all-purpose flour
1 cup unsweetened cocoa powder
2 tsp baking soda
1 tsp baking powder
1 tsp salt
3 large eggs
1½ cups buttermilk
1 cup strong brewed coffee, cooled
¾ cup vegetable oil
1 tsp vanilla
4 oz unsweetened chocolate squares,
    melted and cooled slightly (see tip, page 170)

Frosting

1¼ cups granulated sugar
⅓ cup unsweetened cocoa powder
1 cup whipping (35%) cream
6 oz semi-sweet chocolate squares
2 tsp vanilla
1 pkg (8 oz) light cream cheese, softened
1 cup butter, softened

- Preheat oven to 350°F. Lightly grease bottom and sides of three 9-inch round cake pans. Cut circles of wax paper or parchment paper to fit bottom of pans and place in pans. Lightly grease paper. Set pans aside.

- Combine sugar, flour, cocoa powder, baking soda, baking powder, and salt in a large bowl. Set aside.

- In another large bowl, beat eggs on high speed of electric mixer for about 3 minutes, until they have thickened slightly and are lemon colored. Add buttermilk, coffee, oil, vanilla, and melted chocolate. Mix on low speed until well blended.

- Gradually add dry ingredients to wet ingredients and mix on medium speed until batter is smooth. Divide batter evenly among pans. Bake for 25 to 30 minutes, until a toothpick inserted in center of cakes comes out clean. Cool in pans on a wire rack for 10 minutes. Remove cakes from pans, peel off paper, and cool completely before frosting.

- To make frosting, whisk together sugar, cocoa, and whipping cream in a medium saucepan. Cook slowly over medium heat, whisking constantly, until mixture comes to a gentle boil. Cook 1 minute. Remove from heat and stir in chocolate until melted. Stir in vanilla. Let cool to room temperature.

- In a large bowl, beat cream cheese and butter on high speed of electric mixer until smooth. Add cooled chocolate mixture and beat on medium speed until well blended. Refrigerate frosting until desired spreading consistency is reached, about 1 hour. Important! Don't let it get too firm, or you won't be able to spread it.

- To frost cake, place one cake layer on a pretty plate. Spread 1 cup frosting over top. Repeat with second layer. Place final layer on top. Ice top and sides of cake with remaining frosting. Decorate cake with chocolate curls and/or chocolate-covered strawberries, if desired. Cover and refrigerate. Let cake stand at room temperature for 30 minutes before serving.

Makes 1 cake, 16 servings

	PER SLICE						
calories	total fat	saturated fat	protein	carbohydrate	fiber	cholesterol	sodium
Trust	us	you	do	not	want	to	know!

Metric Conversion

If you are converting the recipes in this book to metric measurements, use the following chart as a guide.

VOLUME		
Conventional Measure	**Exact Metric Conversion (mL)**	**Standard Metric Conversion (mL)**
1/4 teaspoon	1.2 mL	1 mL
1/2 teaspoon	2.4 mL	2 mL
1 teaspoon	4.7 mL	5 mL
2 teaspoons	9.4 mL	10 mL
1 tablespoon	14.2 mL	15 mL
2 tablespoons	28.4 mL	30 mL
3 tablespoons	42.6 mL	45 mL
1/4 cup (4 tablespoons)	56.8 mL	50 mL
1/3 cup (5 1/3 tablespoons)	75.6 mL	75 mL
1/2 cup (8 tablespoons)	113.7 mL	125 mL
2/3 cup (10 2/3 tablespoons)	151.2 mL	150 mL
3/4 cup (12 tablespoons)	170.5 mL	175 mL
1 cup (16 tablespoons)	227.3 mL	250 mL
4 1/2 cups	1022.9 mL	1000 mL (1 L)

WEIGHT		
Ounces (oz)	**Exact Metric Conversion (g)**	**Standard Metric Conversion (g)**
1 oz	28.3 g	30 g
2 oz	56.7 g	55 g
3 oz	85.0 g	85 g
4 oz	113.4 g	125 g
5 oz	141.7 g	140 g
6 oz	170.1 g	170 g
7 oz	198.4 g	200 g
8 oz	226.8 g	250 g
16 oz (1 lb)	453.6 g	500 g
32 oz	907.2 g	1000 g (1 kg)

OVEN TEMPERATURES	
Fahrenheit (°F)	**Celsius (°C)**
175°	80°
200°	95°
225°	110°
250°	120°
275°	140°
300°	150°
325°	160°
350°	175°
375°	190°
400°	205°
425°	220°
450°	230°
475°	240°
500°	260°

Index

We're No Geniuses, But These People Sure Are...

Andrews, Sam S., MD, Luis A. Balart, MD, Morison, C. Bethea, MD, and H. Leighton Steward.
Sugar Busters!: Cut Sugar to Trim Fat.
Ballantine Books, 1998.

Austin, Denise.
Shrink Your Female Fat Zones.
Rodale Inc., 2003.

Balch, Phyllis A., CNC, and Balch, James F., MD.
Prescription for Nutritional Healing, Second Edition.
Avery Publishing Group, 1997.

Balch, Phyllis A., CNC.
Prescription for Dietary Wellness, Second Edition.
Avery Publishing Group, 2003.

Bateson-Koch, Carolee, DC, ND.
Allergies: Disease in Disguise.
Alive Books, 1994.

Batmanghelidj, F.
Your Body's Many Cries for Water.
Global Health Solutions, 1998.

Beck, Leslie, RD.
Leslie Beck's Nutrition Encyclopedia.
Prentice Hall Canada, 2001.

Cass, Hyla, MD, and Holford, Patrick.
Natural Highs.
Avery, 2002.

Colbin, Annemarie.
Food and Healing.
Ballantine Books, 1996.

Colgin, M.
Antioxidants: The Real Story.
Apple Publishing, 1998.

Corriher, Shirley O.
CookWise.
William Morrow and Company, Inc., 1997.

Cruise, Jorge.
8 Minutes in the Morning.
Rodale Inc., 2001.

Edelman, Joe, and Samson, David.
Useless Knowledge.
St. Martin's Press, 2002.

Enig, Mary, MD, and Fallon, Sally.
Eat Fat, Lose Fat.
Hudson Street Press, 2005.

Erasmus, Udo.
Fats That Heal, Fats That Kill.
Alive Books, 1993.

Fallon, Sally.
Nourishing Traditions: The Cookbook that Challenges Politically Correct Nutrition and the Diet Dictocrats.
NewTrends Publishing Inc., 1999.

Graci, Sam.
The Power of Superfoods: 30 Days That Will Change Your Life.
Prentice Hall Canada Inc., 1997.

Kendall-Reed, Penny, ND.
The Naturopathic Diet.
Quarry Press, Inc., 2001.

King, Brad J., and Schmidt, Dr. Michael.
Bio-Age: Ten Steps to a Younger You.
Macmillan Canada, 2001.

King, Brad J.,
Fat Wars Action Planner.
John Wiley & Sons Inc., 2003.

Kleiner, Susan M., PhD, RD.
High-Performance Nutrition, The Total Eating Plan to Maximize Your Workout.
John Wiley & Sons Inc., 1996.

Gallop, Rick.
The G.I. Diet: The Easy, Healthy Way to Permanent Weight Loss.
Random House Canada, 2002.

Gittleman, Ann Louise, MS, CNS.
The Fat Flush Plan.
McGraw-Hill, 2002.

Gittleman, Ann Louise, MS, CNS.
The Fat Flush Fitness Plan.
Mc-Graw-Hill, 2004.

Matsen, Jonn, ND.
Eating Alive: Prevention Thru Good Digestion.
Crompton Books Ltd., 2002.

Murray, Michael T., ND, and Beutler, Jade, RRT, RCP.
Understanding Fats & Oils.
Progressive Health Publishing, 1996.

Nelson, Miriam E.,
Strong Women Eat Well.
The Berkley Publishing Group, 2001.

Niven, David, PhD.
The 100 Simple Secrets of Healthy People.
HarperCollins Publishers Inc., 2003.

Perricone, Nicholas, MD.
The Wrinkle Cure.
Warner Books, 2000.

Phillips, Bill.
Body For Life.
HarperCollins Publishers, Inc., 1999.

Rona, Zoltan P., MD, MSc, and Gursche, Siegfried, MH.
Encyclopedia of Natural Healing.
Avery Publishing Group Inc., 1997.

Schmidt, M.A.
Smart Fats.
North Atlantic Books, 1997.

Schwarcz, Dr. Joe.
That's the Way the Cookie Crumbles.
ECW Press, 2002.

Scott-Moncrieff, Dr. Christina.
Detox: Cleanse and Recharge Your Mind, Body and Soul.
Collins & Brown Ltd., 2001.

Sears, Barry, PhD.
The Age-Free Zone.
Regan Books, 1999.

Sears, Barry, PhD.
The Top 100 Zone Foods.
Regan Books, 2001.

The New Food Lover's Companion, Third Edition.
Barron's Educational Series, Inc., 2001.

Vanderhaeghe, Lorna R.,
Healthy Immunity: Scientifically Proven Natural Treatments for Conditions from A-Z.
Macmillan Canada, 2001.

Vanderhaeghe, Lorna R., BSc, and Karst, Karlene, BSc, RD.
Healthy Fats for Life.
Quarry Health Books, 2003.

Walking with the Wise for Health and Vitality.
MENTORS Publishing House, Inc., 2004.

Watson, Brenda.
Renew Your Life: Improved Digestion and Detoxification.
Renew Life Press, 2002.

Weil, Andrew, MD.
Eating Well for Optimum Health: The Essential Guide to Food, Diet, and Nutrition.
Alfred A. Knopf, 2000.

Woodruff, Sandra, MS, RD.
The Good Carb Cookbook: Secrets of Eating Low on the Glycemic Index.
Avery, 2001.

Couldn't Have Done It Without Ya

In 1996, Greta called **Dave Chilton** an "idiot" on national TV. (She meant "cooking idiot," but it didn't quite come out that way!) Who'da thunk that almost 12 years later, the charismatic author of Canada's all-time bestselling book, *The Wealthy Barber*, would still be the president of our publishing company *and* our food company, our dear friend, and our biggest fan. Dave's involvement has propelled our books to heights that we could never have dreamt possible.

While this may seem a little biased, we're pretty darn sure that **Ted Martin** is the world's most brilliant and talented cartoonist. In fact, we challenge anyone else to draw a green onion that looks like Sylvester Stallone (see page 100)! An absolute pleasure to work with, landing Ted for this project ensured smooth sailing.

Mary Lou Core isn't just our book designer, she's a miracle worker! She whipped pages together with Olympian-like speed and brought them to life with her fantastic ideas. (One exception: When she suggested our recipe cards would look great with a leopard-print border!) One of the nicest, most patient people you could ever meet, she never once complained about our fanatical obsession with the smallest details—at least not to our faces!

Leanne Cusack, our "Honorary Chairwoman of the Board," wore many hats during this project: recipe consultant, proofreader, public relations specialist, advanced sales director, moral support provider, and overall great pal. An avid cook herself, we'd be hard-pressed to find a more ideal or more eager recipe tester. This slim, trim farm girl is a bottomless pit who can effortlessly consume half her body weight in a single sitting—and that's just the appetizer!

Truth be told, if it weren't for **Peter McMenemy**, Granet Publishing's Operations Manager, we wouldn't have a single book to our credit. Back in 1994, while gorging himself on a third piece of Greta's famous Mexican lasagna, Pete declared, "If this is low fat, you should write a cookbook!" So we did. *Looneyspoons* was born, thanks to Pete! Another famous comment, "This is the best meal I've ever eaten in a house," inspired us to begin work on our second cookbook, *Crazy Plates*.

Oh, where to begin!? **Doug** "center-part" **Ridge**, founding member of "Penny Pinchers Anonymous," was a great addition to our office for one simple reason: His brain is as twisted as ours! He blurted out silly recipe titles and really bad puns like they were going out of style. Hmm. That's funny. His haircut, loafers, and purple bomber jacket were all going out of style, too!

Our editor extraordinaire, **Fina Scroppo**, polished our words, perfected our prose, and put up with our puns page after page after page. And she even let us start sentences with "and." Zoinks! *(Could not find in Webster's. Suggest, "Wow!" More common expression.)* Thanks to her keen eye, we don't have no grammatical errors or spelling misteaks.

Sharon and Peter Matthews of Matthews Communications Design Inc. were instrumental in getting this book project off the ground. As design consultants, their creativity and expertise were truly appreciated. They didn't even mind leaving our business meetings covered in Greta's dog's hair! Sharon's suggestions were key to the successful incorporation of Colin Erricson's stunning food photography into our zany, cartoony layout.

Our heartfelt thanks to the following people who supported our efforts and contributed to *Eat, Shrink & Be Merry!* in their own special way:

Bob & Marjorie Chilton
Alfreda Podleski & Charlie Roberts
Donna & George Grabowski
Theresa & Barry Eveleigh
Helen & Don Clark
Margaret & Gary Robb
Colin & Charlene Erricson
Terry Schacht
Wayne Rostad
Maureen Ross
Matt Johannsson
Jackie Mustakas
Jill Donahue
Jodi Martin
Kathy & Eric Johnson
Susan Chilton & Ryan McDonald
Aunt Alice
Jennifer Wolle

Greg Vanderburgh
Wayne Mosley
Dawn Martin
Chuck Temple
Christine Ridge
Sue Kollar
Sadie McMenemy
Brad J. King
Cecile Savereux
Joel Haslam
Andrea Bartels
Alla Makarova
Bruce Bonner
Elizabeth Wiggins
Gaye Bennett
Eric & Felicity Brown
LeeAnn Lacroix
John Randall

Gerry & Austin Lepage
Leslie-Anne Barrett
Kathy White
Michelle Valberg
Grits McMullen
Janet Tottle
Steve Andrews
Paul & Cindy Moore
Don Ritza & Donene Grant
Vicky Cusack & Ron Marrs
Carole Filion
Pauline Cusack
Jim Bonner
Valerie Thornburg
Yuri Podtchainov
Emily Ugarenko
Erika Hamilton-Piercy
Sharon Chang Fong

Hungry for More?

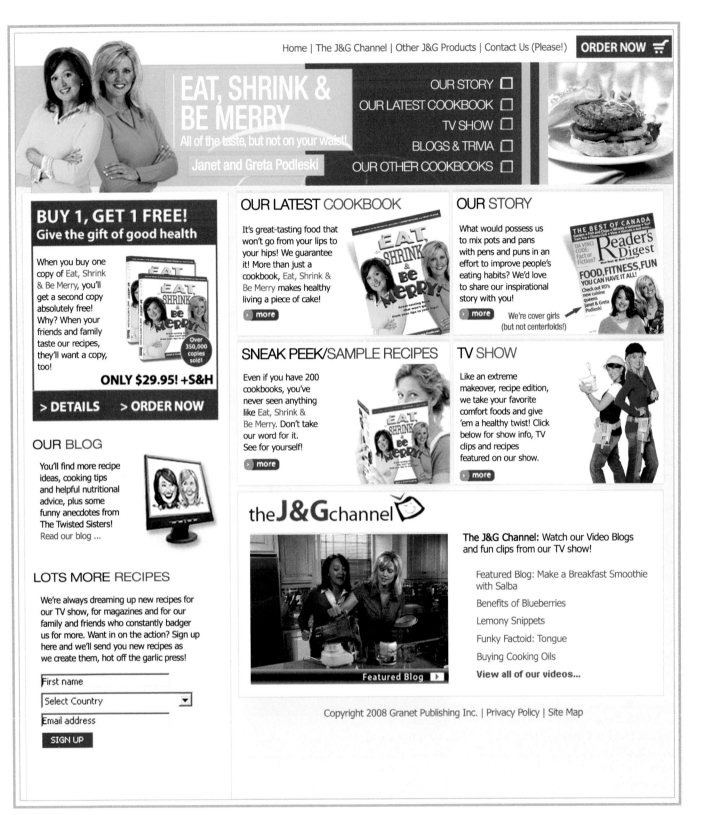

See what's cooking at
www.eatshrinkandbemerry.com